THE BIG BOOK OF ROCK & ROLL NAMES

How Arcade Fire,
Led Zeppelin, Nirvana,
Vampire Weekend,
and 532 Other Bands
Got Their Names

ADAM DOLGINS

ABRAMS IMAGE   NEW YORK

TABLE OF CONTENTS

INTRODUCTION

As Spinal Tap's David St. Hubbins so eloquently put it, "It's such a fine line between stupid and clever." And that certainly holds true for the names of rock bands. Some are brilliant, some are terrible, and some are brilliantly terrible.

When researching the stories for this book, one thing became clear: it's hard to come up with the perfect band name. Or, for some bands, any name at all. When Dennis DeYoung of Styx was asked how they chose their name, his short answer was, "It was the name that no one in the band hated." Said Ed Rowland of Collective Soul, "That's basically the only name we could decide on."

Similarly Albert Hammond Jr. of the Strokes recalled, "We'd come in with all these bad names—the de Niros, the Rubber Bands, the Motels, Flattop Freddie and the Purple Canoes—and no one would agree. One day we're in the studio after practice and Julian said 'The Strokes.' And everyone was like 'That sounds great!'. It was that easy. Five guys agreeing."

Paul Stanley of KISS remembered, "I was driving my '63 Plymouth Grand Fury on the Long Island Expressway, and the name suddenly came to me. I remember thinking to myself, 'God, I know this is the right name, I hope I don't get any grief from the other guys.' I told them I thought the band should be called KISS and I held my breath, waiting for some sort of response, and everybody went, 'Yeah, that sounds pretty good.'"

Beyond the challenges inherent in any democracy, another hurdle for bands is coming up with something unique. As Susannah Hoffs of the Bangles observed, "That's one of the hardest things about being in a band—coming up with a name . . . that hasn't been taken or used in some form already." Her band began as the Bangs, only to learn that another band was using the name, hence the change to the Bangles. For similar reasons, Dinosaur became Dinosaur Jr., the Beat became the English Beat, and Roxy became Roxy Music.

Back in the pre-internet days, the sudden arrival of a cease and desist notice was often a band's first inkling there was another band out there with the same name. Usually by that time the band was established enough to be playing shows and even putting out records, so a name change was inevitably traumatic.

Now, thanks to Google, fledgling bands can avoid such a fate with a thorough web search. But while the web may benefit bands as a research tool, it also holds pitfalls for those whose names are similar to other words or phrases. Chvrches was compelled to use a Roman V when they realized web search results would have them buried under local houses of worship. The Lumineers have been battling for search engine dominance with a company that makes dental veneers with the same name.

One phrase that you'll find throughout this book is "It just stuck." Or, in some cases, "we were stuck with it." This is because many bands never expected to last as long as they did. As Tracey Thorn of Everything but the Girl recalled, "We really thought we'd just be making one single or something and we chose this throwaway, disposable name, and . . . we're stuck with it."

Marcus Mumford of Mumford & Sons noted, "Your name, you never really think about it when you're in the pub. You've done your first rehearsal, you've written your first song, and someone's like, 'You need a band name now.' And we're all, you know, young guns and didn't really think about it very much. And then of course your band name eventually starts preceding you . . . If I'd known it was going to go this way, I would have wanted to call it anything other than my last name. It's a ball-ache. We thought about changing it, but it's a bit late now."

I find these stories endlessly fascinating. Even names that on the surface seem pretty straightforward often have unexpected origins. Some, like the Rolling Stones and Cat Power, are hastily chosen when a show needs to be booked or a song distributed. Others have been in the works for years, like the Arctic Monkeys, Aerosmith, and Smashing Pumpkins, which were all the stuff of youthful daydreams.

For me, some of my favorite stories involve unintended consequences. Nikki Sixx recalled that Motley Crüe's unconventional use of umlauts caused confusion on their first German tour, "where all the kids were going, 'Mutley Cruh!' and we were going, 'Huh?'" Mike Score of A Flock of Seagulls lamented, "Once we'd used the name as a live band, people started making seagull noises—'Arh, arh, arh'—and things like that." When Jimmy Eat World chose their name, they didn't realize it would lead to headlines like the following: "JEW Uses Live Set to Keep Fans Enlivened."

In the end, one can't help but wonder to what degree a band's name helps it succeed, or conversely holds it back in some way. Does the name make the band, or does the band make the name? One name that is mentioned most often by other bands is the Beatles. The Beatles is a pun—a deliberately misspelled reference to beat music, a style that was popular in the UK in the early 1960s. As John Wetton of the band Asia observed, "The Beatles is probably one of the worst names anyone ever came up with, but as soon as you get used to it, it represents the best band that's ever been. What a grotesque pun. It's horrible, a horrible pun. But in fact, once you get past that, it's OK. It's just become a symbol of those four people."

Speaking of Asia, why in the world would four white guys from the UK call themselves that? Read the book and find out.

ABBA The name of the Swedish pop group, which formed in Stockholm in 1972, is an acronym made up of the four members' first initials: Agnetha, Björn, Benny, and Anni-Frid. ABBA was originally intended as a play on words, because it's the name of a well-known fish-canning company in Sweden, Abba Seafood, which sells products like caviar and pickled herring. At the time, the group's manager figured the name would work internationally because Abba Seafood wasn't familiar outside of Sweden. Today many more people have heard of the company, thanks to the Swedish furniture giant IKEA, which sells Abba products in many of its food markets around the world. The company officially granted the group permission to share the name in 1974.

ABC The English pop band began in Sheffield in 1980 as Vice Versa and changed their name when vocalist Martin Fry joined the same year. Fry explains, "I wanted a name that would put us first in the phone directory, or second if you count ABBA; a name that didn't tie us to any one form of music; something big, bold, brash, and vague. It stands for nothing and everything—like the Band."

AC/DC When brothers Malcolm and Angus Young started the band in Sydney, Australia, in 1973, it was their sister Margaret who suggested the name AC/DC after seeing the initials (an abbreviation of alternating current and direct current) on a sewing machine. They liked the name because it fit their "high-voltage" sound, "forgetting," as one bio put it, that the word was also slang for bisexual. This association dogged them for a time, leading publicists to play up the band members' heterosexual adventures whenever possible. AC/DC is pronounced one letter at a time, although in Australia some fans refer to the band as "Acca Dacca."

ACE OF BASE The Swedish group, best known for the hits "All That She Wants," "The Sign," and "Don't Turn Around," had its origins in a band formed by Jonas "Joker" Berggren in 1987 in Gothenburg, Sweden's second largest city. That band went through a series of names, including Tech Noir, after a nightclub in the movie *The Terminator*, when Ulf Ekberg joined them in 1989. The following year they changed their name to Ace of Base. It was rumored that the name was inspired by a subterranean practice room where the four members were "aces of the base(ment)." Berggren told *Entertainment Weekly* in 1994: "Our base is our studio, and an ace is like a master. So we are the aces of our studio." When asked if they had considered spelling it "Ace of Bass," he said, "That would even be more corny." Years later, Ekberg admitted: "We simply made that story up. TV, radio and magazines were constantly asking us about our name so we needed a story to tell. The true story is this one: One day I woke up badly hungover in front of this huge TV. It played music videos and Motörhead's 'Ace of Spades' was on. 'This would make for a cool band name,' I thought, and shortly thereafter Ace of Base was born."

ADAM AND THE ANTS The Ants formed in London in 1977, their name a reference to the Beatles. Of his own name, singer Adam Ant explained: "My real name is Stuart Leslie Goddard. I liked the idea of the 'first man' because I was shaped a bit more like a Renaissance painting, big shoulders and narrow waist, so I decided to enhance that. I think the Tubes wrote a song—'Madam, that's Adam. There's no other woman that's had 'im. He's stronger than a tree and he's freshly molded from clay.' So I thought, 'Oh, that would be good,' and so I became Adam and never looked back." For what it's worth, Atom Ant was the name of a TV cartoon character in the 1960s.

> "I liked the idea of the 'first man' because I was shaped a bit more like a Renaissance painting, big shoulders and narrow waist, so I decided to enhance that."
> —ADAM ANT, ADAM AND THE ANTS

AEROSMITH When the band formed in Boston in 1970, it was drummer Joey Kramer who suggested the name. Kramer said he had first thought of it in high school and would write the word over and over again on his notebooks in class, thinking that one day it would be a cool name for a band. The other members initially balked because they thought it was a reference to the classic Sinclair Lewis novel *Arrowsmith*, which was required reading in English class and therefore not cool. Kramer explained that it was spelled "Aerosmith," and it was inspired by Harry Nilsson's 1968 album *Aerial Ballet*. That album was reportedly named for a circus act performed by Nilsson's grandparents. The cover featured a performer jumping off of a biplane. The band ultimately agreed to the name after considering others, including the Hookers and Spike Jones.

THE AFGHAN WHIGS The Afghan Whigs formed in Cincinnati in 1986. Singer Greg Dulli recalled the band's origins: "I went to this Halloween celebration in Athens, Ohio. I was pissing on a wall and got put in jail, cited for indecent exposure. And in the drunk tank I met Rick McCollum (guitar), who had been selling weed. We had John Curley (bass) in common. I had played with John before. He joined my band the Black Republicans." As for the name Afghan Whigs, Dulli said: "Curley named the band. I still don't know what it means. He did a lot of acid back then." According to Curley, the name is a riff on the Black Republicans. It was not inspired, as rumored, by a little-known, and possibly nonexistent, Florida-based biker gang of white Muslims who were objectors to the Vietnam War.

"As for the name Afghan Whigs, Dulli said: 'Curley named the band. I still don't know what it means. He did a lot of acid back then.'" —GREG DULLI, AFGHAN WHIGS

A-HA The Norwegian trio of Morten Harket, Pal Waaktaar, and Magne Furuholmen formed in Oslo in 1982 and had a global hit with the song "Take on Me" in 1985. According to Furuholmen, "Originally, we were trying to find a Norwegian word that people would be able to say in English." Instead, the name came from a song title that Harket spotted in one of Waaktaar's notebooks. "It was a terrible song, but a great name," Furuholmen said. "I mean, you say it, 'aha,' all the time. Our manager says that this band has been on everybody's lips for years."

ALABAMA SHAKES Singer and guitarist Brittany Howard and bassist Zac Cockrell began playing together when they were high school classmates in Athens, Alabama, and were eventually joined by drummer Steve Johnson. When future guitarist Heath Fogg asked them to open for his band Tuco's Pistol at an area show, they hastily chose the name the Shakes for what they assumed would be a one-time set of cover songs. Howard noted that it was "the most generic name ever," but they stuck with it when they continued playing together and started writing their own songs. As their popularity grew, they were forced to change their name to Alabama Shakes for legal reasons. Howard explained, "The Shakes is trademarked by some kind of milk shake. Every band called the Shakes is probably going to have to change their name if they want to find any point of small success, because there are so many. There's a Shakes out of Athens, Georgia, we keep getting mixed up with. Now there's a Shakes in Nashville, there's a Shakes in Israel, there's a Shakes in probably every state." Coincidentally, in 1931 a duo called the Alabama Sheiks recorded four songs on the Victor label, presumably inspired by the success of the blues/country string band the Mississippi Sheiks, who had a hit the year before with "Sittin' on Top of the World," which would later be covered by the Grateful Dead, Howlin' Wolf, and Frank Sinatra. The Flying Burrito Brothers at one time considered calling themselves the Alabama Shieks.

THE ALARM The band formed in Rhyl, Wales, in 1977 as the Toilets, before changing their name to Quasimodo, Seventeen, and eventually the Alarm. Singer and guitarist Mike Peters recalls: "We sat around a table looking for a name. We were just talking about musical experiences that we'd had, and we were hoping that someone would say a word or a phrase that would become the name of the band. I started telling about a song that I had written called 'Alarm Alarm.' It was the first attempt at writing a song and we all thought, 'Oh, that sounds good—let's call ourselves Alarm Alarm.' So we phoned up (influential BBC disc jockey) John Peel because we were doing a really early show of ours in London—probably one of the first gigs we ever had—and we said, 'Can you plug our gig over the radio?' And he said yeah. So it was, 'Alarm Alarm are playing tonight.' And then he said, 'It's funny, isn't it? There's Duran Duran, Talk Talk, now Alarm Alarm.

Perhaps I should change my name to John Peel John Peel.' And we thought, 'Let's just call ourselves the Alarm.'"

ALICE IN CHAINS When the band formed in Seattle in 1987, they took their name from a glam-metal band that singer Layne Staley had been in called Alice N' Chains, which was formed when the members were still in high school. The origin of that name was a conversation about backstage passes, including one that read "Welcome to Wonderland," which triggered a discussion of the book *Alice in Wonderland*. The band, which began as Sleze, was looking for a name that reflected both glam and metal, soft and hard, so Alice in Chains was suggested, but they changed it to Alice N' Chains in an attempt to allay concerns about female bondage. After Alice N' Chains broke up and Staley was invited to join a band being formed by Jerry Cantrell and Sean Kinney, he suggested the name, which they changed to Alice in Chains.

THE ALL-AMERICAN REJECTS Nick Wheeler and Tyson Ritter formed the band in Stillwater, Oklahoma, in 1999 when they were in high school. The band's name was rumored to be inspired by a line in the Green Day song "Reject"—"So when the smoke clears here I am, your reject all-American"—but Wheeler said its origin is more random: "We were driving around trying to come up with a band name and that was pretty much the first one that wasn't taken. I said 'The All-American . . .' and (Ritter) said 'Rejects.' There's a place called Hastings Books, Music & Video. They've got a little computer, you can pretty much look up every band ever." Ritter said, "We went to Hastings, it wasn't taken." Once they began using the name, however, they discovered there was a punk band in Colorado also called the All-American Rejects. Wheeler and Ritter threatened legal action, claiming they used the name first, and prevailed.

ALT-J Alt-J formed in 2007 when the members met at Leeds University in England. The band's symbol is Δ, the uppercase Greek letter delta. Guitarist Gwil Sainsbury, who suggested the name, noted that "in mathematical equations it's used to show change." The band is most commonly referred to as alt-J, which is how Δ is typed on Mac keyboards, by pressing the alt/option key and the J key. Keyboard player Gus Unger-Hamilton explained, "We were originally called Daljit Dhaliwal, who was a newsreader on British television. But that was a bit tough to spell—even the guys in the band would get it wrong. So we changed it to Films. But there was an American band named the Films so we had to change it again. So we went with Alt-J, which is some keyboard shortcut, so surely no one had already used it." He recalled that "alt-J was the only name we could all agree on. We didn't really bother to think about the name. We were more interested in making music." The cover of their debut album, *An Awesome Wave*, features an image of the largest river delta in the world, the Ganges. River deltas are named for the symbol Δ because they share the same shape. Band members sometimes use the Δ like a heart to sign off on social media posts ("Δ Gus"), and fans sometimes make the symbol with their fingers at concerts.

AMERICA Gerry Beckley, Dewey Bunnell, and Dan Peek—sons of American servicemen stationed in England—began playing together in 1969 while they were students at London's Central High School. Originally part of a five-man band called the Daze, the three took their name from a Wurlitzer-brand Americana jukebox found at a London pub.

THE ANIMALS The Animals began in Newcastle, England, in 1962. Singer Eric Burdon explains: "The story that we were named the Animals because of our wild appearance onstage was just conjured up by some publicity man. The real reason the band was called the Animals was that we were sort of weekend warriors in a street gang. We—John Steel, myself, eventually Alan Price, Chas Chandler—we were part of this street gang. We were the youngest members of the gang. They were mostly older guys—nineteen, twenty, twenty-one. We were like fourteen, fifteen, sixteen, seventeen at the time. We provided them with entertainment, and that's why we survived. We weren't just made hamburger and thrown out of the group because we entertained them. They liked us a lot and took us to heart. One of the main characters in this gang had been demobbed from the British army, who were involved in Cyprus at the time. The British were stuck in the middle—it was kind of like a mini English Vietnam, and there were a lot of vets who came back from that conflict with their minds pretty screwed up. This guy, who we liked a lot, his name was Animal Hogg, and he was the animal of the group. We liked him a lot and he liked us a lot, and we figured it would be good to name a band after him. It was fun to find out in later years that even on *Sesame Street* there was an Animal, a member of the gang called Animal. That's the real straight dope on the band. We named the band after our favorite character in the gang." When asked about being called the Animals because of the way they looked or performed, Burdon explains, "That was just an easy way to tell the story, because then we would've had to've gone into the politics of being a vet, talking about a guy who had been in the conflict. It wasn't good subject matter. In fact, just recently, when I tried to tell that story, in a book that I wrote, Pete Townshend (who was working as an editor at the British publishing house Faber & Faber) wouldn't let me. I went into how this guy, one night around the campfire, broke down and told me how he and his buddies had raped and pillaged in a village on Cyprus and how he had actually raped someone at gunpoint, and that's what destroyed him, he couldn't handle it anymore. Townshend's

Adam Dolgins

reaction was, 'You can't tell a story like that, you'll offend female readers. It'll be offensive to readers.'" When asked about what came of Animal Hogg, Burdon says, "I have no idea. We left town shortly after that. We started traveling." Burdon said he liked the name "because it stuck in people's minds. I remember George Harrison and Georgie Fame on separate occasions, after watching our show at the Flamingo and the Ham Yard where the Who started out as the High Numbers—everybody played there—coming up and going, 'Hey, you guys are crazy calling yourselves the Animals.' It was pretty outrageous then. Pretty tame now, but back then it was pretty outrageous. We'd get people on the phone wanting to book us asking, 'What's the name of the band?' 'The Animals.' 'The Animals? Jesus, we can't put that on a poster.' I think only the French really understood what we were getting at with the name. We were really pissed off when we came to America because the American pop press would go, 'OK, guys, get down on your hands and knees and growl like animals.' And kids would ask, 'Which one's the tiger?' 'Who's the elephant?' Y'know. But in the French press, we got reviews that said, 'This music lives up to the title. It's raw, it's animalistic, it has a wild soul.' They approached it in a different way. That's pretty much it."

"'The Animals? Jesus, we can't put that on a poster.'"
—ERIC BURDEN, THE ANIMALS

ANTHRAX Anthrax formed in New York City in 1981 and were one of the pioneers of thrash metal. Guitarist Scott Ian thought of the name, which the American Heritage Dictionary defines as "an infectious, usually fatal disease of warm-blooded animals, especially of cattle and sheep, caused by *Bacillus anthracis*. It is transmissible to man, capable of affecting various organs, and especially characterized by malignant ulcers." "I learned about the disease in science class in high school," recalled Ian, who grew up in the Bronx. "It sounded like a great name for a band." In 2001, the name brought the band unexpected attention when, in what was the nation's first bioterrorist attack, envelopes containing anthrax spores were mailed to several media outlets and two US senators, killing five people and sickening seventeen others. The *New York Times* reported that as a result "the aging metal band from Bayside, Queens . . . has become more famous for its moniker than its music. . . . Anthrax, whose members once reveled in how coolly evil the band sounded, has been humbled by its ironic association with terrorism, even as many of its older records have been selling at double their usual, albeit modest, pace—perhaps the first time that a biological attack has prompted a spike in heavy-metal album sales."

"I learned about the disease in science class in high school..... It sounded like a great name for a band."
—SCOTT IAN, ANTHRAX

APHEX TWIN Richard D. James took his stage name from Aphex Systems, a company that traffics in professional music technology including audio processing equipment and effects pedals, which are used to change how musical instruments or other audio sources sound. The company reportedly gave permission to use the Aphex name, which is a contraction of "analog effects." James has said that Twin is in memory of his brother who was born three years before he was, but who died at birth: "He has the same name as me. It's not like I have a big hang-up about it. I just think it's tight because my mum was so upset about it when he died that she kept his name on but forgot about him, thinking, 'The next boy I have, that'll be him.' So I sort of took his place as if he didn't exist." A photo of what is alleged to be his brother's gravestone was used as the cover for the 1996 Aphex Twin *Girl/Boy* EP.

ARCADE FIRE Win Butler formed the band in Montreal in 2000, their name inspired by a story told by an older boy who'd bullied him: "The first kid who beat me up when I was twelve was a high school kid who always used to talk about how the old arcade burned down and all these kids died." Butler doubts the truth of the story: "It's not an actual event, but one that I took to be real. I would say that it's probably something that the kid made up, but at the time I believed him." Given the story, Butler's recollection of one of the band's early shows is a bit eerie: "I remember doing a show at our old second-floor loft, where I hung coatracks and got a bunch of coats from the thrift store and then had people hang their coats when they got there, so when you arrived you had to push your way through all these coats. It was a horrifying fire risk, basically a death trap."

ARCTIC MONKEYS The band formed in 2002 in High Green, a suburb of Sheffield, England. Their name was suggested by guitarist Jamie Cook. Drummer Matt Helders said of the name, "It's just a name. Jamie came up with it at school before we were in a band. He just always wanted to be in a band called Arctic Monkeys." Singer Alex Turner recalled, "I've no idea where it came from. It was Jamie's fault—he came up with it, and he's never even told us why. If he even knows, he's keeping it a secret from me." Unlike most other bands, it was the first name they chose and the only one they've used. Turner continued, "There might have been other ideas for offshoots at the time, but the Monkeys was the first one. It sounds like a first band name, doesn't it? It's so bad that the tribute bands don't sound worse." At one point they considered renaming the band Bang Bang because Artic Monkeys was too "silly."

> "The Beatles is probably one of the worst soon as you get used to it, it represents grotesque pun. It's horrible, a horrible pun.
> —JOHN WETTON, ASIA

ART OF NOISE The intentionally faceless British techno-pop group Art of Noise met as part of Trevor Horn's production team in London in the early 1980s. Their name was coined by ex–music critic Paul Morley, who ran ZTT Records with Horn, after a sociomusical manifesto, *The Art of Noises*, published in 1913 by the Italian futurist Luigi Russolo.

ASIA Asia formed in London in 1981 by ex–UK lead singer and bassist John Wetton; Emerson, Lake and Palmer drummer Carl Palmer; and two former Yes men, guitarist Steve Howe and keyboard player Geoff Downes. According to Wetton, the name was suggested by their manager, Brian Lane: "The name game is one that everyone dreads, y'know? 'What are we going to call it?' All the good names have been had long ago. Basically you know that the name is only sort of unusual for the first three months. As soon as people get used to it, you can be called anything. The Beatles is probably one of the worst names anyone ever came up with, but as soon as you get used to it, it represents the best band that's ever been. What a grotesque pun. It's horrible, a horrible pun. But in fact, once you get past that, it's OK. It's just become a symbol of those four people. We were doing the name game in the office, and our manager came up with

names anyone ever came up with, but as the best band that's ever been. What a But in fact, once you get past that, it's OK."

the name Asia. He said, 'No one's ever used that.' And everyone said, 'Oh, yeah, right, Brian, shut up.' Everyone told him to shut up and carried on. And about an hour later, I said, 'That's not a bad idea— four guys, four letters, graphically pretty strong, yeah, OK.' It wasn't intentionally a place name. It could have been any word that had four letters and was graphically strong." When asked about the rumor that they chose the name in part because it would put them at the beginning of the record bin up in the A's, Wetton says, "No, that's a little bit obvious. I mean, we could have done better than that. We could have done Aardvark. Then we could have guaranteed that we would have been at the top. It wasn't that at all."

THE ASSOCIATION When the Association formed in Los Angeles in 1964, all but one of the original members belonged to a folk-rock group called the Men. After disagreements over the band's direction, keyboard player Terry Kirkman walked out of rehearsal one day and was joined by five of the other members. Kirkman recalls, "We all went back to my apartment in the afternoon and sat down with a glass of wine and some joints. We thought, 'We just took eight and a half months of really hard work, just trying our hardest, our absolute fucking hardest, and threw it away. What are we going to do?' We're in that post-separation shock when one of the guys said, 'Don't look now, but

The Big Book of Rock & Roll Names

there's six of us in this room and there's two tenors, two baritones, and two basses.' I said, 'Well, fuck, I'm game if you are. We've already got this work ethic. We already know what we're doing. We're obviously all in agreement.' And we decided that we would try to become a group right there. And then we jokingly started to muse over what we would call ourselves. There was this really despicable joke I loved a lot at the time in which a family group comes in to audition for a show business agent and he says, 'Great. What is it you do?' And the joke went something like, 'Well, first I stick it in my wife's butt, and then my little kid jumps on me and the little sister does this.' The answer is this horrible, incestuous daisy chain of interlocked family sex. And the agent is totally aghast and says, 'That's so fantastic. What do you call yourselves?' And the guy says, 'We call ourselves the Aristocrats.' We all started laughing, and Brian Cole said, 'I'm for it. Why don't we call ourselves the Aristocrats.' We were fairly whacked by that time, and somebody said we better make sure of the true, true meaning. So while Judy, my wife, was looking for 'aristocrat' (in the dictionary), she said, 'Here's a word that I think defines what you are.' The definition that she read was 'a group of people gathered together for a common cause.' And we went with that. We were named and formed within two hours." Was Kirkman glad they went with the Association? "No. I wish we had stuck with the Aristocrats."

AVERAGE WHITE BAND The band formed in Dundee, Scotland, in 1972 and topped the charts in 1975 with "Pick Up the Pieces." Like Vanilla Fudge, their name was a joking reference to the fact that they were a white band that played black music. The band's saxophonist Malcolm "Molly" Duncan, recalled, "A friend heard us jamming and said, 'This is too much for the average white man.' When we'd all stopped laughing, the name just stuck." That friend was American singer Bonnie Bramlett, who began her musical career at the age of thirteen as a backup singer for blues singers such as Albert King and Little Milton and the R&B singer Fontella Bass and was the first white woman to sing with Ike and Tina Turner as one of the Ikettes. In 1979, Bramlett made news when she punched Elvis Costello in the face at a hotel bar in Columbus, Ohio, after a drunk Costello used a racial slur to describe James Brown and Ray Charles. In the 1980s, Bramlett had a recurring role on the ABC sitcom *Roseanne*, playing a co-worker and friend, also named Bonnie, of Roseanne Barr's character Roseanne Conner.

AZTEC CAMERA Roddy Frame formed the pop/new wave band Aztec Camera in 1980 in East Kilbride, outside of Glasgow, Scotland. The name was rumored to have been inspired by the Baghdad Battery, a set of three ancient artifacts found together—a ceramic pot, a tube of copper, and a rod of iron—that some researchers hypothesized functioned together as a galvanic cell, possibly used for electroplating or some kind of electrotherapy. Not so according to Frame: "No, it was in one of my deep-thinking, psychedelic periods when I was about fifteen. You know, that sort of acid rock thing. We used to wander around East Kilbride wearing pink nylon paisley and cravats and red shoes with massive trousers and great big overcoats. And because the bands we were listening to had names like the 13th Floor Elevators and all that ridiculous crap, we came up with the name Aztec Camera."

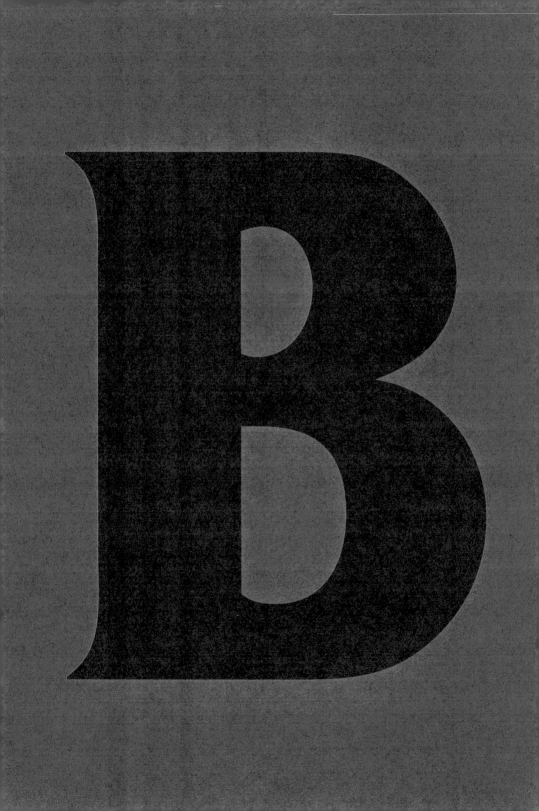

THE B-52'S The band, which formed in Athens, Georgia, in 1977, took their name from the Southern term for the towering bouffant hairdos worn at the time by band members Kate Pierson and Cindy Wilson. Those hairstyles were named for B-52 bombers, whose noses they were thought to resemble.

BAD BRAINS Bad Brains formed in 1977 in Washington, D.C., as a jazz fusion group called Mind Power before turning to hardcore punk. The rumor they took their name from the Ramones' song "Bad Brain" was denied by guitarist Dr. Know: "No, Bad Brains as in good brains. We were called Mind Power and we flipped it, we said, what's the opposite of Mind Power? Bad Brains. Do you know what I mean about 'bad' being 'good'? Bad Brains, it sounded better. It made more sense."

BAD COMPANY The hard rock supergroup was formed in Westminster, London, in 1973 by two members of the band Free—singer Paul Rodgers and drummer Simon Kirke—along with Mott the Hoople guitarist Mick Ralphs and King Crimson bassist Boz Burrell. When asked if the 1972 Western film *Bad Company* inspired the band name, Kirke said, "Well, it did and it didn't. I've been asked this question many times and I can only tell you what I remember. When we were putting the band together in late 1973 we didn't have a name. We were playing in Paul Rodgers's little studio, and I remember him coming home one day. He'd been to Guildford, which is this town just outside London. He'd been walking down the street and saw an advert for this Jeff Bridges film called *Bad Company*. It became sort of a cult movie. But I remember him saying, 'That's a great name for the band,' and I agreed. We'd just signed to Swan Song Records, Led Zeppelin's record label, and we had to get them to ask Warner Bros. if we could use the name. We weren't sure if it was trademarked and all that stuff. And I believe everything was cleared for us to use the name. Now, fast forward many years, and I remember Paul saying in another interview about the derivation of the name, that he was reading an old Victorian book and he maintains that there was an image in it that sparked the idea. I always remember the name as coming from the movie, but Paul Rodgers would question that." Rodgers said, "No. I've never even seen the movie, actually. The name came from my childhood days. I saw a book on Victorian morals with a picture of this Victorian punk. He was dressed like a tough, with a top hat and the spats and vests and the watch in the pocket and the tails and all of that. But everything was raggy. The shoes were popped out at the soles, and the top of the hat was popped out. And the guy is leaning on the lamppost with a bottle in his hand and a pipe in his mouth, obviously a dodgy person. And you've got this little choirboy kind of guy—a little kid, actually—looking up to him. And underneath it said, 'Beware of bad company.'"

BADFINGER The band formed in Swansea, Wales, in 1961 and were signed to the Beatles' record label, Apple, in 1968 as the Iveys, named after Ivy Place, a street in Swansea. It was decided that the name the Iveys was too old-fashioned for the new modern era. John Lennon suggested the names the Glass Onion, the Cagneys, and the Prix, which would be pronounced "the Pricks." Neil Aspinall, who ran Apple Records, came up with the name Badfinger, inspired by "Bad Finger

Boogie," an early working title of a Lennon-McCartney composition that would eventually become "With a Little Help from My Friends." "Bad Finger Boogie" was so named because Lennon had injured his finger while working on the song. George Harrison would later claim that Badfinger was actually named for Helga Fabdinger, a stripper the Beatles had met in Hamburg, Germany.

BAD RELIGION When asked how they got their name, Greg Graffin, lead singer of this seminal Los Angeles punk band, said, "We've been asked this question at least a thousand times. It's worse for us because we've been around for so long. Well, in 1980, we were a bunch of teenagers. I was fifteen years old when the band started. And if you think back to what was going through your mind when you were fifteen, you'd think about pissing off adults more than anything. And we thought Bad Religion would accomplish that goal. Back then, I gotta say, the motivation for the name was pretty juvenile. However, if you remember, it was a time when there was a lot of televangelism, so it was sort of timely, that we would poke fun at some aspect of American culture. And it turns out that the name, although it started out on a juvenile foundation, became actually a pretty good name over the years, because we use religion as a metaphor for organized, dogmatic thought—really the opposite of what punk rock is all about, which stresses independence and individuality more than anything else. And so, actually, the name is still thought-provoking, because we have to combat dogma for our entire life." When asked whether he was happy with the choice, he said, "It's not a name I have to be embarrassed about, which is nice. We almost went with Bad Family Life. Then we almost went with Head Cheese."

BANANARAMA Singers Sara Dallin, Siobhan Fahey, and Keren Woodward formed the pop music vocal group in London in 1981.

Their name did not come from *The Banana Splits* children's TV series from the late 1960s, as has been reported. It was instead inspired by the group's first recording, "Aie a Mwana," a cover of a song by Black Blood, an African group based in Brussels. Fahey recalled, "We just wanted a silly name that expressed enjoyment and lightheartedness. Our first single was sung in Swahili, so we thought of something tropical—bananas—and added 'rama' 'cause it sounded silly." Fahey noted that "rama" was inspired by Roxy Music's "Pyjamarama," a favorite song of theirs. "Sometimes we've regretted calling ourselves that," she said. "It's not the easiest name to spell or pronounce, around the world." Dallin said, "I don't even notice the word now. It's like saying 'the Tower of London' or 'Buckingham Palace.'"

> "When we were working with Bob Dylan and we moved to Woodstock, everybody referred to us as 'the band.' He called us 'the band,' our friends called us 'the band,' our neighbors called us 'the band.'" —ROBBIE ROBERTSON, THE BAND

THE BAND The band members first met in rockabilly singer Ronnie Hawkins's backing group the Hawks, which they joined individually between 1958 and 1963. After they split from Hawkins in 1964, they used several different names, including Levon Helm & the Hawks, the Canadian Squires, and eventually simply the Hawks. Guitarist Robbie Robertson recalled, "Everything was fine, we were sailing along, and all of a sudden, one day the Hawks meant something else altogether (as in 'warmongers,' this being the height of the Vietnam War)." They eventually opted to call themselves simply the Band because, Robertson explained, that's how everyone referred to them: "When we were working with Bob Dylan and we moved to Woodstock, everybody referred to us as 'the band.' He called us 'the band,' our friends called us 'the band,' our neighbors called us 'the band.'"

THE BANGLES The band started in Los Angeles in 1980 as the Colours before changing their name to the Supersonic Bangs, which was inspired by an article in the July 1965 issue of *Esquire*. Singer and guitarist Susanna Hoffs recalled, "I had an issue of *Esquire* magazine with Ed Sullivan on the cover wearing a Beatle wig, and it was a whole thing on hairdos and hairstyles." The name was soon shortened to the Bangs. "We liked the double-entendre of the name," Hoff explained. "You can read a lot into it. There was something kind of gutsy about it." After they put out their first single under the name and were preparing to release a follow-up EP, their manager received a call from a band in New Jersey called Bangs. Hoffs remembered, "The artwork was done, everything was ready, and . . . we had to change our name. They basically said, 'Pay us X amount of dollars if you really want to use the name,' dollars which we of course didn't have at the time, and we had, like, 48 hours to think of a new name. We were not happy about having to rethink the name, because that's one of the hardest things about being in a band—coming up with a name, one that hasn't been taken or used in some form already. So we were just thinking of a thousand different possibilities, but in the end, when we came up with Bangles, it kind of had a ring to it that we liked. There was a little bit of Beatles," you know, being Beatlemaniacs. And then we were looking up the definition of bangles in the dictionary, and there was one definition that said 'to hang loose,' and we sort of thought that was kind of groovy and '60s. In the end, I think it's a better name for the band, weirdly. I would never have thought that back then, 'cause there was a kind of toughness to the Bangs. We were garage-pop. We were firmly rooted in the garage, so we liked the tough aspect of it. Having come out of a sort of post-punk movement in LA of pop bands, it was still a lot of the punk energy in the scene. Those were the reasons why we liked the Bangs, but in the end, I think the Bangles was a better name for us."

BARENAKED LADIES The name Barenaked Ladies predates the band, which was formed by Ed Robertson and Steven Page in Scarborough, a suburb of Toronto, in 1988. The pair first met in grade school and bonded over their love of music. They came up with the name at a Bob Dylan concert they attended as teens, where they amused themselves by pretending to be rock critics and make up backstories about the members of Dylan's band, including fictional band names, one of which was Barenaked Ladies. Later, Robertson entered a cover band he had formed into a local battle of the bands contest, but they broke up and he forgot about the show. When one of the organizers contacted him to confirm details, Robertson claimed he had a new band called Barenaked Ladies and then asked Page if he would play the show with him. Page couldn't believe he had used the name but agreed. Recalling the name's origins, Page explained, "It made us laugh and reminded us of when we were eight years old and would look at the women's underwear section of the Sears catalog. When Ed got our first gig, he told them we were called Barenaked Ladies, and after that there was no backing out. Because if we changed our name, how would the seven people that were there find us again?"

BAUHAUS The band formed in Northampton, England, in 1978 after singer Peter Murphy joined guitarist Daniel Ash, bassist David J, and drummer Kevin Haskins, who were performing as the Craze. They changed their name to Bauhaus 1919, named after the German institute founded that year for the study of art, design, and architecture and known for its development of a style of functional architecture and its experimental use of building materials. Bauhaus is German for "architecture house."

THE BAY CITY ROLLERS In an effort to give the Scottish pop rockers an American-sounding name, manager and producer Tam Paton randomly stuck a pin in a map of the US and put a hole in Bay City, Michigan, a city of about forty thousand residents near the southern end of Saginaw Bay.

THE BEACH BOYS The band members called themselves the Pendletones—a reference to the plaid Pendleton-brand shirts popular with West Coast surfers—when they cut their first single, "Surfin'," in 1961. The single was released by the regional label Candix Records, which wanted to call the band the Surfers, despite the boys' wish to remain the Pendletones. When it was discovered that there already was a band called the Surfers, Candix called them the Beach Boys, which was coined by Candix executive Russ Regan. The band wasn't aware of the name change until they opened up a box of the singles and saw it on the label. Brian Wilson remembers that when his father called to complain, he was told it was too late to change the name back to the Pendletones: "The records had already been pressed, the labels printed, and the whole kit and caboodle shipped. It was a small-time operation. Low budget. Reprinting the labels was too costly, my dad was informed. There was nothing we could do except shrug it off."

BEACH HOUSE Victoria Legrand and Alex Scally formed the group in Baltimore in 2004. Scally remembered, "We'd been writing music, and we had all these songs, and then there was that moment where you say, 'What do we call ourselves?' We tried to intellectualize it, and it didn't work. There were different plant names: Wisteria, that kind of thing. Stupid stuff. But, once we stopped trying, it just came out, it just happened. And it just seemed perfect. One thing Victoria and I can agree on is that our music is its own world. And I think that's very much what the 'beach house' feel is: going off to a different world. It just felt right." Legrand noted, "We were trying to describe the sounds we were hearing in the little world where we exist. It always sounded strange, haunted, and potentially weird, like a house somewhere else."

THE BEASTIE BOYS Adam Yauch (MCA, for "Master of Ceremonies Adam"), Adam Horovitz (King Ad-Rock), and Michael Diamond (Mike D) formed the Beastie Boys in 1981 as a hardcore band with Kate Schellenbach and John Barry. Prior to the Beastie Boys, Schellenbach and Diamond were in the Young Aborigines, and Horovitz was in the Young and the Useless. Schellenbach recalls that the name first appeared on a button made and worn by Yauch, and she seemed to think that the double B in the name was a takeoff on Bad Brains, as was the band's mock-reggae song, "Beastie Revolution" from the *Cookiepuss* EP. Yauch, however, gave credit to Barry for coming up with the name and denied that it has any link to Bad Brains. "It was more like a goof on the Angry Samoans," said Yauch. "It was like me and John sitting around my room in Brooklyn, just kickin' around names. It was like Beastie this, or Boys that. And we just said, 'Let's go with that one—it sounds pretty stupid, like some Angry Samoans hardcore shit.' Then we started making buttons and writing it on the back of our jackets with masking tape."

> "It was like Beastie this, or Boys that. And we
> pretty stupid, like some Angry Samoans hard
> and writing it on the back of our jackets with

THE BEATLES The Beatles began as the Quarrymen, a band John Lennon formed when he was a fifteen-year-old student at the Quarry Bank High School in 1956. Paul McCartney joined the band the following year, and after a brief stint as Johnny & the Moondogs, they became the Silver Beatles in 1959. The band members were fans of Buddy Holly and the Crickets, and Lennon, a lover of wordplay, appreciated the fact that the name the Crickets could refer to the British sport, which of course was not intended. Lennon recalled, "I was sitting at home one day, just thinking about what a good name the Crickets would be for an English group. The idea of beetles came into my head. I decided to spell it BEAtles to make it look like beat music, just as a joke." Beat music was a genre that developed in the UK in the early 1960s, and was also known as Merseybeat, which was named for bands from Liverpool and nearby areas close to the River Mersey. Beat music was a fusion of early rock and roll influenced by Chuck Berry and Buddy Holly mixed with doo-wop, rhythm & blues, and skiffle, a blend of folk, blues, and jazz that was popular in the 1950s. Many of the bands that were part of the British Invasion had their roots in the beat music scene. When Lennon told a friend, Casey Jones of the group Cass and the Casanovas, about the name

just said, 'Let's go with that one—it sounds core shit.' Then we started making buttons masking tape." —ADAM YAUCH, THE BEASTIE BOYS the Beatles, Jones said it was too short and plain. He suggested they call themselves Long John and the Silver Beatles. They didn't love the name but decided to use the Silver Beatles for a brief time before shortening it. It's worth noting that the Beetles was the name of the motorcycle gang led by Lee Marvin in the 1954 biker movie *The Wild One*, starring Marlon Brando, whose leather-clad look John Lennon, Paul McCartney, and George Harrison affected early on.

> "I was sitting at home one day, just thinking about what a good name the Crickets would be for an English group. The idea of beetles came into my head. I decided to spell it BEATles to make it look like beat music, just as a joke." —JOHN LENNON, THE BEATLES

THE BEE GEES First called the Rattlesnakes, and later Wee Johnny Hayes & the Blue Cats, the Gibb brothers—Barry, Maurice, and Robin—were renamed by Bill Good, a racetrack promoter they met while performing at Brisbane's Speedway Circus in Australia in 1960. Spotting their talent, Good introduced them to Bill Gates, a disc jockey on the local radio station 4KQ, who began to play their tapes on the air. When interest in their music started to build, Good magnanimously rechristened them the B.G.'s after his and Gates's initials, not for the "brothers Gibb," as some assume.

BELLE AND SEBASTIAN When Belle and Sebastian formed in Glasgow, Scotland, in 1996, they took their name from a popular children's TV series based on the French novel *Belle et Sébastien* by Cécile Aubry. Sebastian was a young boy who lived in the French Alps with his dog Belle. The live action series was shot and aired first in France in 1965 under its original name and then appeared on British television starting in 1967, dubbed into English with an anglicized title. The theme of the series was the power of love.

BETTER THAN EZRA The band formed at Louisiana State University in Baton Rouge in 1988 and refuse to reveal the exact origin of their name. Bassist Tom Drummond explained, "It's just that the true meaning behind the band name is so lame you wouldn't even want to print it." The most common assumption is the band took their name from a reference to poet Ezra Pound in *A Moveable Feast*, Ernest Hemingway's memoir of Paris in the 1920s: "I had heard complaining all my life. I found I could go on writing and that it was no worse than other noises, certainly better than Ezra learning to play the bassoon." The passage appears in the chapter "Birth of a New School," in which Hemingway describes being interrupted while attempting to write at a café.

BIG AUDIO DYNAMITE Singer and guitarist Mick Jones formed Big Audio Dynamite after leaving the Clash in 1984. Jones said that it was Tony James of Sigue Sigue Sputnik who suggested the letters B.A.D. He admitted that it was only later that he tried to come up with the right words to make the acronym. Two of the names he considered were Before Alien Domination and Black and Decker.

BIG STAR Cult favorites Big Star pioneered power pop in the 1970s. The band formed in Memphis in 1971, where ex–Box Tops singer/songwriter Alex Chilton joined Ice Water, a trio composed of guitarist Chris Bell, bassist Andy Hummel, and drummer Jody Stephens. One evening, as the band left the Ardent recording studio, they noted the name of the Big Star supermarket across the street. And thus Big Star was born.

BIKINI KILL When they began in Olympia, Washington, in 1990, Bikini Kill borrowed the name of a short-lived band formed by fellow riot grrrls Lois Maffeo and Margaret Doherty several years earlier. Maffeo took the name from the 1967 British spy B-movie *The Million Eyes of Sumuru*. In the movie, Sumuru is a beautiful supervillain who plans to take over the world by having her sexy all-female soldiers eliminate male leaders and replace them with her female agents. The movie was based on books by Sax Rohmer, who is best remembered for his series of novels featuring master criminal Dr. Fu-Manchu.

THE BLACK CROWES The band began as Mr. Crowe's Garden in 1984 with brothers Chris and Rich Robinson in their native Atlanta. The name came from a favorite children's book, *Johnny Crow's Garden*. After they were signed to Def American Records in 1989, A&R man/producer George Drakoulias convinced them to change their name. Chris Robinson recalled, "Everyone just called us the Crowes when we hung out. And we came up with Black Crowes—blackbirds. That was it."

BLACK FLAG Black Flag emerged from southern California in the late 1970s to become one of America's first and most influential hardcore bands. According to guitarist Greg Ginn, the name was inspired by both the international symbol of anarchy and the bug spray brand, which was advertised on TV at the time: "It was really a combination of reasons—the connotations of anarchy and also the aggressiveness of the bug spray. I think it came from the anarchist angle, but we liked the fact that there was a fun aspect too, with the spray can. The third thing was just the sound of it— 'Black Flag.' Y'know, Black Sabbath is one of my big influences. So, really, those three things were about equal. It wasn't really triggered by one particular event. The name just came up, and after thinking about it, it stuck."

THE BLACK KEYS Singer and guitarist Dan Auerbach and drummer Patrick Carney, friends from childhood, started the band in 2001 in their hometown of Akron, Ohio. Their name was inspired by an expression used by Alfred McMoore, a local outsider artist befriended by Auerbach's father Chuck, an art collector who helped McMoore sell his unique drawings. Chuck Auerbach introduced McMoore to Carney's father Jim, a staff writer at the *Akron Beacon Journal*. Patrick Carney said of McMoore, "He was schizophrenic, and lived in a halfway house, and really liked to draw with crayons and pencil on five-foot by fifty-foot scrolls of paper, and he was constantly calling both of our houses when we were kids, asking our dads to bring him pipe tobacco, Diet Coke, and crayons. He would always end the message with, 'Don't be a black key. Don't be a B-flat.' It was his way of saying that the black keys sounded dissonant, or insulting someone." After McMoore died in 2009, the band started a fund in his name to help finance the local nonprofit organization that helped him and others who struggle with mental illness.

BLACK SABBATH When they first got together in Birmingham, England, in 1968, they called themselves the Polka Tulk Blues Band, a name inspired by an inexpensive brand of talcum powder that came in a polka dotted canister used by singer Ozzy Osbourne's mother. He recalled the idea came to him one night while he was sitting on the toilet, "So I'm on the shitter . . . and I'm looking straight ahead at this shelf in front of me. My mum's put a tin of talcum powder on there, right? She loves that stuff. When you go to the bog after she's taken a bath it looks like Santa's fucking grotto in there. Anyway, it's that cheap brand of talc, the one with the black and white polka dots on the side." After lineup changes, the band switched their name to Earth. When they learned there was another band with a similar name, they became Black Sabbath, the title of one of their songs inspired by a low-budget 1963 horror anthology film that featured Boris Karloff.

BLEACHERS Jack Antonoff started Bleachers as a solo side project while on tour with his band fun. in 2013. The band is named for the kind of seating frequently found at high school sporting events. "I knew I didn't want to call it 'Jack Antonoff,'" he recalled, "'cause I wanted it to have its own identity. There's something suburban and disconnected about the word 'bleachers.' It reminds me of the shitty parts of being young that ended up being the most important moments in my life."

BLIND FAITH Blind Faith, composed of Eric Clapton, Steve Winwood, Ginger Baker, and Ric Grech, only stayed together long enough to produce one album and one arena tour in 1969. The band's name, coined by Clapton, was an ironic commentary on the hype surrounding the "instant supergroup" in the music press, which had "blind faith" that they could live up to it.

BLIND MELON While famed comic stoners Cheech & Chong do have a song titled "Blind Melon Chitlin," the *New York Times* claimed in the obituary of lead vocalist Shannon Hood that the band's name was inspired by a moniker that unemployed hippies who were neighbors of the group's bassist, Brad Smith, used to call each other.

BLINK-182 Formed in Poway, California, a San Diego suburb, in 1992, this irreverent trio performed under a variety of names, including Duck Tape, Figure 8, and American Blink, until guitarist Tom DeLonge suggested they simply go by Blink. Bassist Mark Hoppus explained how they ended up with 182: "We were just Blink, and there was another band called Blink, and so the label called us up and said you have to change your name. And we said, 'OK, let us think about it; we'll call you back.' An Irish band that formed in 1991 had derived the name from the song "Iceblink Luck" released by the

Cocteau Twins in 1990. So two weeks later they called us back, and we said, 'We haven't decided yet; call us back.' They called us back again. Finally, it got to the point where they said, 'If you don't choose the name of your band on this phone call, we're gonna choose one for you.' So we were like, 'All right, Blink, uh . . . 182.' And we just made up the 182, and ever since then we've made up different stories all the time about what 182 means. It was my ideal weight. . . . It was the ship number that my grandfather worked on in World War II. . . . It was the number of times Al Pacino says fuck in *Scarface*. . . ." (According to the *Family Media Guide*, which monitored profanity, sexual content, and violence in movies, the 1983 film actually featured 207 uses of the word.)

BLOC PARTY Russell Lissack and Kele Okereke first met in London in 1998 and decided to form a band the following year when they ran into each other at the Reading Festival. After considering a variety of names, including Union, the Angel Range, and Diet, they chose Bloc Party, which was both a play on "block party"—a party for the residents of a city neighborhood, typically held on a closed-off street and often featuring local bands as entertainment—and a merging of Eastern "blocs" and Western "parties" in the political sense.

BLONDIE Blondie formed in New York City in 1974. Bleached-blonde singer Debbie Harry recalled, "Nineteen seventy-four was the non-period of punk. Television, the Ramones, and us, either as Angel and the Snake (for two gigs) or with no name, were just playing around. Then we did two or three gigs with a couple of girls, Julie and Jackie, and we all had blonde hair, so that's when we started fooling around with the name Blondie. I had always been called 'blondie' by assorted motorists and truck drivers and thought it was a good name, a natural (HA!), so easy to remember."

"When asked about other names they considered at the time, he recalled, 'Catharsis was one. Herpes Simplex was another. Those were the two working names. We ditched Catharsis because no one could pronounce it, and we ditched Herpes Simplex because they probably wouldn't have let us use it anyway.'"

—AL KOOPER, BLOOD, SWEAT & TEARS

BLOOD, SWEAT & TEARS Al Kooper formed Blood, Sweat & Tears in New York City in 1967 as an experimental rock band that would incorporate jazz, blues, folk, and classical elements into its sound. Kooper remembered, "I was playing in an all-night jam session, and I had cut my finger and I didn't know it. When they turned the lights on at the end, the organ keyboard was covered with blood. So I called everybody over, and I said, 'Wouldn't this make a great album cover, for a band called Blood, Sweat & Tears?' And so we called it that, except we didn't use that picture because no one had a camera." The phrase, Kooper noted, is "borrowed from a Winston Churchill speech. That's where it originated." When asked about other names they considered at the time, he recalled, "Catharsis was one. Herpes Simplex was another. Those were the two working names. We ditched Catharsis because no one could pronounce it, and we ditched Herpes Simplex because they probably wouldn't have let us use it anyway."

BLUE CHEER The band, best known for their crunching cover of Eddie Cochran's "Summertime Blues," formed in Boston in 1967 and took their name from a particularly high-quality strain of LSD.

BLUE ÖYSTER CULT An early version of the group was launched at the State University of New York at Stony Brook on Long Island in 1967 by Sandy Pearlman, who would later become a writer for the rock magazine *Crawdaddy*. One day in 1971, when Pearlman was trying to come up with a new name for the band, he found himself standing outside a New York City restaurant with fellow music journalist Richard Meltzer, who had been in an earlier version of the group. Pearlman glanced at a menu in the window and Blue Point oysters caught his eye: "I said, 'Why don't we call it Blue Oyster Cult?' And Richard said, 'And we'll add an umlaut over the O!' And I said, 'Great.' (The umlaut) was meant to bring all sorts of ambiguous implications to the name."

BLUR The band formed in 1988 in Colchester, England, as Seymour, named for the J.D. Salinger character Seymour Glass who appeared in a number of Salinger's stories. When they signed with Food Records in 1990, the label insisted they change their name and gave them a list of alternatives. From that list, which included the names the Shining Path, the Government, Sensitize, and Whirlpool, they chose Blur.

BON IVER Singer-songwriter Justin Vernon took his stage name, Bon Iver, from the French phrase *bon hiver* (pronounced "bone ee-VARE"), meaning "good winter." It was a greeting he heard on the TV series *Northern Exposure*. In 2006, he left Raleigh, North Carolina, to spend the winter in a cabin his father owned in Dunn County, Wisconsin, Vernon's home state. While recovering from mononucleosis, he began watching *Northern Exposure* on DVD. In one episode of the show—season five, episode ten, to be exact—the residents of the fictional town of Cicely, Alaska, take to the streets as the first snow of the season begins falling and wish each other "bon hiver." Vernon wrote the phrase down as "boniverre." When he learned the correct spelling, he chose not to use the H in "hiver" because it looked too much like "liver," the epicenter of his illness.

THE BOOMTOWN RATS Ireland's Boomtown Rats had a hit in the US in 1980 with "I Don't Like Mondays," but they're best known for the charitable activities of front man Bob Geldof, who organized Live Aid in 1985. When the band first formed, they went through a variety of names before settling on the Boomtown Rats. Geldof explained, "I had been reading Woody Guthrie's autobiography, *Bound for Glory*. I had reached the part where, at the age of about eleven, oil was discovered in his hometown in Oklahoma. Teams of casual laborers moved in, and the place became a boomtown. A split had developed between the native kids and the children of the newcomers. Excluded from existing gangs, the new kids formed their own. It was called the Boomtown Rats. Even at that tender age Woody could spot the moral discrepancy and left his old friends to join the new gang. As a result, the two gangs eventually merged."

BOSTON Guitarist and keyboard player Tom Scholz formed Boston in 1976. When asked who came up with the name, Jim Collins, who worked for the management company that represented the group, said it wasn't Scholz: "He says he doesn't know exactly who thought up the name. It wasn't Tom, and there are about five or six people who claim that they made it up, all of whom would have some varying levels of credibility. He says all that he recalls is that he approved the name. There was a list of about eighty names going around and that was one that he liked, but he was a lot more concerned about the music than he was about the name. He likes it now, though. I was trying to think of some really good story to tell you, like that he wanted to use Chicago but it was already taken. The truth of it is kind of lost in the pages of history, as it were."

DAVID BOWIE Born David Robert Jones in 1947, he changed his surname to Bowie in 1966 to avoid confusion with Davy Jones of the Monkees. He chose the new moniker in honor of the hunting knife frequently referred to in American films.

BOW WOW WOW Sex Pistols manager Malcolm McLaren formed Bow Wow Wow in 1980, after pairing Adam Ant's original backup band with singer Annabella Lwin, a fourteen-year-old native of Burma whom he discovered working at his local dry cleaner. McLaren got the band signed to EMI, the label that had signed and then dumped the Sex Pistols in 1977. He named them Bow Wow Wow in honor of Nipper, the dog who was known to Americans as the trademark of the RCA Corporation, but in England was the mascot of HMV (His Master's Voice) Ltd., the music retailer owned by EMI.

THE BOX TOPS Led by Alex Chilton, the band formed in Memphis, Tennessee, in 1967 and had a series of hits, including "The Letter," which went to number one that year. Wayne Carson Thompson, who wrote the song, recalled the group hadn't decided on a name by the time they recorded it: "One of the guys said, 'Well, let's have a contest (to name the group) and everybody can send in fifty cents and a box top.' Dan (Penn, the song's producer) looked at me and I looked him, and he said, 'Hell, that sounds great,' and named 'em the Box Tops."

BREAD The soft-rock band Bread formed in Los Angeles in 1969 and in three years released eleven Top 40 hits and earned six gold records. The band chose the name Bread after getting stuck in traffic behind a Barbara Ann bread delivery truck.

THE BREEDERS Twin sisters Kim and Kelley Deal first formed the Breeders in their native Ohio, before Kim moved to Boston and joined the Pixies in 1986. Kim recalled, "My good friend is gay, and we were in a bar together one night. I commented on some guy, and all I remember my friend saying was 'Oh'—in disgust—'he's a breeder.' I thought, 'Wow, we're like little rats in the corner copulating.' It was funny, kind of turning the tables. For so long, heterosexuals, especially guys, would say things like 'Homos gross me out, man.' But now it was a homosexual saying, 'Oh, well, they're breeders.' And one of the girls in the band, Josephine Wiggs, is a lesbian, so it's particularly funny in that way." Some music journalists not in on the joke initially took the band's name at face value. "They thought we're like cows. The Mother Earth cow crap or something—like we're motherhood. I hope they don't think that anymore."

BRIGHT EYES No, Conor Oberst did not take his band's name from the line in the Bonnie Tyler song "Total Eclipse of the Heart" that goes, "Turn around bright eyes, every now and then I fall apart." Nor was it from the name that Charlton Heston's character is given by talking chimps in *Planet of the Apes*. But it was, in fact, inspired by a movie. Oberst explained, "I was staying up late one night watching Turner Movie Classics. I can't remember the name of the movie, but the main Humphrey Bogart–type dude kept calling the girl 'bright eyes,' a term of endearment."

> "I was staying up late one night watching Turner Movie Classics. I can't remember the name of the movie, but the main Humphrey Bogart–type dude kept calling the girl 'bright eyes,' a term of endearment." —CONOR OBERST, BRIGHT EYES

BROKEN SOCIAL SCENE Kevin Drew and Brendan Canning formed the band in Toronto in 1999. Drew recalled, "I went on tour ... playing keyboards for a friend's band, and I had this really elaborate setup with lots of different keyboards. I was a keyboard freak back then. When the tour was over, I came back to Toronto and played a Sunday night show under the name John Tesh Jr. and the Broken Social Scene. The John Tesh Jr. part was because of the keyboards (a nod to the smooth musical stylings of the former *Entertainment Tonight* cohost). The Broken Social Scene part just sort of popped into my head, I think. But Brendan said that the Broken Social Scene was a great name for a band and that's what we went with. A writer friend of mine told me to drop 'the,' though, and just have it be Broken Social Scene. I was kind of thinking of using the name Broken Membership for a while, but Brendan wasn't feeling it."

BROWNSVILLE STATION The band formed in Ann Arbor, Michigan, in the early seventies and had a big hit in 1973 with "Smokin' in the Boy's Room." Guitarist Cub Koda recalled: "It was a week before our very first gig and we still didn't have a name for the band yet. Every guy in the band seemed to want to call it something else. One guy wanted to call it the City. We thought that was too ominous for the style of music that we played. Another guy wanted to name it after that Moby Grape song, 'Omaha.' We nixed that right away. I wanted to call it the Amazing Pelicans, which got vetoed like right quick. Our drummer at the time, T.J. Cronley, was a major-league hitchhiker. The guy would hitchhike to gigs and beat us there, and he said, 'Well, you know, boys, we're playing a lot of Southern rock 'n' roll, rockabilly, that kind of music where it all comes from the South—we should name it after the southernmost city in the United States, which is Brownsville, Texas.' We thought, 'Well—Brownsville? I don't know.' Then it got back to sort of generic names, and someone decided to call it the Station. Then we started thinking that was too bland, it should have more pizzazz to it. What would be, like, the funkiest place on earth? To which T.J. again said, 'Why, that's simple, lads—the Greyhound bus station in Brownsville, Texas. Irresponsible border guards, naked kids running around with flies attached to them, sensational ambience in the men's room—it's wonderful.' Well, we were all on the floor laughing, and it just seemed obvious. So we said, 'That's it.' We didn't realize that five, six, seven, eight years down the line, with eleven letters in Brownsville, most of our marquee appearances at rock/ hippie theaters would have our name reduced down to 'Brown Sta.'"

BUFFALO SPRINGFIELD Buffalo Springfield helped pioneer country rock during their brief career from 1966 to 1968. Originally called the Herd, the band changed their name after spotting the words Buffalo Springfield on a steamroller. Dewey Martin recalled, "I lugged my drums over to this old house on Fountain Avenue. They were paving the streets, I remember. And there was this steamroller out front with a big sign on the side that read "Buffalo-Springfield." When I walked into the house, the guys were already talking about taking that as a group name, and I thought, 'Yeah, what a great name—Buffalo Springfield.'"

BUSH The band took their name from the Shepherd's Bush area of London, where they formed in the mid-nineties. The fact that bush is also British slang for marijuana was also a factor, as was, perhaps, its reference to pubic hair.

BUTTHOLE SURFERS Butthole Surfers formed in 1980 in San Antonio, Texas. Guitarist Paul Leary recalled: "It gets complicated. We started out as the Dick Clark Five back in San Antonio, Texas. We had this deal about wanting to change the name of the band for every show that we did, so the next show we were the Dick Gas Five, and then we were Nine Foot Worm Makes Own Food. Then we started playing in Austin as that, and then we were the Vodka Family Winstons, and we were Abe Lincoln's Bush. Then we were the Inalienable Right to Eat Fred Astaire's Asshole, and then the

"I can't remember who it was that got up
At the end of that night we got paid a
we were going to get rich, and we stuck

next show we were just plain the Right to Eat Fred Astaire's Asshole. Then one night we were playing as something really ridiculous, I think it was Independent Worm Saloon. We had a song that Gibby (Haynes, the singer) wrote called 'Butthole Surfer,' and we were getting ready to play as Independent Worm Saloon, and some guy got up—I think it might have been Chris Gates from the Big Boys, or somebody, I can't remember who it was that got up—and introduced us as 'the Butthole Surfers.' At the end of that night we got paid a hundred and fifty bucks, so we thought we were going to get rich, and we stuck with that name and, well, here we are."

THE BUZZCOCKS Pete Shelley and Howard Devoto decided to form their band after seeing the Sex Pistols play twice in one weekend in London in February 1976. The band's name came from a review in British magazine *Time Out* of *Rock Follies*, a TV sitcom about an all-girl rock band that concluded, "Get a buzz, cock." In American vernacular, this roughly translates to "Check it out, dude."

and introduced us as 'the Butthole Surfers.'
hundred and fifty bucks, so we thought
with that name and, well, here we are."
—PAUL LEARY, BUTTHOLE SURFERS

THE BYRDS The Byrds were called the Jet Set when they first got together in 1964, named by group leader Roger McGuinn, who was fascinated by airplanes and flight. When they signed to Columbia Records later that year, the band—all hard-core anglophiles—had become the Beefeaters, after the royal guard in England, in an effort to pass themselves off as British. They renamed themselves the Byrds on Thanksgiving Day that year, misspelling their name like the Beatles, whom they would soon be compared to. Drummer Michael Clarke recalled: "It was over Thanksgiving dinner, and everything was happening at the moment with the letter B—the Beach Boys, the Beatles. We decided on Birds and then changed the 'i' to a 'y.' It gave it a bit of flair, I think."

CABARET VOLTAIRE Sheffield, England's prolific Cabaret Voltaire took their name in 1973 from the Zurich café that served as headquarters for Swiss dadaists in the years before World War I. It was the band's intention to apply the dadaist aesthetic doctrine of irrational disturbance to music, using found sounds and tape manipulations.

CAGE THE ELEPHANT The band got their start in Bowling Green, Kentucky, in 2006. Singer Matt Shultz remembered: "We played as Perfect Confusion for a while. That was a terrible name. We thought of it in high school. It was our version of a trippy band name. New Young Lovers is another one I remember being thrown around." According to Shultz, the name Cage the Elephant was inspired by an incident outside of an early show: "We were in Knoxville, Tennessee, hanging outside a club after a show—this is probably in 2006—and we saw this guy with a shaved head and a long goatee yelling and screaming and talking to himself. I'm pretty sure he had some mental issues going on. He all of a sudden beelined towards us. Everyone jumped into our car and shut the doors. But I didn't make it into the car. I was stuck outside. I thought for sure the guy was gonna stab me or something, but then he came up to me and gave me a hug. The whole time he was saying, 'You have to cage the elephant, you have to cage the elephant.' Afterwards, I was like, 'We gotta name the band that.'"

CAKE Alt-rock band CAKE formed in Sacramento, California, in 1991. Singer John McCrea explained, "It was chosen mostly for its phonetic power. It just has a lot of phonetic momentum. It's a four-letter word but without all the other baggage. Do you know what I mean? It's very abrupt sounding. It looks good on a poster. I used to make all of our posters in the early years, and there's nothing like a four-letter word just sort of juxtaposed with some sort of two-dimensional iconic graphic beneath it to confuse people and generate curiosity. In the back of my mind, I thought, 'Marie Antoinette' ("Let them eat cake"), but we were more thinking about 'cake' as a verb than as a noun—as if you were to find some dried banana caked on your corduroy trousers. Or mud caked on your shoe sort of thing. Or layers of culture or whatever."

CAMPER VAN BEETHOVEN Camper Van Beethoven made their mark in the eighties by combining an absurdist sense of humor and an eclectic musical style. The name was suggested by David McDaniel, one of the band's original guitarists. Lead singer David Lowery noted that "McDaniel was into this stuff that would sound like it made sense, but really it didn't. He'd watch a lot of TV, accept all this mass media stuff, and spit it out all chopped up." The name is a cross between a camper van and composer Ludwig van Beethoven.

CAN The krautrock band formed in Cologne, West Germany, in 1968, first as Inner Space, then the Can, and finally Can. The band allegedly liked the name because it meant different things in a variety of languages: the Turkish word *can*, pronounced "chan," means life or soul; the Japanese word *kan* means feeling or emotion; and the Japanese word *chan* means love when used in salutation. Keyboard player Irmin Schmidt has said that the name is an acronym for "communism, anarchism, nihilism."

CAPTAIN BEEFHEART When he was thirteen, Don Van Vliet moved with his family from Los Angeles to Lancaster, California. There he met Frank Zappa, a classmate at Antelope Valley High School, who nicknamed him Captain Beefheart because he seemed to have a "beef in his heart" against the world.

THE CARS The band's name was suggested in 1976 by drummer David Robinson. Singer and guitarist Ric Ocasek liked the name because, he said, "It's so easy to spell. It doesn't have a Z on the end. It's real authentic. It's pop art, in a sense."

CAT POWER Cat Power is the stage name of singer Charlyn "Chan" Marshall and was originally the name of her first band. The name is not a reference to cats but to Caterpillar, the company that makes heavy-duty construction vehicles. When the band formed in 1990, Marshall was living in Atlanta and playing music with a loose collective of local musicians. When they were invited to open for another band, they quickly needed to come up with a name. Marshall recalled that she was working at a pizzeria when guitarist Mark Moore called her to discuss the name: "There was a line of people. Mark was yellin', 'We need a name!' This old man came in wearing a 'Cat Diesel Power' cap. I was like, 'Cat Power!' and hung up the phone."

> "There was a line of people. Mark was yellin', 'We need a name!' This old man came in wearing a 'Cat Diesel Power' cap. I was like, 'Cat Power!' and hung up the phone." —CHAN MARSHALL, CAT POWER

THE CHAINSMOKERS Alex Pall originally formed the Chainsmokers with fellow New York University student Rhett Bixler in New York

City in 2012. After Bixler left the group, he was replaced by Andrew Taggart. Their name was inspired by Pall's marijuana usage and chosen because the domain name thechainsmokers.com was available. Pall explained, "At the time of conception it was totally just like, I was in college. You know, I enjoyed smoking weed and you know it was just like such a 'Yeah, the domain's open, I don't have to have any, like, underscores.'" Noted Taggart, "Honestly, we never thought it was all going to be this big. Alex used to smoke, it seemed clever, and the domains were open. We do love it . . . but no baby formula advertisements for us sadly 'cause of it."

THE CHAMPS The band formed in Los Angeles in 1957 when the members, working as session men for the Challenge label that was founded by singing cowboy Gene Autry, got together to record instrumental tracks for another artist. Using some leftover studio time, they decided to lay down some additional tracks and release their own single. Needing a group name, someone suggested the Champs in honor of Gene Autry's horse, Champion. "Train to Nowhere" bombed, but then DJs discovered the B side, "Tequila," which became a huge hit.

CHEAP TRICK The band formed in Rockford, Illinois, in 1974. An early incarnation was known as Sick Man of Europe, from a term for a European country in economic decline that was first used by Tsar Nicholas of Russia to describe the Ottoman Empire in the mid-nineteenth century. The name Cheap Trick was inspired by a concert by the band Slade. Bass player Tom Petersson recalled, "Rick (Nielsen, the guitarist) and I were in Philadelphia and we were at a Slade concert. We didn't have much money, but we blew it on going to see Slade. They came out and they had glitter platforms, they had glitter in their teeth, they were doing everything. It was comical, we knew that. And I looked at Rick and I said, 'God, these guys are doing every cheap trick in the book.' Which was true. And then he goes, 'Wow, that would be a great band name.' And I go, 'Ah, I don't know about that.'"

CHICAGO Originally called the Big Thing, the band was renamed the Chicago Transit Authority by James Guercio when he took over the band's management in 1967. Guercio recalled: "I came up with the name because I grew up on the northwest side of Chicago and I had a hell of a time getting to school. I used to have to take the bus. It was called the Chicago Transit Authority. I said, 'This is the name, this is what the band'll be called,' and that was it. There wasn't much discussion. Where there was discussion was, after the first album, Mayor Daley and the City of Chicago were threatening litigation. I was not authorized to use the name of the Chicago transit system to name a band, and I hadn't copyrighted it, I hadn't paid them a royalty, so we would've gotten sued. The group is not aware of a lot of this because I was in control of all the marketing and was producing and managing the band. And I was a little too autocratic. . . . Anyway, I did not want to change the name from the Chicago Transit Authority. But people were saying, 'It's too long. So you're from Chicago, so you took the bus—nobody's going to remember it. You ought to just shorten it to Chicago.' And I really wasn't responding to the arguments, but I was convinced by David Geffen. He and I were old friends from when he was in the mailroom (at the William Morris Agency). Geffen talked me into it. He just said, 'Call them Chicago. We can remember Chicago. Why are you hanging on to CTA? You're getting sued.' I've got to give David the credit. I talked to the band and said, 'Boys, we'll shorten the name and call ourselves Chicago.' I had designed all those logos. The minute they fired me, they put their picture on the cover."

THE CHIPMUNKS The Chipmunks, a novelty animated band, were created in 1958 by Ross Bagdasarian, who, as David Seville, had a number-one hit earlier that year with "Witch Doctor," a novelty song that featured sped-up voices. Bagdasarian said he was driving through Yosemite National Park in California when he came upon a chipmunk who refused to budge from the road. Inspiration struck. (The car did not.) Bagdasarian recorded "The Chipmunk Song" and named the trio of singing cartoon rodents after executives at his record label, Liberty. Alvin was named for company president Al Bennett, Simon for his partner Si Waronker, and Theodore for recording engineer Ted Keep. "The Chipmunk Song" hit number one that year and sold millions.

CHUBBY CHECKER Chubby Checker was born Ernest Evans and got the nickname Chubby from a friend at the poultry market where he worked. After Evans was signed to Philadelphia's Cameo-Parkway label, Dick Clark's wife, Bobbie, suggested he call himself Chubby Checker, a pun on Fats Domino, whom he was adept at impersonating.

CHUMBAWAMBA The band formed in Leeds, England, in 1982. Lead guitarist Allan Mark "Boff" Whalley explained: "There's a theory that an infinite amount of chimpanzees sitting at an infinite amount of typewriters will eventually, hitting the keys at random, lead to one of them writing the entire works of Shakespeare. Several scientists have tested this logic in order to try to put some kind of context of time and possibility into it. There was an article in something like *The Enquirer* or *The English Observer* in the late seventies which printed a list of words which a chimpanzee had actually typed. Predictably enough, none made any sense whatsoever. So in the quest to avoid finding a name which had immediate pigeonhole possibilities, in 1982 Danbert (Nobacon, vocals and keyboards) was blindfolded and placed in front of a typewriter: an Olivetti Dora, in fact, with a green case. He typed a list of words, filling an A4-size piece of paper, and from that resulting list we found the word 'chumbawamba.' Really. That's it. Sounded good to say, looked weird, so we kept it."

CHVRCHES The Scottish trio chose the name Churches when they came together in Glasgow in 2011 because they liked the way it sounded and said it has no religious connotation. They changed the U to a Roman V so the band would be easier to find in an Internet search. Observed lead singer Lauren Mayberry, "It's a strange concept: 'This is what you should refer to us collectively as, and we will answer to nothing but that.' It's quite silly if you think about it. I think we just wanted something that had a strong visual element and that was short and powerful, and I think that's what we came up with. But I maintain that any names of great bands are quite silly when you think about them. Like Radiohead is quite a silly name, but it's a great name, you know what I mean? I think names take on their own meaning when you listen to the music of the band."

CIRCLE JERKS Singer Keith Morris formed the band in Los Angeles in 1979 after he left Black Flag. He remembers: "Greg (Hetson, the guitarist) and I were over at Raymond Pettibon's house—he's the guy that did all the artwork for Black Flag in the beginning. We were over there getting the artwork for some flyers, and we didn't have a name for the band. We were originally going to call ourselves the Plastic Hippies or the Runs, and we decided those names weren't really anything particularly outstanding. Pettibon had an American slang dictionary there. We started flipping through it and I came across 'circle jerk,' and I thought, 'Wow, that's kind of interesting.' I looked at Greg, and he looked at me, and he kind of said, 'Yeah, this looks like something that we could use; this looks like something that could be permanent.'"

When asked if he was glad they chose it, Morris said, "Yeah, I mean, it never bothered me, when I found out what it meant. It was really—it was just a really stupid name. If you look at all these band names, they're just really stupid names, and the more stupid the name, the more outstanding it is, I guess. Or the more memorable. We weren't able to be mentioned in a lot of newspapers, say in the Bible Belt. We were referred to as the C.J.'s. Just like the Dead Kennedys and the Butthole Surfers. Even the *L.A. Times* won't put Butthole Surfers in the newspaper; it's the B.H. Surfers. We've told people that it meant like six guys in a van driving around in circles—which happened to us quite a bit. Say like we would pull into a city, say like in Boston, the way the streets are set up, it's very easy to get lost. We just kind of made up things like that."

"'Yeah, I mean, it never bothered me, when I found out what it meant. It was really—it was just a really stupid name. . . . We weren't able to be mentioned in a lot of newspapers, say in the Bible Belt.'" —KEITH MORRIS, CIRCLE JERKS

THE CLASH The Clash formed in London in 1976. Bassist Paul Simonon recalled, "We had plenty of names that only lasted five minutes before being chucked out the window. There was the Weak Heart Drops, after the Big Youth record, the Outsiders, and Psycho Negatives, and the Mirrors. . . . I was looking through the *Evening Standard* with the idea of names on my mind, and I noticed that the word 'clash' appeared a few times. I thought the Clash would be a good name. So I suggested it to the others."

CLEAN BANDIT The band members met in 2008 when they were undergraduates at Cambridge University. Grace Chatto and Jack

Patterson studied in Moscow for a year, where they picked up the Russian phrase *chistaya banditka*, which translates to "clean bandit" and is meant as an affectionate insult. Chatto explains, "A 'clean bandit' is a total bastard. A Russian friend of ours used the phrase to describe my sister and we found it funny and took it for our band name."

THE COASTERS The Coasters, considered one of the most influential vocal groups of the rock 'n' roll era, began as the Robins in Los Angeles in the late forties. In 1955, after two of the Robins left the group, the remaining members changed their name to the Coasters, in honor of their West Coast origins.

COBRA STARSHIP Gabe Saporta launched Cobra Starship as a solo project in New York City in 2006. He eventually enlisted other members, including guitarist Ryland Blackinton, who explained that the name "came from two jackets that Gabe owned. One said 'Cobra' on the back and the other said 'Starship Disco,' so he just put two cool things together." The fact that one of their first hits was featured on the soundtrack for the movie *Snakes on a Plane* was purely coincidental.

COCTEAU TWINS When the band formed in Grangemouth, Scotland, in 1973, they took their name from the song "Cocteau Twins" by fellow Scotsmen Johnny and the Self-Abusers, who later renamed themselves Simple Minds. The song was eventually released by Simple Minds as "No Cure."

COLDPLAY Lead singer and pianist Chris Martin and lead guitarist Jonny Buckland met at University College London in 1996 when they were introduced by fellow student and musician Tim Crompton. Martin and Buckland formed a band they called Pectoralz. They eventually re-named themselves Starfish. Crompton suggested the name the Coldplay, which he had used briefly for his own band. Drummer Will Champion, who had joined the band by this point, remembered, "Tim had a band that used to go through six names every week, and the Coldplay was one of the ones he came up with, so we just took it." The name came from a little-known book of poems called *Child's Reflections, Cold Play*, published in 1997. The book is described on Amazon as a "stark collection of poetry (that) escapes the stylistic and structural conformity to explore the psychological realms, combining the surreal with the natural which results in a startling and provocative ambiguity."

COLD WAR KIDS The group formed in Fullerton, California, in 2004 and adopted the name Cold War Kids after considering the Reds and the Nudes. Bassist Matt Maust explained: "I had the name six or seven years before the band started—so probably since 1997. I was traveling in Eastern Europe with my brother. There's this big park in Budapest where they dumped all these statues that had been removed after Communism fell. Now it's just a place where people can go and have picnics. There's a playground there. So being in that environment just made the phrase 'cold war kids' pop into my head. I may have heard it before. I'm a cold war kid too—I was born in 1979. Originally, I used the name for a website I had where I posted art and poems. Then when I started playing music with the guys, they thought it would be a good name for the band too."

COLLECTIVE SOUL The band formed in Atlanta in the early nineties. Guitarist Ed Roland explained: "I was reading the book *The Fountainhead* by Ayn Rand, and I just came across a part that said 'collective soul.' We were in a little transitional period, trying to rename the band. We were called Marching Two-Step, and everyone thought we were a country act. So we decided to change the name and that's basically the only name we could decide on."

THE COMMODORES The Commodores began as a funk band in 1970 after meeting at the Tuskegee Institute as freshmen. At first called the Jays, they became the Commodores after horns player William King picked the name out of the dictionary. They later joked that they were almost called the Commodes.

> "Michael Stipe of R.E.M. came up with the name, and I don't even think he knows what it means. And I've never asked him." —JOHNETTE NAPOLITANO, CONCRETE BLONDE

CONCRETE BLONDE The band originally formed in Los Angeles in 1982 as Dream 6. Singer Johnette Napolitano said of the name Concrete Blonde, "Michael Stipe of R.E.M. came up with the name, and I don't even think he knows what it means. And I've never asked him."

ALICE COOPER Before there was Alice Cooper the man, there was Alice Cooper the band. Cooper was born Vincent Damon Furnier, the son of a minister, in Detroit in 1948. He formed a band called the Earwigs in Phoenix in 1965, which he later changed to the Nazz, only to learn that there was another band using the name on the East Coast—Todd Rundgren's group. He said he doesn't know where the name Alice Cooper came from: "I have no idea. I really don't. It was one day, just boom. We needed a new name and I said, 'Why don't we call ourselves . . .' and I could have said 'Mary Smith,' but I said 'Alice Cooper.' And that was the name. But think about it—Alice Cooper has the same kind of ring as Lizzie Borden and Baby Jane. 'Alice Cooper.' It's sort of like a little girl with an ax. I kept picturing something in pink and black lace and blood. Meanwhile, people expected a blond folk singer." Cooper eventually adopted the band's name as his own.

ELVIS COSTELLO Born Declan MacManus (not McManus, as sometimes reported) in Liverpool, England, he changed his name at the
insistence of manager Jake Riviera when he signed to Riviera's Stiff
Records in 1976. Costello explained, "I hadn't picked the name at
all. Jake just picked it. It was just a marketing scheme. 'How are we
going to separate you from Johnny This and Johnny That?' He said,
'We'll call you Elvis.' I thought he was completely out of his mind."
Costello is a family name on his mother's side.

> "I can remember being eight years old and having infinite
> possibilities. But life ends up being so much less than we
> thought it would be when we were kids."
> —ADAM DURITZ, COUNTING CROWS

COUNTING CROWS Formed in San Francisco in 1991, the band took
their name from a line in the 1989 independent film *Signs of Life*, also
known as *One for Sorrow, Two for Joy* that starred Vincent D'Onofrio
and featured singer Adam Duritz's real-life love interest Mary-Louise
Parker. D'Onofrio's character says, "It's something my mom used to
say, 'counting crows.' She used to say, 'It's one for something, two for
something, three for something,'" but he can't remember the details.
"One for Sorrow" is a traditional children's nursery rhyme about
magpies, which are birds in the crow family. According to an old
superstition, the number of magpies one sees determines whether one's
luck will be good or bad. A common version goes:

> One for sorrow,
> Two for joy,
> Three for a girl,
> Four for a boy,

Five for silver,
Six for gold,
Seven for a secret,
Never to be told.
Eight for a wish,
Nine for a kiss,
Ten for a bird,
You must not miss.

The phrase "counting crows" is referenced in the band's song "Murder of One" from their debut album:

Well, I dreamt I saw you walkin' up a hillside in the snow,
Casting shadows on the winter sky as you stood there counting crows

Duritz said of the song, whose theme echoes that of the movie *Signs of Life*, "I can remember being eight years old and having infinite possibilities. But life ends up being so much less than we thought it would be when we were kids, with relationships that are so empty and stupid and brutal. If you don't find a way to break the chain and change in some way, then you wind up, as the rhyme goes: a murder of one, for sorrow." A group of crows is called a "murder."

COUNTRY JOE AND THE FISH Formed in San Francisco in 1965, Country Joe and the Fish were one of the most political of the Bay Area psychedelic bands. Guitarist Joe McDonald explains, "In 1965 I was working on a magazine called *Rag Baby* with a guy named Ed Denson, who owned Takoma Records along with John Fahey. We didn't have any copy for an issue, and so we decided to put out a "talking issue" of the magazine. I had written 'Fixing to Die Rag' a little bit earlier, and it was popular, so we decided we would put 'Fixing to Die

Rag' on there, and a song, 'Superbird,' and two songs by Peter Krug, one about the Watts riots, which had just happened. So we recorded it all, and it was the first recording of 'Fixing to Die Rag'—skiffle band, kind of washboard, and washtub bass and stuff. . . . Afterwards, Ed realized that we had to have some label copy and decided that, because he was into folk music and politics, he would call the group that we had assembled and recorded that day Country Mao and the Fish. I asked him why, and he said, 'Because Mao Zedong had said that the revolutionaries move through the people like the fish through the sea.' And I said, 'Hmm, wow, that's a little bit . . . dumb.' And he said, 'Well, OK, we'll call it Country Joe and the Fish after Joseph Stalin.' And I had been named after Joseph Stalin coincidentally, and I said, 'OK, well, Country Joe and the Fish sounds at least not as dumb as Country Mao and the Fish.' Then it was released, and that was really the beginning of Rag Baby Records, and the beginning of Country Joe and the Fish. I was the only Joe in the group, and I was the lead vocalist, so people began calling me Country Joe. Ultimately what happened was that people left the group and sold out their interest in the name, and by the end—'69 I believe it was, or '70—we, Barry Melton and myself, finally signed a piece of paper which he interprets as saying that he is the Fish. So when we play together in a week or so, it'll be 'Country Joe' McDonald and Barry 'the Fish' Melton. It's evolved to that. He's become a lawyer, so we don't argue with him anymore."

THE CRAMPS Singer Lux Interior and guitarist Ivy Rorschach met in Cleveland in the mid-seventies. They chose the Cramps, Rorschach explained, because it sounded like a street gang and had a variety of meanings: "It's an involuntary physical reaction. It's something that your mind can't control. In France, it's a sexual disturbance for men—it's slang for hard-on—so it applies to men and (to) women" in regards to menstrual pains."

THE CRANBERRIES The band formed in Limerick, Ireland, in the late eighties. Their name was originally the Cranberry Saw Us, with the last two words occasionally hyphenated, a play on "cranberry sauce." It was suggested by the lead singer at the time, who was replaced in 1990 by Dolores O'Riordan. The new lineup eventually shortened their name to the Cranberry by the time they mailed demo tapes to several English record labels. The cassettes were marked "The Cranberry's," and when they received their first response, an otherwise encouraging rejection letter from Rough Trade, it was addressed to the Cranberries. The name stuck. Cranberries are not native to Ireland.

CRASH TEST DUMMIES The group started in the mid-eighties as a loose circle of friends who gathered at an after-hours club in Winnipeg, Canada, to play what lead singer and songwriter Brad Roberts said were "ridiculous cover tunes, everything from cheesy Irish traditional to TV theme songs to acoustic versions of Alice Cooper hits." They chose the name Crash Test Dummies as a joke, after considering the Chemotherapists and Skin Graft. "Eventually," Roberts recalled, "the band transformed into something other than just a weekend band. But the name stuck, because it had been written down so many times."

CREAM The short-lived supergroup, formed by Eric Clapton, Jack Bruce, and Ginger Baker in 1966, took the name Cream because the trio reportedly considered themselves the cream of the crop of British blues players.

CREED The band's original name when they first formed in Tallahassee, Florida, in 1993, was Naked Toddler, which was suggested by guitarist Mark Tremonti. Lead singer Scott Stapp recalled, "One night when we were jamming, Mark pulled a newspaper clipping out of his wallet that said something about the abduction of a naked toddler.

'I always thought that would be a great name for a band,' he said. We thought it was funny and teased him about it, but Mark wasn't the kind of guy who liked to be teased. Our first gig, at a club called Yanni's, was coming up, and to avoid conflict we called ourselves Naked Toddler. The name didn't go over well." After considering names like Backbone and Spine, the band asked bassist Brian Marshall about the names of his previous bands. One of them, Mattox Creed, caught their attention. "At that moment, Creed was born. I wasn't thinking in terms of a religious creed. My goal was simple: to create a rock 'n' roll band. The dictionary defines 'creed' as a system of Christian and/or other beliefs. But believe me, if any of the other guys had thought I had God in mind when the name came up, they would have shut it down—and I would have too. We didn't have the slightest intention of introducing anything spiritual into our music. Our ambition was to be a big-time rock band like Def Leppard or Metallica."

CREEDENCE CLEARWATER REVIVAL Begun in El Cerrito, California, in 1959 by guitarist John Fogerty, bassist Stu Cook, and drummer Doug Clifford, the band had a much less earthy-sounding name at first. Clifford rememebered: "Initially, we started as an instrumental trio called the Blue Velvets. Then Tom Fogerty (John's older brother) started coming to our gigs, and he used us to back him up on recordings to try and get a record deal for himself as a singer-songwriter. When he was doing that, we were Tommy Fogerty and the Blue Velvets. After that, we were the Visions for one week, until we found out that there was another Visions out there, and we didn't want to have problems with them. That's when (our) manager named us the Golliwogs." The band hated that name and decided they needed a new one, as well as a new direction. "In 1967, we decided not to be a part-time band—everybody was either a student or had a job. We decided that we were going to go for broke and be full-time musicians, so we had to quit everything else we were doing. At that time we also decided to change our name from the Golliwogs. We knew a fellow named Credence Newball and liked his name, but we thought if we had a hit, he'd probably sue us. So that didn't work, but we liked the idea of 'credence,' as in truth and justice and all that. We were very young and certainly idealistic. So we added an E to Credence to make it totally different, to indicate we were going to do our own thing and we weren't going to play acid rock anymore. Clearwater came from an Olympia beer commercial, and it had a great image—you know, the stream coming down, and it also had significance in the scheme of things in that it meant we had a clear direction. The revival was a revival of ourselves—we weren't going to wear the uniforms that this manager had for us, we weren't going to do things that we didn't want to do, we were going to take this thing and run with it, so to speak." Clifford said that "revival" didn't have anything to do with a more "rootsy" approach, "but a lot of people thought that. There were a lot of misconceptions, I guess, but that was really it. It was a revival of the four of us, a personal revival, if you will."

BUDDY HOLLY AND THE CRICKETS Buddy Holly formed the Crickets in 1957 with Jerry Allison on drums, Niki Sullivan on rhythm guitar, and Joe B. Mauldin on bass. Sullivan recalled, "We were at Jerry's house, and everything we thought of had been used or didn't fit. So Jerry got an encyclopedia, and somehow we got started on insects. There was a whole page of bugs. We thought about Grasshopper and quickly passed that over. And we did consider the name Beetles, but Jerry said, 'Aw, that's just a bug you'd want to step on,' so we immediately dropped that. Then Jerry came up with the idea of the Crickets. He said, 'Well, you know, they make a happy sound, they're a happy type of insect.' I remember him saying too, 'They make music by rubbing their legs together,' and that cracked us up. So we kept going and tried some other names, but finally we settled on the Crickets. You know, though, we really weren't happy with that name. In fact, at some point, we were laughed at—might have been the Cotton Club, just after our record was released. People kidded us about the name, about how dumb it was."

"In fact, at some point, we were laughed at—might have been the Cotton Club, just after our record was released. People kidded us about the name, about how dumb it was."
—BUDDY HOLLY AND THE CRICKETS

CROWDED HOUSE The band, which originally formed in Melbourne, Australia, in 1985, took their name from the cramped bungalow they shared in Hollywood, California, where they had come to record their debut album.

THE CULT The band began as the Southern Death Cult in 1982, became the Death Cult in 1983, and was finally reduced to the Cult in 1984. Their original name came from a headline that singer Ian Astbury spotted in a newspaper.

CULTURE CLUB Culture Club was formed in London in 1981 by singer Boy George, born George O'Dowd. After a very brief stint singing in front of Bow Wow Wow under the name Lieutenant

Lush, George formed his own band called In Praise of Lemmings, which evolved into Sex Gang Children. When drummer Jon Moss joined the band, he convinced George to change the name, arguing that it was too negative. The initial suggestion of Caravan Club became Can't Wait Club, and finally Culture Club, to reflect their diverse lineup.

THE CURE The band, led by singer and guitarist Robert Smith, was formed in Sussex, England, in the mid-seventies. They performed as Obelisk, Goat Band, and Malice, before becoming Easy Cure in 1977. Smith explained: "We decided we needed another name if we were going to start playing again, so one night in the middle of January 1977, we sat around in my kitchen discussing it. One of our songs was called 'Easy Cure,' a song written by Lol (Tolhurst, the band's drummer at the time), and eventually, in desperation, we settled on that." A year later, following the departure of original guitarist Porl Thompson, the band decided to change their name again. Smith remembered: "I had always thought Easy Cure was a bit hippyish, a bit American sounding, a bit West Coast, and I hated it, which put Lol's back up, as he'd thought of it. Every other group we liked had 'the' in front of their name, but the Easy Cure sounded stupid, so we just changed it to the Cure instead. It upset a few old fans but, well, there you are. I thought the Cure was much more it." The story that Smith named the band the Cure because his father was a pharmacist is false.

DAFT PUNK In 1992, the year before they became Daft Punk, electronic music stars Guy-Manuel de Homem-Christo and Thomas Bangalter started a short-lived indie rock band with future Phoenix member Laurent Brancowitz called Darlin' that was after the Beach Boys song of the same name. A review of two of their songs released on the *Shimmies in Super 8* compilation was referred to as "a daft punky thrash" by critic Dave Jennings in the May 1, 1993, issue of the British music publication *Melody Maker.*

THE DAMNED The seminal British punk band took their name in 1976, inspired by singer Dave Vanian, a gravedigger who often performed in a vampire outfit. They were originally called the Doomed.

DAMN YANKEES Guitarist Ted Nugent formed Damn Yankees in 1989 with former Styx guitarist Tommy Shaw, ex–Knight Ranger bassist Jack Blades, and drummer Michael Cartellone. Nugent explained: "(We) were in our early hours of discovery, jamming, when I called home to Michigan to see how my hunting buddies were doing. My friend asked what the hell Ted Nugent and Tommy Shaw could possibly sound like together, and I immediately responded that we sounded like a bunch of damn Yankees to me. I felt right away that we all shared a sense of origin, blues and American R&B in our preferred musical attitude, overtly Americana."

DANGER MOUSE Producer and musician Brian Joseph Burton took his stage name from *Danger Mouse*, an animated series that debuted on British television about a mouse who worked as a secret agent in a parody of English spy shows and movies. Burton used to DJ in a mouse outfit to conceal his identity. He co-founded the group Gnarls Barkley and has produced songs for U2, Beck, the Black Keys, Iggy Pop, and Parquet Courts, among others.

DASHBOARD CONFESSIONAL Chris Carrabba started Dashboard Confessional in Boca Raton, Florida, as a solo side project in 1999 while he was in the band Further Seems Forever. The name Dashboad Confessional was inspired by the opening lines to his song "The Sharp Hint of New Tears," which appeared on the debut album *The Swiss Army Romance*: "On the way home/This car hears my confessions/I think I'll take the long way."

THE DAVE MATTHEWS BAND The band formed in Charlottesville, Virginia, in 1991. Singer-songwriter and guitarist Dave Matthews observed, "It's pathetic that it ended up the Dave Matthews Band. I think it's a sign of laziness. And for a couple of years it was a sign of tension in the group—the idea that it was my band as opposed to a band. But it was the fault of everyone in the band. None of us had an idea. I'd like to take this chance to apologize, but it's served us well. It seems like a small victory that the not-very-creative name has carried us pretty fucking far. I hate to admit it, but we're pretty badass."

DEAD KENNEDYS Dead Kennedys formed in San Francisco in the late seventies. Singer Jello Biafra recalled: "I thought we should call ourselves Thalidomide, but nobody else really wanted that. (Guitarist East Bay) Ray suggested the Sharks—he was very conscious of wanting to survive and figured a record contract was the way to do it. My second choice for a name was Dead Kennedys. A couple of different people back in Colorado (in Boulder, where he lived before moving to San Francisco) came up with that but didn't have the nerve to use it. That was the one that seemed to provoke the most reaction—positive or negative—so I just began telling people that was the name of the band."

DEATH CAB FOR CUTIE The band began as a solo project of singer, guitarist, and keyboard player Ben Gibbard in 1997 when he was a student at Western Washington University in Bellingham, Washington. Death Cab for Cutie is named after a song from the Beatles' 1967 TV movie *Magical Mystery Tour* that was performed by the Bonzo Dog Doo-Dah Band. The song was itself a reference to a fictional pulp crime magazine story referenced in Richard Hoggart's 1957 cultural studies book *The Uses of Literacy*. When asked if he wished he had picked a better Beatles reference, Gibbard replied, "The name was never supposed to be something that someone was going to reference fifteen years on. So yeah, I would absolutely go back and give it a more obvious name."

THE DECEMBERISTS The name of the band, which formed in Portland, Oregon, in 2000, is a play on words. It's derived from the Decembrist revolt, a rebellion by Russian army officers and soldiers against Tsar Nicholas that took place on December 26, 1825. But according to lead vocalist, guitarist, and principal songwriter Colin Meloy, it's also "an allusion to the month of December and imagining the drama and melancholy of winter."

DEEE-LITE The name of the New York-based group, best known for their 1990 hit "Groove Is in the Heart," was inspired by the song "It's De-Lovely" from the 1936 Cole Porter musical *Red, Hot, and Blue*.

DEEP BLUE SOMETHING The band got its start in 1991 at the University of North Texas as Leper Messiah, a name taken from a line in David Bowie's "Ziggy Stardust." They decided to change their name because too many people assumed that they were a heavy metal band. The new name was coined when lead singer Todd Pipes asked his bandmates what they should call an instrumental that he had composed. Drummer John Kirtland recalls, "I said 'Deep Blue Something,' expecting him to fill in the last word. Instead, he said, 'That's pretty cool,' and it became the name of the band."

> "I said 'Deep Blue Something,' expecting him to fill in the last word. Instead, he said, 'That's pretty cool,' and it became the name of the band." —JOHN KIRTLAND, DEEP BLUE SOMETHING

DEEP PURPLE When the band took shape in 1968, they considered the name Concrete God but settled on Deep Purple at the urging of guitarist Ritchie Blackmore's grandmother after her favorite song, "Deep Purple," a number-one hit for Nino Tempo and April Stevens in 1963. If this seems like an unlikely inspiration for an act whose trademark was the hard-rocking sound characterized by their 1973 hit "Smoke on the Water," it's worth noting that their first two hits in 1968 were mellow revivals of Joe South's "Hush" and Neil Diamond's "Kentucky Woman." The name is not a reference to hickeys, as sometimes rumored.

DEERHOOF The band, formed in San Francisco in 1994, took their name from a recording of improvised bass and harmonica solos by original bassist Rob Fisk. The recording was released on tape in an edition of five copies, packaged in recycled Billy Squier promotional cassettes decorated with leaf fragments and spray painted black and gold. When asked why they chose the name, drummer Greg Saunier said, "If it had struck me as a strange band name at the time I probably would have vetoed it, but I thought it was a great name, nice and simple and cute. I guess I never understood what was odd or interesting about it, so I never know how to answer that question. Forgive me."

DEER TICK The indie rock band formed in Providence, Rhode Island, in 2004 as My Other Face. Lead singer and principal songwriter John J. McCauley says that the name was inspired by a hike in the Morgan-Monroe State Forest near Bloomington, Indiana, in the summer of 2005, when he found a deer tick on his scalp. It was the first time he had come in contact with one, despite having gone camping and fishing since childhood.

DEF LEPPARD The heavy metal band formed in Sheffield, England, in 1977. Singer Joe Elliott explained, "In 1975, when I was idling my time away in art class in school, instead of painting or drawing the obligatory bowl of fruit or vase with a rose in it, I used to design posters for rock bands and concerts, such as Led Zeppelin, the Beatles, the Who, the Rolling Stones. After a while, I ran out of bands, so I started making names up. I invented various names of bands, one of which was Deaf Leopard. When I left school, I took my art folder home, and somehow the badly put-together poster for the mythical band Deaf Leopard ended up on my bedroom wall. So when we all got together in my room to discuss the forming of a band and what we could call it, it was suggested, I think by Sav (bassist Rick Savage), 'Why don't we call our band Deaf Leopard?' He had seen the school-drawn, shitty poster. We all decided then and there—the majority of us, I don't think (guitarist) Pete Willis was too keen on it—that we thought it sounded good. Once we got into our little rehearsal space and were firing up, learning our new songs, the original drummer for the band, Tony

Kenning, suggested that we change the spelling of the name Deaf Leopard to Def Leppard because it didn't look good as it was. It was a little too 'punky' looking. There were a lot of punk bands out at the time with animals in their names—Boomtown Rats, Flying Lizards, Slaughter and the Dogs—and we didn't want 'spikies' showing up at our gigs. So Tony crossed the 'A' out of Deaf with a pen and stuck a stick on the 'O' to make a 'P.' But it wasn't until we rewrote the name without the 'A' that someone pointed out that it looked a bit like Led Zeppelin, but we couldn't be bothered with changing it by then. We'd rather be linked to Led Zeppelin than to Slaughter and the Dogs or the Flying Lizards. So we stuck with it. Any relevance to similarities between Def Leppard and Led Zeppelin are absolutely, 100 percent coincidence, even though we really are big fans of theirs."

DEFTONES The alternative metal band formed in Sacramento, California, in 1988. Vocalist and guitarist Chino Moreno remembered, "I always imagined being in a band, but I could never pick out a name. I was like, 'How do bands just pick their names?' You know, some bands, you got these metal bands that try to make their name all ugly and whatever. I wanted to pick a cool name, something that would just stand out but, you know, not be all cheeseball at the same time. Well, I was really into old classic music, like from the 1950s and shit like that. I was like, 'Tones,' you know, there's a lot of bands from that era that has 'the Tones' in it. And 'Def,' just 'cause I listen to a lot of LL Cool J, Public Enemy, you know, like Def Jam (Records) and all that. Then I thought, 'Deftones,' that would be kinda cool. 'Def' would be mean 'cool' and 'Tones' would be like the sound of the old days but being vague, 'cause we didn't do just one kind of music."

THE DEL FUEGOS The band formed in Boston in 1980. Singer and guitarist Dan Zanes named the band after Tierra del Fuego, the southernmost point in the world before Antarctica. Says Zanes, "We were looking for something as low down as you can get. Del Fuegos sort of said it all."

DEPECHE MODE In 1980, vocalist David Gahan joined synthesizer players Vince Clarke, Martin Gore, and Andy Fletcher, who were performing as Composition of Sound, to form a new band. Gahan remembers: "We were rehearsing for gigs in the spring of 1980 but were yet to agree on a name. I was attending Southend Technical College at the time, studying fashion, and I would sometimes refer to fashion magazines for ideas. One of these magazines was a French publication called *Depeche Mode* (which means 'fast fashion'), and the name just kind of stood out. I took a copy along to the next rehearsal, and the other three agreed that we should take the name."

DEREK AND THE DOMINOES Eric Clapton's band made its debut at the Lyceum in London in June 1970. He remembered: "Tony Ashton (of the group Ashton, Gardner & Dyke) suggested we call ourselves Del and the Dominoes because he always used to call me Del. So it became Derek and the Dominoes. It was the last minute in the dressing room before we went onstage at the Lyceum. We didn't have a name up to that point. You don't think of that when you're forming a group. In fact, when someone suggests to you that you get a band title, that's when you really start to worry about whether you should have a band at all, because you realize so much hinges on the name and you've blown the whole gig no matter what the gig is like."

MITCH RYDER AND THE DETROIT WHEELS Originally known as Billy Lee and the Rivieras in 1963, William Levise Jr. changed the name of his Detroit band in 1965, after landing a record deal. He picked his new stage name, Mitch Ryder, out of a phone book and rechristened the band the Detroit Wheels to make them sound more up-to-date.

DEVO Devo got their start in Akron, Ohio, in 1972, and were named after the band's philosophy of "de-evolution." Bassist Jerry Casale explained: "We thought that there wasn't progress, there was regression, and that things were falling apart. We called it 'de-evolution' and took the name and contracted it to Devo since it was more catchy."

DINOSAUR JR. The band was formed in 1984 in Amherst, Massachusetts, as Dinosaur. Guitarist J Mascis said he can't recall how he came up with the name: "I don't really remember, to tell you the truth. We just kind of thought it was cool." He said it was not a joking reference to classic rock, which is sometimes referred to as dinosaur rock, but that was indeed the intention of a Bay Area supergroup called the Dinosaurs made up of members of Big Brother and the Holding Company, Quicksilver Messenger Service, Jefferson Airplane, the Grateful Dead, and other bands from the psychedelic era. When the Dinosaurs threatened to sue Dinosaur, they forced a name change. Mascis lamented, "They just wanted us to change our name so their hippie buddies wouldn't go see us and think it was them. The guy, the Fish, Barry Melton (of Country Joe and the Fish), he's the lawyer, and his office is on Haight Street, so I guess that he became a lawyer after he became the Fish. . . . So we just thought of some stuff and came up with Junior, and that was OK with them." Mascis said he had no particular fondness for dinosaurs, but "now I get tons of dinosaur paraphernalia from my relatives, though I keep telling them no. My sister gave my dad a sweatshirt she made for his birthday that said Dinosaur Sr." When

"Some people still won't even say ['Junior']. It bothers them."
—J MASCIS, DINOSAUR JR.

asked if he regrets the name, he said, "I don't think about it. I mean, it bummed us out at the time to have to change it. Everyone hated the junior part. They'd all go, (singsong) 'Junior, Junior' . . . make fun of us . . . thought it was lame. Some people still won't even say ('Junior'). It bothers them."

DIRE STRAITS Guitarist Mark Knopfler launched Dire Straits in London in 1977, originally calling the band the Café Racers. Under that name, the band debuted at a festival headlined by Squeeze. A friend of drummer Pick Withers observed their sorry financial condition and suggested they call themselves Dire Straits, which they did for their second gig.

DISHWALLA The band formed in Santa Barbara, California, in 1993 and used several names before settling on Dishwalla. In September of that year, the *L.A. Times* noted: "First there was Life Talking, then dish and now dish walla. As the band keeps changing its name, they hope they can make the big time, and, perhaps, afford some capital letters." The band was forced to change their name from dish because another band with the same name threatened to sue. According to bassist Scot Alexander, "First off, no, I had nothing to do with it! Ha-ha, never liked it. The only thing that makes me OK with the name is the fact that many of my favorite bands—the Beatles, U2, Arctic Monkeys, etc.—have had stupid names, and it just goes to show how much it doesn't really matter. The 'walla' portion of the name was supposed to be a temporary fix. We were contacted by an attorney for a band called Dish (the name by which we were also called at the time). We were served a cease and desist letter and had to change the name. The keyboard player at the time, Greg Kolanek, was a tech nerd. Reading *Wired* magazine one day, he stumbled across an article about people pirating satellite television in India, calling them "dish-wallahs," and so we added the 'walla' on the end to get us through for a while till we found something better. The idea was we had a solid following growing and didn't want to change the name too much. Things happened quickly for the band, industry types started to take interest, and the rest is history!" The 1993 *Wired* article by Jeff Greenwald, titled "DISH-WALLAHS," begins: "Before the Gulf War, one of the most culturally prudish countries in the world had a choice of exactly one channel, Indian National Television. Then came the dish-wallahs." Greenwald says the band contacted him to get permission to use the name and gave him a little cash.

DR. FEELGOOD John "Wilko" Johnson started the band in 1971 in Canvey Island, England, taking the name from the 1962 song "Doctor Feel-Good" by bluesman Willie "Piano Red" Perryman, which was recorded under the name Dr. Feelgood and the Interns. The band did not take its name from a song by Johnny Kidd & the Pirates, as has been reported.

DOG'S EYE VIEW Singer-songwriter Peter Stuart formed the band in 1994, and they're best known for the 1995 hit "Everything Falls Apart." He explained, "I lived in a basement apartment in Chicago, and all I could see were fire hydrants and feet walking by . . . so I decided that I had a dog's eye view of the world."

THE DOORS The name the Doors grew out of conversations singer Jim Morrison had with his roommate Dennis Jakob at UCLA. Discussing names for an imaginary rock band, they agreed that a good choice would be the Doors, which came from a poem by William Blake: "There are things that are known and things that are unknown, in between the doors. If the doors of perception were cleansed, everything would appear to man as it is, infinite." Aldous Huxley used the line for the title of his book on mescaline experimentation, *The Doors of Perception*.

THE DRIFTERS When they began in New York City in 1953, they chose the name the Drifters because the members had drifted from one group to another. Today, over three dozen people can legitimately claim to have been full-fledged members of the Drifters at one time, and many of them have performed in various touring versions of the group.

DURAN DURAN Duran Duran formed in Birmingham, England, in 1978. The name was inspired by a villain played by Milo O'Shea in Roger Vadim's 1967 science-fiction spoof *Barbarella*, which starred Jane Fonda. Bassist John Taylor recalled: "I remember sitting at home one night watching *Barbarella* on BBC TV. I'd always liked the film, thinking it was so sexy, but this time was struck more by the words 'Durand Durand,' which kept getting repeated. A man's name, in fact, was what it was. Well, I had a little combo of extrovert nature happening at the time centered at our Birmingham City Art School. There was myself, Nick Rhodes, Stephen Duffy, and a forgotten clarinetist Simon Colley. The sounds we were making were quite out of the way and required an out-of-the-way moniker. After some small deliberations, the shoe fit."

BOB DYLAN Born Robert Allen Zimmerman in Duluth, Minnesota, in 1941, Dylan changed his name in 1962. When asked by a reporter from the *Chicago Daily News* in November 1965 whether he changed his name from Zimmerman to Dylan because he admired the poetry of Dylan Thomas, as was popularly believed, he replied: "No, God, no. I took the name Dylan because I have an uncle named Dillon. I changed the spelling, but only because it looked better. I've read some of Dylan Thomas's stuff, and it's not the same as mine." This myth persisted, prompting Dylan to ask Robert Shelton, author of the biography *No Direction Home: The Life and Music of Bob Dylan*, to "straighten out in your book that I did not take my name from Dylan Thomas."

THE EAGLES The Eagles began as Linda Ronstadt's backing band
in 1971. Drummer Don Henley recalled that the name was originally
suggested by singer Glenn Frey: "I think he was the one who came
up with the name, for a number of reasons. I think we all agreed that
we wanted a name that wouldn't go out of date, like we didn't want
Strawberry something or other. We wanted something that was all-
American and would be sort of timeless, and not be subject to the
fads and fashions and whimsies of the day. We were all very interested
in Indian lore and Indian mythology and Indian religion at the time,
and the eagle was a sacred symbol in the Native American world.
It was the animal that flew closest to the sun and carried the prayers
of people on the ground up to the gods, according to Indian legend.
We had a habit of going out to the Southern California desert and
doing various kinds of ceremonies that were associated with the Native
Americans. We'd go out as a band with a friend of ours who was
sort of our teacher. He's dead now, but his name was John Barrick.
We did the peyote rituals and threw up a lot. Glenn was and is a
very big sports buff, and the Eagles also sounded like a sports team.
In fact, we've been confused with the Philadelphia Eagles several
times." When asked if he was pleased they chose the name, Henley
said, "Yeah, well, it's always really hard picking a name, it's really
difficult. But in retrospect I guess it sort of stuck. I guess the band

makes the name. I mean, just looking at Beatles without attaching it to that group, it's kind of a silly name. I guess you sort of make the name, whatever it is, so that's what happened. It turned out to be OK. I mean, you're always apprehensive when you pick a name. You go, 'Oh, God, is this ridiculous? Or is it cool?'" Glenn Frey recalled, "We had this sort of name meeting over at Henley's apartment on Camrose in Hollywood, and as I recall we were all sitting around trying to talk about names and stuff. There was a time, when J.D. Souther and I were together as Longbranch Pennywhistle, we thought about calling ourselves Double Eagle. Part of it was that we are both Scorpios, and Scorpio evolves from the spider to the lizard to the eagle. Just some astrological mumbo jumbo. So that word was around. The thing that clicked for us, about the Eagles, was that it was a simple name, it did relate to Native American mythology, it did also sound like a car club, a sports team, things of that nature. It was on the dollar bill, and every country has an eagle—the German eagle, there's an eagle on the flag of Mexico, every nation has one. Also, it's the only bird of prey that does not prey on other birds. It had all of that. It seemed to be sort of a 'cover all the bases' kind of name. It could mean what you wanted. You could take it any way—there was a lot of latitude for interpretation. That's really how it came to be, and everybody thought it was a good name. We've been stuck with it ever since." When asked about being confused with the football team, Frey confirmed, "I would introduce myself, 'Hi, I'm Glenn Frey from the Eagles,' and they would just look at me like, 'Well, you must be the placekicker, because you're not big enough to play football.'"

"I would introduce myself, 'Hi, I'm Glenn Frey from the Eagles,' and they would just look at me like, 'Well, you must be the placekicker, because you're not big enough to play football.'" —GLENN FREY, THE EAGLES

Adam Dolgins

EARTH, WIND & FIRE The band began as the Salty Peppers
in Chicago in 1969, led by Maurice White, who had recently left
the Ramsey Lewis Trio. White had developed an interest in
astrology and Egyptology while touring the world with that group,
and this fascination inspired him to rename his band Earth,
Wind & Fire the following year after the three elements in his
astrological chart.

ECHO & THE BUNNYMEN The band made its debut in November
1978 in Liverpool, England, as a trio—vocalist Ian McCulloch,
guitarist Will Sergeant, and bassist Les Pattinson—plus a drum
machine. The name was coined by McCulloch's roommate, Paul
"Smelly Elly" Ellenbach, whose initial suggestions included Glycerol
and the Fan Extractors, as well as Mona Lisa and the Grease Skins.
Echo referred to the band's beatbox, in addition to the Liverpool
evening newspaper. In September 1979, Echo the beatbox was
replaced by flesh-and-blood drummer Pete de Freitas. McCulloch
has said that they chose the name to make sure they'd never take
themselves too seriously. Manager Martin Kirkup told *Rolling Stone*
that he thought the name had limited their exposure on US radio:
"Program directors have said they don't want to play a band named
Echo & the Bunnymen. They think the name is silly or something.
They deliberately ignore them."

EINSTÜRZENDE NEUBAUTEN The German industrial rock band's
name means "collapsing new buildings," chosen because it conveyed
their desire to make music from the sounds of destruction.

THE ENGLISH BEAT The English Beat formed in Birmingham,
England, in 1979. Singer and guitarist Dave Wakeling remembered:
"I was looking in the music section of *Roget's Thesaurus*, and

I think there's a part that had harmony on one side and discord on the other. This was 1979, so there was lots of discord in punk music. I noticed the word 'clash,' then I noticed the word 'slam,' but at first look I thought it said 'sham,' and I was like, 'My God, all the groups get their names out of here!' So looking over from the discord side, I thought, 'Well, I wonder what there is in the harmony side. That would be nice.' Because we were going for a kind of harmony—musical, racial, social, etc. And more or less the first thing I saw was 'beat,' and I just thought, 'Of course!' I just wandered around for a few days saying to people, 'What about the Beat?' And they all said, 'Of course! Why hasn't anybody done it?' I suppose because of the Beatles everybody had kept away from it for a little while, the Merseybeat and that sort of thing. So that was that." Not long after they decided to call themselves the Beat, they learned there was another band already using the name: "We got a phone call, I think from Bill Graham's management company, that said—I think they'd seen us in the *New Musical Express* or something—they wanted us to be aware that they had a group called the Beat. Then we got another message saying that if we'd like to consider Bill Graham Management as representation for the band, we could probably call ourselves the Beat, which was a nice introduction to the music industry. We said no. We wanted to call ourselves the Beat Brothers first. We thought that was—well, we'd never been to America, but we thought that sounded very American. And then somebody said no, the people who owned the name the Blues Brothers would object—they found it too similar to them. So by that time we'd realized that people in America for some reason seem to love the word 'English.' They didn't really like the words 'British' or 'UK' that much, but something about English was kind of cute—muffins or something. So we decided on the English Beat. So that was how that turned up."

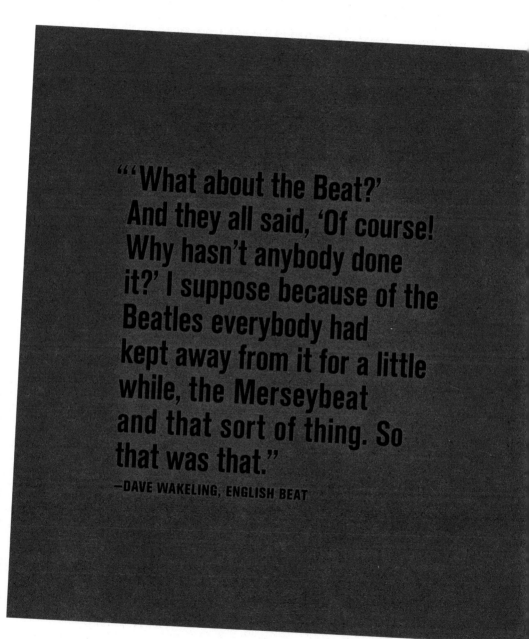

"'What about the Beat?' And they all said, 'Of course! Why hasn't anybody done it?' I suppose because of the Beatles everybody had kept away from it for a little while, the Merseybeat and that sort of thing. So that was that."

—DAVE WAKELING, ENGLISH BEAT

BRUCE SPRINGSTEEN AND THE E STREET BAND Before landing a record deal as a solo artist, Bruce Springsteen played in a number of bands, including Steel Mill and Dr. Zoom and the Sonic Boom. When he went on tour in 1973, after the release of his debut studio album *Greetings from Asbury Park, N.J.*, his backing band didn't have a name. They ultimately chose the E Street Band after the location of the family home of original keyboard player David Sancious, where the band sometimes practiced: 1105 E Street in the town of Belmar on the Jersey Shore.

"I had the band name before I had the band. I always thought the name Everclear would be a great name for a really intense rock band. Because I really got sick on it. The dichotomy of it is so funny. It looks like water, but it's pure spirit."
—ART ALEXAKIS, EVERCLEAR

EVERCLEAR Led by Art Alexakis, Everclear formed in Portland, Oregon, in the early nineties. He recalled, "I had the band name before I had the band. I always thought the name Everclear would be a great name for a really intense rock band. Because I really got sick on it. The dichotomy of it is so funny. It looks like water, but it's pure spirit. So I thought it would be a good name for a rock band, and open-ended, so the band could change within it." Everclear is a brand of grain alcohol. Alexakis explained, "We called them (the company) a long time ago. The guy just asked me not to do anything with any other alcohol company and he didn't mind. Then I found out about a year after I took the name that about the same time American Music Club had a record called *Everclear*. A lot of people tried to read into that. But I had the name way before they did on their album."

EVERYTHING BUT THE GIRL Tracey Thorn and Ben Watt met in 1982 while studying at Hull University in England. Thorn recalled: "We were living in a town in the north of England called Hull, and they had a furniture shop called Turner's Furniture Store, and they had a big slogan along the front of the shop which basically said that they could sell you everything but the girl, you know, to make your home complete. And when Ben and I got together we really thought we'd just be making one single or something and we chose this throwaway, disposable name, and . . . were stuck with it." Watt added: "It was really kind of cheap and vulgar and pop. I think people at the beginning were really intrigued, and I think they still are. There was a lot of questions in the early days about 'Is there a girl? Isn't there a girl?' It came out of that period in the early eighties when a lot of bands had slightly sort of obscurist names like Echo & the Bunnymen and the Teardrop Explodes, you know, Orchestral Manoeuvres, all these kinds of things. It was just that sort of period."

THE FALL Formed in Manchester, England, in 1977, the prolific, influential band took their name from the novel *The Fall* by Albert Camus.

FALL OUT BOY The band formed in Wilmette, Illinois, a suburb of Chicago, in 2001. When they asked the audience at an early show for name suggestions, someone shouted "Fallout Boy," the name of the sidekick to *Radioactive Man*, a fictional superhero on *The Simpsons*. On the series, Fallout Boy first appeared in a 1950s *Radioactive Man* film serial shown at a comic book convention in the episode "Three Men and a Comic Book," from the show's second season. Fallout Boy's signature catchphrase is "Jiminy jillickers!"

FATHER JOHN MISTY After leaving Fleet Foxes in 2012, singer-songwriter Josh Tillman changed his stage name from J. Tillman to Father John Misty. He explained, "The whole purpose of this name is that it's just some dumb shit I would call myself, and it looks hilarious on a marquee—it looks like some Christian Science puppet show."

THE FEELIES The Feelies formed in New Jersey in 1977. Their name comes from what Aldous Huxley called the futuristic movies in his classic novel *Brave New World*.

FIERY FURNACES Siblings Matt and Eleanor Friedberger formed the band in 2000 in New York City. Matt explained, "The name comes from *Chitty Chitty Bang Bang*. I was watching and the dad (the inventor Caractacus Potts, played by Dick Van Dyke) says he's going to put the car in the fiery furnace, and I knew it was a biblical reference. The idea of fire and brimstone I just thought sort of fit for a rock band, plus my last name is Friedberger and there are two of us, so you have the two F's. And the plural of furnace just when you say it seems sort of hard and tongue-twisting." About the biblical reference, he noted, "In the Book of Daniel, 'the fiery furnace' means staying constant in difficult situations and not giving up your God. But what sealed it was *Chitty Chitty Bang Bang*. That movie, it's us, a mix of menace and silliness."

FINE YOUNG CANNIBALS The band was formed in 1984 by bassist David Steele and guitarist Andy Cox following the breakup of the English Beat. After recruiting singer Roland Gift, they took their name from the 1960 film *All the Fine Young Cannibals*, starring Natalie Wood and Robert Wagner, which none of them had seen at the time.

FIREHOSE Following the 1985 death of Minutemen guitarist D. Boon in an automobile accident, bassist Mike Watt and drummer George Hurley added Ed Crawford to the lineup and changed the band's name to fIREHOSE. Watt says the name was inspired by the 1966 documentary *Don't Look Back*, in which Bob Dylan flashes a placard that says "FIRE HOSE" to accompany the line "Carry round a fire hose" from the song "Subterranean Homesick Blues."

FISHBONE The band started in 1979 when the members were in junior high school. When they started booking shows they were using the name Megatron, until they found themselves on a bill with two metal bands and decided they needed a name that was less heavy. Drummer Philip Fisher was nicknamed Fish, and that was on the mind of his brother, guitarist Norwood, one day when he was at the Egyptian Theater on Hollywood Boulevard. The movie theater's faux-ancient design, including sarcophagus replicas, got him thinking about fossils, which led to "fishbone."

FITZ AND THE TANTRUMS Lead singer Michael Fitzpatrick's nickname is Fitz. A friend suggested the Tantrums because of the pun (one can throw a tantrum or a fit). Fitzpatrick said they liked it because "it's a name that captures what we are all about."

THE FIXX The band was briefly called Jungle Bunny and the Banana Boat Boys until, as drummer Adam Woods told *Rolling Stone*, "we realized some people were insulted." Their choice of the Fix, a drug reference, was amended to the Fixx to placate their record label.

THE FLAMING LIPS Wayne Coyne, lead singer and guitarist for the Oklahoma City-based band, said of their name, "It's such a dumb name that it doesn't matter. There are some great band names out there, like Fugazi, where you get an idea what's it about, but still it's mysterious enough to make you wonder. But the Flaming Lips? It's just fucking silly."

FLEET FOXES Robin Pecknold and Skyler Skjelset met in high school in Kirkland, Washington, a suburb of Seattle. When they formed a band in 2006, they first went by the name the Pineapples until representatives of another local band sent them a cease and desist email. Pecknold remembered, "I'm like, 'You can take it, we're not really using it anyway.' He chose the name Fleet Foxes because he said it was "evocative of some weird English activity like fox hunting." He explained, "I just love the word 'fleet' as an adjective, and I love England. So much English music is just so great—Fairport Convention, Pentangle, Steeleye Span, they're so good, I can't get enough of them."

FLEETWOOD MAC In 1967, drummer Mick Fleetwood, bassist John McVie, and guitarist Peter Green, all veterans of John Mayall's Bluesbreakers, formed Peter Green's Fleetwood Mac. Green got top billing because of his fame as an extraordinary bluesman. The band released three albums before Green left in 1969 to record a solo album and then disappeared. Fleetwood and McVie then became simply Fleetwood Mac.

FLESH FOR LULU The band formed in the Brixton area of London in 1982. According to member Derek "Del Strangefish" Greening: "Basically, the name came from Lulu, the Scottish singer. She was in a film called *To Sir With Love* with Sidney Poitier. She was a little schoolgirl and a little rock singer, and she had a hit with a cover of 'Shout.' All the band is vegetarian, and we saw her buying a (burger at) McDonald's one day, and we just thought, 'flesh for Lulu,' and that was it." When asked why they were at McDonald's, he explained: "Victoria Station is a big open-plan station, and McDonald's actually doesn't have a wall outside it. You can just see in and people walk in and out really quickly—the fast-food thing." The band were not fans of Lulu's: "No, no, she's really rubbish now. She sells clothes in mail-order catalogs—that's about her only claim to fame now."

FLIPPER The San Francisco punk band formed in the early 1980s. In a roundabout way, their name is a reference to the television adventure series starring Flipper the dolphin that aired on NBC from 1964 through 1967. Singer and bassist Bruce Loose elaborated: "I left to go to Portland for a couple of months, and they got this other singer, this guy Rick Williams, who sang with the Sleepers, and he had come up with the name Flipper or suggested it, and then everybody had their own variations on the reasons for (using) it. He did it because it was the only thing he could remember from having pets and stuff like that named by the same name. There'd be, like, a dog that had three legs, or a turtle with a couple of fins missing, or something like that, and he called them all Flipper. Then Ted (Falconi, the guitarist) and his reasoning, from thalidomide babies, and with girls, if you flip her over they're all the same—things like that. In Europe, they liked it because it was always on pinball machines—it always says 'flipper.' It's really strange. They'd send us Xeroxes of pinball machines and things that said 'flipper' on them."

> "Once we'd used the name as a live band, people started making seagull noises—'Arh, arh, arh'"
> —MIKE SCORE, FLOCK OF SEAGULLS

A FLOCK OF SEAGULLS When the band formed in Liverpool, England, in 1980, singer Mike Score recalled, "The name of the band originally came because I read the book *Jonathan Livingston Seagull* (by Richard Bach). I thought it was a great book. I felt like I was, you know, flowing against the grain of society or whatever, and the book kind of said, 'You're not alone doing this. If you keep doing it you'll eventually arrive at the point you wish to be at.' So I thought that that would be a great name for a band. And also I was into the Stranglers, and they have a song called 'Toiler on the Sea' in which he yells out, 'A flock of seagulls.' So the two things together just cemented the name. Once we'd used the name as a live band, people started making seagull noises—'Arh, arh, arh'—and things like that, and we became known as the Seagulls no matter what we tried to do."

"Toward the end of the Second World War, US Air Force flyers patrolling the German skies would encounter a number of strange aerial phenomena … in the Rhine Valley. Similar to modern reports of UFOs, or so-called 'flying saucers,' these objects would come to be referred to as 'Foo Fighters.'"

—DAVE GROHL, FOO FIGHTERS

FOGHAT Foghat formed in London in 1971. Singer and guitarist "Lonesome" Dave Peverett recalled: "The name originates from when I was a kid. My brother and I, long before I was in music, were playing this word game, kind of like Scrabble. It had tiles in it—it wasn't actually Scrabble, but it was that kind of game. We were making up silly words, and 'foghat' was one of them. We thought it was hilarious. We used to laugh about this sort of nonsensical word. Years later, we tried to use it in one of the early blues bands I was in. We tried to get the singer, Chris Jordan, who was in Savoy Brown with me later on, to change his name to Luther Foghat and he wouldn't do that. Then, when we formed the band (that would become) Foghat, and we had the album finished and we had the artwork done, we were going to be called Brandywine, which is a horrible name for a band. At the last minute, I suggested the name Foghat. I did a drawing of a guy in a hat with fog coming out of it and brought it up to the artist that was doing the album cover. The label said, 'All right, that's fine,' and the band agreed to it and said, 'At least we've got a logo.' So that's it— no real deep meaning to it. It was just kind of a nonsensical word. We liked it because it had no meaning really, it was just a name, and it didn't tie the band to anything. We liked that because at that time we weren't really sure what the direction of the band was going to be, although the first album kind of set the mold for it really." When asked if he's glad they chose it, he said, "Yeah, because it's become what it is. I mean, you say the word 'Foghat' and there's only one meaning for that really. I think it's worked."

FOO FIGHTERS Former Nirvana drummer Dave Grohl formed the band in 1994. The name, as explained in an official band biography, stems from his interest in unexplained phenomena: "Toward the end of the Second World War, US Air Force flyers patrolling the German skies would encounter a number of strange aerial phenomena in the area between Hagenau in Alsace-Lorraine and Neustadt an der Weinstrasse in the Rhine Valley. Similar to modern reports of UFOs, or so-called 'flying saucers,' these objects would come to be referred to as 'Foo Fighters' ('foo' being slang for the French *feu*, fire) or, by those who believed the highly maneuverable balls of light to be a newly developed German weapon, 'Kraut Balls.' One incident reported on November 23, 1944, had Foo Fighters tailing an American plane over the Rhine Valley for some eighteen miles. Four days later, two pilots logged an encounter with a large, glowing, orange mass moving approximately 250 mph. They followed it briefly before sudden, inexplicable radar malfunctions forced their return to base. Naturally, pilots who made official reports regarding Foo Fighters were subject to skepticism if not outright ridicule. An imposed silence ensued, only to be broken a month later by two flyers from the 415th Squadron who reported a December 22 pursuit by two Foo Fighters. Two nights later the same pilots were 'attacked' by a glowing red object while flying over the Rhine. Disturbed by the frequent and vivid nature of these reports, authorities attempted to dismiss them as St. Elmo's Fire, a naturally occurring by-product of mutual electrostatic induction caused by the very planes being 'attacked.' Theoretically, the im-material nature of St. Elmo's Fire would account for its radar invis-ibility, while the charges present in these energy bodies could explain interference in the planes' radar functions. Yet reports of Foo Fighters persisted, climaxing in May 1945 with the sighting of five orange balls traveling in a triangular formation near the eastern edge of the Pfälzerwald. With the conclusion of the war, however, decreased air activity in this region logically led to fewer sightings of Foo Fighters. Eventually, they would be forgotten until their reemergence in 1950, heralding the modern age of UFO sightings." Grohl's own label, Roswell Records, is named for the town in New Mexico where some allege an alien craft crash-landed in the fifties.

FOREIGNER The band was formed in New York City in 1976 by guitarist Mick Jones after he left the Leslie West Band. The band was originally called Trigger, but when it was discovered that another band was using the name, Jones chose Foreigner because of the dual nationality of the original lineup: He, Dennis Elliott, and Ian McDonald were British, and Lou Gramm, Ed Gagliardi, and Al Greenwood were American.

FOSTER THE PEOPLE When lead singer Mark Foster formed the band in Los Angeles in 2009, he first considered calling it Foster and the People. But one night when he was out with a friend watching another band perform and mentioned the name, it was misheard. Foster recalled: "It was loud in there and he's like, 'Oh, it's Foster the People? That's awesome!' And I was like, 'No, no, it's Foster and the People." When he saw his friend's expression change when told the correct name, Foster thought to himself, "Foster the People. That means something totally different." The idea of "nurturing the people" appealed to Foster: "Early on, we played some charities, kind of our first shows, and that was kind of right around the same time that we were discussing our band name." They decided to go with Foster the People because, in addition to making music, they would also "be of service to people."

FOUNTAINS OF WAYNE Adam Schlesinger and Chris Collingwood first met at Williams College in Williams, Massachusetts, and eventually formed the band in New York City in 1996. The name came from a lawn ornament and outdoor furniture store in Wayne, New Jersey, near where Schlesinger grew up in Montclair. The shop was next door to the Department of Motor Vehicles office where he got his driver's license. They chose the name, he said, because "we just thought it was funny." Other names considered included Woolly Mammoth, Are You My Mother?, and Three Men Who When Standing Side by Side Have a Wingspan of Over Twelve Feet. Although perhaps meant as a joke, the name also represented the band's suburban roots. Schlesinger recalled, "We found our style only when we started honestly reflecting on how we'd grown up. We have a little bit more of an outer-borough or suburban perspective, and that made more sense than trying to be the Velvet Underground or Sonic Youth, which would've rung really false." As the band became popular—thanks to songs like "Stacy's Mom"—the store Fountains of Wayne found itself the focus of unexpected attention. At the time, the store's owner, Don Winters, didn't mind the association because "they're not doing anything profane or racist." One downside: "Our site, fountainsofwaynenj.com, is a disaster because of thousands of hits that are not about anything we sell." The band's site is the same, minus "nj." Winters considered changing the name but figured, "Next week there will be a band with that name." The store closed in 2009 but was immortalized in the *Sopranos* episode "Another Toothpick."

> "We have a little bit more of an outer-borough or suburban perspective, and that made more sense than trying to be the Velvet Underground or Sonic Youth, which would've rung really false." —ADAM SCHLESINGER, FOUNTAINS OF WAYNE

THE FOUR SEASONS Frankie Valli began his career as a solo singer in 1952 and then joined the Variatones, which renamed themselves the Four Lovers. The group went through several name changes during the next decade, recording as Frank Valle & the Romans, the Village Voices, and Billy Dixon & the Topics. In 1962, their recording of "Bermuda" was released by Gone Records under the name the Four Seasons, after the landmark restaurant on East Fifty-Second Street in Manhattan opposite the label's offices.

THE FOUR TOPS The group formed in Detroit in 1954 as the Four Aims. To avoid confusion with the Ames Brothers, they changed their name to the Four Tops because they were "aiming for the top."

FRANKIE GOES TO HOLLYWOOD The band formed in Liverpool, England, in 1980, taking their name from a newspaper headline referring to the film plans of a young Frank Sinatra.

FRANZ FERDINAND The Scottish band formed in Glasgow in 2002. The name was inspired by a racehorse called Archduke Ferdinand, which won the Northumberland Plate, an annual race in the UK, in 2001. The horse led to a discussion about Archduke Franz Ferdinand, whose assassination in 1914 triggered a series of events that led to World War I. Explained bassist Bob Hardy, "Mainly we just liked the way it sounded. We liked the alliteration." Lead singer and guitarist Alex Kapranos noted, "He was an incredible figure as well. His life, or at least the ending of it, was the catalyst for the complete transformation of the world, and that is what we want our music to be. But I don't want to over-intellectualize the name thing. Basically a name should just sound good . . . like music."

THE FRAY When the band came together in Denver in 2002, they considered a variety of names, including Belladonna, Street Fighters, and Brick Top Derby. Recalls singer Isaac Slade, "We had 200 name ideas and we kept going online to see if they were already being used. I liked Belladonna because it was a poisonous plant that looked really pretty, but when we looked it up, we found that a pretty successful, regional hair-metal band used that name. So, we let that one go. We thought about using the Street Fighters. I told the guys that name would invite the wrong clientele." Ultimately, the Fray was selected from suggestions made by guests put into a bowl at a family celebration. Slade said, "It was a fishbowl, actually. It was after our second performance, a graduation party. We were asked for a name, so we grabbed this fishbowl and put in five name suggestions." The name the Fray was picked at random. They say they don't know who suggested it.

FREE The name was suggested by Alexis Korner, an influential figure on the British rhythm and blues scene in the sixties, after his own group Free At Last. In addition to serving as a mentor for Free founder Paul Kossoff, Korner had a hand in the formation of Led Zeppelin. His pioneering Blues Incorporated group included the founders of the Rolling Stones and Cream.

FUGAZI Ian MacKaye named the band after army slang for "Fucked Up, Got Ambushed, Zipped In." He found it in the book *Nam*, a collection of Vietnam veterans' war stories.

THE FUGS The satirical Fugs formed in New York City in 1965, led by poets Ed Sanders and Tuli Kupferberg. Kupferberg explained: "Well, it was Ed's idea to form the band because we thought we would raise the level of rock lyrics. I think we did a little. I picked the name from Norman Mailer's *The Naked and the Dead*. He used it as a disguise for the word 'fuck.' There's a story—it may be apocryphal—that when Dorothy Parker was introduced to Norman Mailer at a party, she said, 'So you're the young man who doesn't know how to spell "fuck."' So that's about it, I guess."

FUN. The band formed in New York City in 2008. According to lead singer Nate Ruess, "The name came up because we were coincidentally having dinner with a comedian friend of ours in New York. He was excited about the new group, so he was like, 'What are you guys going to call it?' After his set, we had dinner at the Comedy Cellar. We're all sitting around talking about band names. Someone said 'Ice Cream?' That was a terrible one. So I think one of us was like, 'I like the image that it conjures up.' I think Jack (Antonoff, lead guitarist) said, 'What about Fun?' It seemed so obvious. But we still waited another six months." The band ended up tweaking the name slightly when they learned there was another band with the same name. Ruess explained, "We found out there was a Scandinavian death-metal band named Fun, and they asked us to do something subtle to change it up. So we added a period and lowercased the F." Ruess said he liked the period because "it's so uneventful. That allows us to remain apathetic."

FUTURE ISLANDS The synth-pop band began in Greenville, North Carolina, in 2006. It grew out of a krautrock parody band called Art Lord & the Self-Portraits. Singer Sam Herring played Locke Ernst Frost, an arrogant artist from "Germany, Ohio," who dressed in a 1970s-style white suit with slicked-back hair and had a heavy German accent. According to guitarist and bass player William Cashion, the band "had been talking for a while about how we wanted to get rid of the gimmick. We wanted to be taken seriously. Our songs had outgrown the gimmick that the band was made on. The songs were starting to deal with bigger, personal, universal themes. We wanted to be taken seriously." When choosing a new name, the band sought something deliberately vague. Cashion noted, "We were either gonna be called Already Islands or Future Shoes. Because, seriously, you don't know what future shoes look like, but you know you'd want a pair, you know? So after deciding Already Shoes was a bad name, we combined them to Future Islands. That's the boring truth, sorry!"

GALAXIE 500 The band, which formed in Boston in the mid-eighties, took its name from a sixties Ford muscle car.

GANG OF FOUR Careening funk-rock sound and politically incisive lyrics made Gang of Four one of the most exciting post-punk bands of the late seventies and early eighties. Their name is a play on words. It's a reference to the fact that there were four band members and also the name given to the widow of Mao Zedong and three other Chinese government officials accused of counterrevolutionary activities by Hua Guofeng and the post-Mao government. Singer Jon King explained, "I don't know that much about Maoism—I know that it's a branch of Chinese communism. We knew exactly who they were, but it was suggested because it was a good name for a band." Guitarist Andy Gill said, "Obviously, it was chosen in the first place because it was naming what we were, and in the second place because it had associations with a radical group. It was a joke in a sense and serious in a sense." "The irony of it now," King noted, "is that in England, the people who are called the Gang of Four in the papers are the Social Democrats, the right-wing pull-offs from the Labour Party. So now we're asked, 'Did you name yourself after the Social Democratic Party?'"

THE GAP BAND The Gap Band, one of the most successful funk bands in the eighties, was formed in the early seventies by brothers Ronnie, Charlie, and Robert Wilson, cousins of Parliament Funkadelic's Bootsy Collins. They named the band using the first initials of three streets in the Tulsa, Oklahoma, neighborhood where they grew up: Greenwood, Archer, and Pine.

GARBAGE Drummer Butch Vig, bassist Steve Marker, and guitarist Duke Erikson played together in the bands Spooner and Firetown before forming Garbage with Scottish vocalist Shirley Manson in Madison, Wisconsin, in the mid-nineties. The name was suggested by Pauli Ryan, a local musician, upon seeing the mess of tape from some of the band's early recording sessions.

GENERATION X The pioneering punk band, fronted by Billy Idol (born William Michael Albert Broad), took its name from a pop sociology paperback that examined the behavior of English teenagers in the sixties, specifically the Mods and Rockers.

GENESIS Genesis formed at the Charterhouse School in England where the original members were students in the mid-sixties. Peter Gabriel, Tony Banks, and Chris Stewart called themselves the Garden Wall, and Mike Rutherford and Anthony Phillips were in a band with several others called the Anon. In 1966, the two bands merged and recorded a demo tape, which they gave to Charterhouse alumnus Jonathan King, who signed them to Decca Records in 1967. It was King, who went on to become a well-known producer and label executive, who named the band, as he did 10cc. King said he thought of the name Genesis "because it was right at the start of my career in the business. I'd just written and recorded a record called 'Everyone's Gone to the Moon' that went to number one. I was up at Cambridge University at the time and had decided to go back to my old school, Charterhouse, as a sort of old boy for the Old Boys Day, as you can imagine, rather triumphantly returning to my old school, sort of flaunting the fact around that I'd been number one in the charts. And I was approached by this kid who had a cassette of his band who didn't have a name or anything, but were the local school band. And as of course they were a year or so younger than me at school—I'm sure you realize that somehow at school you never talk or even become aware of people either a year younger or a year older than you—I didn't actually know them as people, but I listened to the tape and liked it, decided to record them, and gave them the name Genesis because it was sort of the beginning of my production career. I had actually produced a couple of hits before—I produced a record called 'It's Good News Week' that I also wrote, by a band called Hedgehoppers Anonymous. But since this was the first band I felt was a serious band, I wanted to call them Genesis, as the beginning of my production career. So Genesis was the name they got, and we immediately discovered that there was a soul band in America called Genesis, and the American record company wanted us to change the name, and I refused to do so. So we put the first album out without an artist name, just calling it From Genesis to Revelation. Then the soul band folded or something, so we managed to keep the name and the name stuck with them."

THE GERMS The band formed in Los Angeles in 1977. Guitarist Pat Smear recalled: "Well, Darby (singer Darby Crash, who died of a drug overdose in 1980) came up with it. We originally called ourselves Sophistafuck and the Revlon Spam Queens, and there were a couple of others. But he liked the Germs. He was always thinking about the future. He liked the Germs because it was like, 'Well, this is the start of something new.' Y'know, the germ of an idea or something like that, and I just liked it because it was silly. We considered ourselves a band, but we hadn't played anything—we hadn't gotten the instruments or even the songs, for that matter. But we considered ourselves a band. We picked the name and immediately went out and had T-shirts made at the iron-on lettering T-shirt place and strutted around for a couple of months saying we were a band. We would go to record stores, in-store appearances and stuff, and just cause trouble and make a mess and get all drunk and screw with people while we were wearing our T-shirts and say, 'We're the Germs, we're the Germs.' And someone finally said, 'There's a show, why don't you play?' We were drunk enough to do it, and we went and played. We didn't have any songs or know how to play our instruments or anything like that. We just went and made a bunch of noise, and they threw us off after five minutes."

"It sounds really pretty, and what it represents is something really quite ugly and sort of disgusting. What a gin blossom is literally—what it symbolizes, I suppose, is loss of control."
—ROBIN WILSON, GIN BLOSSOMS

GIN BLOSSOMS The band was formed in Tempe, Arizona, in the early eighties by guitarist Doug Hopkins and bassist Bill Leen. The band's name is a deceptively pretty term to describe an ugly condition. Robin Wilson, the Gin Blossoms' lead singer, explained: "It's those things when old men drink too much, they have a sugar disorder and their nose, the capillaries on their nose explode—they get a big, red nose. It's a great name. We're very fortunate. I like the fact that it's got this really twisted duality to it. It sounds really pretty, and what it represents is something really quite ugly and sort of disgusting. What a gin blossom is literally—what it symbolizes, I suppose, is loss of control." It was founder Doug Hopkins's excessive drinking that got him kicked out of the band in 1992.

GNARLS BARKLEY CeeLo Green and Danger Mouse formed Gnarls Barkley in 2003. The name, which was suggested by a friend, is a reference to retired NBA legend Charles Barkley. The dictionary definition of "gnarls" is: "rough, knotty protuberances, especially on a tree," but in this instance it's derived from "gnarly," slang for either "very good" or "very bad." Danger Mouse has said of the name, "It's just a name that we liked. It's a name and that's it. There's not really some big thing to it. . . . "It just made its way into being." CeeLo recalled, "In retrospect, I can see clearly why we didn't call our new musical partnership CeeLo Green and Danger Mouse—or Danger Mouse and CeeLo Green, for that matter. Which one of our names would have come first anyway? Trust me, that subject alone is something we could have argued over for hours if we had wanted to. Instead, we just got down to what was most important—the music—and the name came second. From what I've heard, while Brian (Burton, aka Danger Mouse) was tossing around names with some of his friends, he almost called the group Bob Gnarley, but he liked the sound of Gnarls Barkley better. For my money, Gnarls Barkley is as absurd as any other memorable rock 'n' roll name, from the Goo Goo Dolls to Oingo Boingo to Kajagoogoo. Yes, our name sounded weird, but it's also immediately unforgettable. With all due respect to Charles Barkley, I didn't immediately like our name when Danger Mouse first mentioned it. Honestly, I immediately hated it. OK, for the record, I still don't like it. But however goofy it may be, the name Gnarls Barkley is pure quirk, and I have found that quirk works—at least it works for me. Although for a long time after our albums came out, people walked up and called me Mr. Barkley. A lot of them still didn't get that we were a group." Charles Barkley has said that he was "flattered and honored" by the name.

GOOD CHARLOTTE The band formed in Waldorf, Maryland, near Washington, D.C., in 1996 after the members met at La Plata

High School. They took their name from the children's book *Good Charlotte* by Carol Beach York, about an orphan, which was part of the Butterfield Square series. Lead singer Joel Madden explained, "It's the name of a children's book I had. It's really old. It was one of my favorites when I was younger. We were looking for a name and it was sitting there. Good Charlotte—it just fit." When asked if the book's theme has any significance, Madden said, "It kinda does, but when we were going over names, we weren't thinking of that. It's about a little girl. Everyone thinks she's bad. She's always getting in trouble and has bad luck. At the end of the book, everyone finds out she's really good."

GORILLAZ The virtual band was created by Blur front man Damon Albarn and artist Jamie Hewlett. There are several explanations of how the band got their name. One is that it was a joking reference to a snide comment made by Noel Gallagher of Oasis when asked about his band's rivalry with Blur in the April 1996 issue of *CMJ New Music Monthly*: "The thing that gets me is people will say (Blur's) the Beatles and we're the Stones. The fact of the matter is we're the Beatles and the Stones, and they're the fucking Monkees." The Monkees, like Gorillaz, were a manufactured band. Another story is that the name was inspired by the fact that Albarn and Hewlett were both born a few weeks apart in 1968, the year of the monkey in the Chinese zodiac related to the Chinese calendar. Another explanation is that it's a playful reference to the fact that a group of gorillas is called a "band." The Gorillas was a 1970s rock group from Hammersmith in the UK.

GOTYE Wouter "Wally" De Backer was born in Brugge Belgium, in 1980 and moved to Australia at the age of two. The name Wouter is Flemish, from the Dutch-speaking part of Belgium, but when he was young his mother used to call him Gaultier, the French version of the name. He eventually decided to use it as his stage name, but changed the spelling to Gotye. He explained, "When I settled on the sound of it as a name, I didn't like the resonance of the fashion world that it had with designer Jean-Paul Gaultier, so I came up with my own spelling." It's pronounced "gore-ti-yeah." The English equivalent of Wouter and Gaultier is Walter.

GRAHAM CENTRAL STATION The name of the seventies funk group, launched by former Sly and the Family Stone bassist Larry Graham, is a pun on New York's Grand Central Station, which, to be precise, is actually called Grand Central Terminal.

GRAND FUNK RAILROAD The band, which formed in Flint, Michigan, began as Terry Knight & the Pack and released a single called "I (Who Have Nothing)" that almost reached the US Top 40 in 1967. The following year, Knight stepped down to become the group's manager and renamed them Grand Funk Railroad, after Canada's Grand Trunk Railroad.

THE GRATEFUL DEAD Dennis McNally, the band's official publicist, explained: "The Grateful Dead were called the Warlocks, and in November 1965 they were sitting around (bassist) Phil Lesh's apartment, in Palo Alto, California, considering the fact that there was apparently some other band called the Warlocks and they'd have to come up with a new name. They came up with various ideas, all of which got sillier and sillier, and in the end, literally, God's truth, they picked up the dictionary that was lying there, which was a Funk & Wagnalls dictionary, opened it up, and Jerry Garcia stabbed a finger in and it landed, honest to God, on 'grateful dead.' The entry was a reference to a motif in folklore specifically explored by Francis Child, a turn-of-the-century British ethnomusicologist who classified ballads. You know, those sort of English folk ballads. There was this kind of ballad, that kind of ballad, and there was a grateful dead ballad. In the grateful dead motif, a traveler is going along the road, finds a body that's not being given a proper burial (usually because it owes money), resolves the debts of the body, and puts its spirit to rest, as it were. The body is then given a decent burial and the guy goes along his way. Usually he then encounters a representation of that spirit, usually in the form of an animal, which helps him in his own quest. The whole meaning, of course, is the notion of the resolved spirit of the dead and the whole idea of good karma and a cycle—death and life and rebirth and all that good stuff. I think the dictionary definition may have been something as short as 'a type of myth in folklore.' Expanded, that's what it is. They found it, and they looked at each other, from all accounts, and at least three band members said, 'No, that's too intense, that's too heavy, I don't like it.' But it's also one of these things that once you get it, how can you not go with it? And it has obviously served them well. A punch line to this story is that the first time they played, their first significant gig, was for Bill Graham at the Fillmore Auditorium on December 10, 1965, and Bill loathed the name. He thought it was a terrible name that would drive people off. It was a benefit for the San Francisco Mime Troupe and Bill's first show at the Fillmore. There were many acts, so they had a little easel at the side of the stage with placards with the name of each act. And Bill was so mad about the name change he put 'The Grateful Dead, formerly the Warlocks' up on the sign. But obviously he came to appreciate the name."

GREEN DAY Guitarist Billie Joe Armstrong and bassist Mike Dirnt (born Michael Pritchard) formed the band Sweet Children in their hometown of Rodeo, California, in the late eighties. They renamed themselves Green Day after one of their own songs, an ode to hanging out and smoking pot.

GRIZZLY BEAR The band began in Greenpoint, Brooklyn, in 2002, as a solo project by front man Ed Droste. He explained, "It (Grizzly Bear) was a nickname I had for an (ex-boyfriend) and kind of a joke. Anyone who knows me knows I'm not a camping kind of guy." The band was not named after drummer Chris Bear, who Droste had yet to meet, as is sometimes assumed.

GUNS N' ROSES When the band formed in L.A. in 1985, they considered a variety of names, including Heads of Amazon and AIDS. Guns N' Roses was chosen by combining the names of two bands that the members had previously played in, L.A. Guns and Hollywood Rose.

GWAR While they say they're the evil spawn of visitors from Uranus who were stranded in Antarctica, the theatrical shock-rock group GWAR actually consists of musicians, dancers, and artists who met at Virginia Commonwealth University in Richmond in 1985. Their name is reportedly an acronym for "God What an Awful Racket," although band members have also said that it came from a comic book titled *Gay Women Against Rape*.

GYM CLASS HEROES The band formed in 1997 when singer Travis "Travie" McCoy met drummer Matt McGinley in high school in Geneva, New York. McGinley remembered, "(When we started) we didn't have a name or a real idea of what we wanted to do. Travis and I had our gym and math classes together. We had our first show and we needed a name. Travis said, 'Gym Class Heroes. That's the name, that's it.' We never really questioned it or looked back on it. We also didn't plan on it lasting as long as it did."

HAPPY MONDAYS Formed in Manchester, England, in 1981, Happy Mondays were one of the pioneers of that city's influential rave scene. Guitarist Mark Day dubbed the band Happy Mondays in 1983 after the New Order hit "Blue Monday," a song reportedly inspired by the 1980 suicide of Joy Division vocalist Ian Curtis.

HAWKWIND Hawkwind formed in London in 1969. Bassist Lemmy (born Ian Kilmister) joined the band in 1971. After he was thrown out of Hawkwind in 1975 following an arrest in Canada on drug charges, he formed Mötorhead. Lemmy explained, "The reason for Hawkwind was that (sax and flute player) Nik Turner had a big nose and he farted all the time. He had a fuckin' nose like a beak and he farted all the time, so we called it 'Hawkwind.' When asked if the band was first called Hawkwind Zoo, he confirmed, "Yeah, that was the original name, but it was the same reason—a nose like a hawk's beak and he farted all the time." Lemmy said there is no such place as Hawkwind Zoo. Why Zoo then? "I wasn't with them then," he said, "but believe me, it fitted. Believe me."

HEART The band now known as Heart, famously featuring Ann and Nancy Wilson, actually began without the sisters as a group called the Army, and was formed by bassist Steve Fossen and guitarist Roger Fisher in Bothell, Washington, near Seattle, in 1967. Fossen said they meant "an army of art, music, and goodness, and stuff like that," but it was the height of the war in Vietnam and the name proved controversial. As they were talking about renaming the band, Fossen said they discussed how "Steppenwolf came from a title of a novel and that was a cool name." Friends had formed a band called White Hart named after the book *Tales from the White Hart*, a collection of short stories published in 1957 by science-fiction writer Arthur C. Clarke, author of *2001: A Space Odyssey*. The White Hart in the title was a pub. The Army asked if they could use the name from the other band and were given permission. They added an "e" and became White Heart. Fossen said, "That was as good as any other name," but after a while they grew tired of being mistakenly called the White Heart or White Hearts or being asked, "What's a 'white heart?'" They opted to shorten the name to Heart. Fossen noted, "Heart had a lot more meaning. It's the center of your emotions and feelings." He said he's never read *Tales from the White Hart*.

THE HEARTBREAKERS Guitarist Johnny Thunders (born John Genzale) and drummer Jerry Nolan formed the Heartbreakers in New York City after leaving the New York Dolls in 1975. Former Dolls bandmate Sylvain Sylvain claimed credit for the name: "Just before the Dolls broke up in 1975, we were with (manager) Malcolm McLaren in the car—this was in Florida—and 'Heartbreak Hotel' came on the radio. We were all sitting together in the car, driving from Tampa to who knows where, y'know, and I turned around to Johnny and Jerry, and I said, 'Wow, that would be a great name for a band, the Heartbreakers.'"

TOM PETTY AND THE HEARTBREAKERS The band formed in Gainesville, Florida, in 1976, and was originally made up of Tom Petty and several other members from a group called Mudcrutch. Petty recalled, "We decided that we would be a group and needed a name. My choice was the King Bees. The guys didn't much like that. I thought it sounded good—you know, Tom Petty and the King Bees. Where the Heartbreakers came from I'm not sure. It was probably (producer) Denny Cordell." Keyboard player Benmont Tench concurred, "I think it was our producer, Denny Cordell. We couldn't come up with a name. We had some terrible names. I just remember I got a call at some point. Tom said, 'What about the Heartbreakers?' I thought it looked great written out. And it was just about the last thing you'd say about us. I thought it was tongue-in-cheek." When told he'd been credited with suggesting the name, Cordell said, "Really? I must have nicked it off Johnny Thunders in that case." Johnny Thunders and the Heartbreakers had formed the year before in New York City. Petty remembered, "The band thought the name had a good ring to it. Later on we were really shocked because there was a band called the Heartbreakers. They were fairly big in New York. But we thought, 'We're not changing our name just because of this other group.' They thought the same thing. We figured we'd watch and see who wins this contest."

> "My choice was the King Bees. The guys didn't much like that. I thought it sounded good—you know, Tom Petty and the King Bees. Where the Heartbreakers came from I'm not sure."
> —TOM PETTY, TOM PETTY AND THE HEARTBREAKERS

HEAVEN 17 The band was formed in 1980 after synthesizer players Ian Craig Marsh and Martyn Ware left the Human League to establish the British Electric Foundation. The B.E.F. was a production unit whose first project was Heaven 17, for which they recruited vocalist Glenn Gregory. The name came from a group in the Anthony Burgess novel *A Clockwork Orange*.

HERMAN'S HERMITS Herman's Hermits began in Manchester, England, in 1963. Vocalist Peter Noone recalled: "We were originally called Pete Novak and the Heartbeats, and I was Pete Novak and wore this silver lamé suit, which I bought from another guy in another band in town. It didn't really fit, but it was cheap. We won this competition and I became 'The Crown Prince of the Twist.' But by 1963, it was getting a bit tired—you know, even my mum could do the Twist by now, and I was never going to be Chubby. So we were looking for another name and we used to have meetings, like those fifteen-year-old-boy-serious meetings: 'Let's call a meeting.' We used to rehearse in this place called—I can't remember the name of the place, like the Golden Garter or something, in Manchester. We were rehearsing there and *The Bullwinkle Show* came on. It was a bar and it was closed. The pubs were always closed. We used to offer to play one free date a week to get free rehearsals there. I went to school so we rehearsed from four to five thirty for free. In the bar was a television, and *The Bullwinkle Show* was on at four thirty every day. It was sort of going on in the background and

> "'Hey, Herman and the Hermits. Brilliant.' The drummer's mother made us some sackclothes so we'd look like hermits. But I wouldn't wear mine because it was abrasive, you know."
> —PETER NOONE, HERMAN'S HERMITS

we were very amused by it—it was so way ahead of its time. And there was a guy in it that we thought was named Herman. And I said, 'Herman—that would be great!' I had seen an American cartoon with this really wimpy-looking guy with glasses. I borrowed the guitar player's glasses, and I looked like Buddy Holly when I wore these glasses. I said, 'Great! We can do Buddy Holly songs and I'll call myself Herman.' You know, it was so sort of anti–rock 'n' roll, so sort of anti–Elvis Presley.

'Cause everybody was being called George and Paul suddenly, and Fred. Nobody in England was called Herman in those days, nobody. We'd never, ever heard of anyone named Herman, so it was totally unique. So we were all excited about me being Herman and we were looking for a name to go with it, and the barman says, 'Call yourselves Herman and the bloody Hermits.' We said, 'Hey, Herman and the Hermits. Brilliant.' The drummer's mother made us some sackclothes so we'd look like hermits. But I wouldn't wear mine because it was abrasive, you know. We did an afternoon show at the Plaza Ballroom in Manchester, and the guys walked onstage in these sackclothes. I had on this blue suit. My manager took me and bought me a suit on credit—I wouldn't wear the sackclothes. Everybody laughed in the audience and that was the one and only time we wore them." When asked what other names they considered, Noone recalled, "Herman and the Supermen was one of them. Herman and the Supermen would have been a disaster, especially for four white, wimpy English guys. Then we thought to call ourselves Watkins and the Dominators because we had an amplifier, which was a Watkins Dominator. So we thought 'Watkins and the Dominators!' Then we thought dominator sounded like something in a book with men with whips and men in leather underwear, you know. So we dropped that one. Herman's Hermits was the perfect name for our band. Couldn't have been a better name. It was totally different. And for years everybody called me Herman. I remember John Lennon always used to call me Herman and it amused me." Noone eventually discovered the animated character was named Sherman, not Herman: "We told my sister that we were calling our-selves after the guy on *The Bullwinkle Show* and she said, 'Well, his name is Sherman.' But we stuck with it. We had already printed the cards. In those days every band had a card. You know: 'The Beatles: weddings, bar mitzvahs, anything, money, call us.' We'd done the cards. It was like nine pounds for a thousand cards, which we'd give to anybody, even other guys in school."

THE HIVES The band formed in Fagersta, Sweden, in 1989. The name has nothing to do with beehives. According to lead singer and pianist Per "Howlin' Pelle" Almqvist, "it's definitely a rash. We once considered it might be the haircut (the beehive hairstyle), but it is the rash. We irritate people. We get under their skin."

HOLE Hole began in Los Angeles in 1990. Singer Courtney Love said she named the band after a line in the play *Medea* by Euripides: "There's a hole burning deep inside me." She says she chose it because she "knew it would confuse people," who would assume the name was an arch reference to a woman's anatomy.

THE HOLLIES The Hollies formed in Manchester, England, in 1962. Although it has been reported that they were named after the Christmas decoration, guitarist Graham Nash stated, "We were Buddy Holly crazy. So that's how our name came about."

HOOBASTANK The band members met in high school in Agoura Hills, California, and formed the band in 1994. They were originally called Hoobustank. According to lead singer Doug Robb, "It's one of those old high school inside-joke words that didn't really mean anything."

"I was kind of wild in those days, and I
to take a black group and call them the

HOT TUNA Jorma Kaukonen and Jack Casady formed a splinter group from Jefferson Airplane in 1968, originally calling the band Hot Shit before renaming it Hot Tuna at their record label's insistence.

THE HUES CORPORATION The disco-soul group got their start in Los Angeles in 1969 and had a hit in 1974 with "Rock the Boat." Group leader Wally Holmes recalled: "I wanted to call the group the Children of Howard Hughes, because I knew Hughes was single and he represented a conservative element. I was kind of wild in those days, and I thought a fantastic thing would be to take a black group and call them the Children of Howard Hughes." To avoid legal complications, Holmes "came up with the idea of the Hues Corporation," a veiled reference to Hughes and, perhaps, the group's racial identity, as in hues of skin tone.

THE HUMAN LEAGUE The Human League originated in Sheffield, England, in 1977, and took their name from Starforce, a science-fiction board game. Synthesizer players Martyn Ware and Ian Craig Marsh left the band in 1980 to form Heaven 17. Vocalist and synth player Phil Oakey and Adrian Wright, who handled "stage visuals," recruited new members and had several hits, including "Don't You Want Me" in 1982 and "(Keep Feeling) Fascination" in 1983.

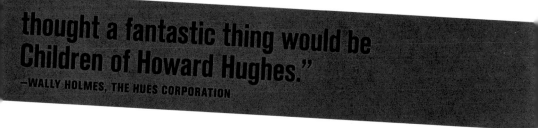

thought a fantastic thing would be Children of Howard Hughes."
—WALLY HOLMES, THE HUES CORPORATION

"We walked into his dressing room, which he'd made into his little photographic studio, and there were four plates and a big pie. You can imagine where the pie ended up—on the photographer and on the wall. We weren't about to—that really wasn't what Humble Pie was about." —PETER FRAMPTON, HUMBLE PIE

HUMBLE PIE After he left the Small Faces in 1968, guitarist Steve Marriott formed Humble Pie in Essex, England, with ex–Herd guitarist Peter Frampton. Frampton recalled: "Well, when we all got together and rehearsed, we didn't have a name, so one night we decided we'd all go home and think about it and call each other on the phone. And we did, and the one that we went for was one that Steve had thought of, which was Humble Pie. That was it. He was very, very clever with words and names in general." When asked why Marriott chose the name, Frampton explained, "I think the fact that we knew that we were already being called a super-group because Steve was from the Small Faces and I was from the Herd—I think that the (phrase) 'you eat humble pie,' it was sort of a reverse on the way people were thinking of us, so it was sort of downplaying the supergroup image. The only thing was, the first time we did *Top of the Pops*, the big English TV show—you always used to go to the BBC photographer's room either before or after the show because they take a picture of you to put on the credits for next week. If your song went up in the charts, they played the video again of what you just did. We walked into his dressing room, which he'd made into his little photographic studio, and there were four plates and a big pie. You can imagine where the pie ended up—on the photographer and on the wall. We weren't about to—that really wasn't what Humble Pie was about."

HÜSKER DÜ The influential Minneapolis trio began in the early eighties and took their name from a board game popular in the fifties, which means "Do you remember?" in Swedish. It was chosen so the band wouldn't be easily categorized. Guitarist Bob Mould noted, "Back in '79 there were a lot of bands picking really punky and power-pop names. We wanted to grab hold of a name that was timeless, ambiguous, and that would not label us."

IMAGINE DRAGONS Lead singer Dan Reynolds started Imagine Dragons in 2008 in Provo, Utah, when he was a student at Brigham Young University. By 2010, after all of the original members had left the group, the band relocated to Las Vegas, Nevada, where Reynolds had grown up. Reynolds and the new lineup have all claimed that the band's name is an anagram of another name they originally intended to use. Lead guitarist Wayne Sampson said, "Our original name was a phrase we all liked, and we were gonna make that phrase the band's name until we randomly switched the order of all the letters a few times and came out with Imagine Dragons." The hitch in this story is that when Reynolds first formed Imagine Dragons in 2008 and the group won a series of local battle-of-the-band contests in Utah and recorded an EP under that name, neither Sampson, bassist Ben McKee, or drummer Daniel Platzman was in the group. Nonetheless, the band has stuck with the anagram story and hidden clues, or red herrings, in music videos and liner notes, including the phrases "Ragged Insomnia" and "Amigos in Danger." In the video for the song "Whatever It Takes," a license plate reads "ADEMONISRAGING" ("A Demon Is Raging"). Then again, if you play one section of a Spotify-only version of their song "Cha Ching (Till We Grow Older)" backward, Reynolds repeatedly sings what sounds like "There is no anagram."

INCUBUS The band formed in 1991 in Calabasas, California, when the members were students at Calabasas High School. Lead singer Brandon Boyd remembered, "We were fifteen and we had to think of a name because we had to play a party in someone's backyard. My choice was Spiral Staircase because I was into the trippy, hippy thing when I was fifteen." Bassist Dirk Lance, the stage name of Alex Katunich, suggested Chunk o' Funk. According to Boyd, "And then Mike (Einziger, lead guitarist) looked into the thesaurus. He's all, 'Incubus, right there, that should be our name.' And we're all, 'Uh... all right.'" Mike said the definition was "a spirit that seduces women while they are sleeping." Brandon said, "We were like, 'Yeah, all right!' We're all, 'Sex in the name—let's go.'"

INDIGO GIRLS Amy Ray and Emily Saliers met at Shamrock High School in Decatur, Georgia. Ray said of their name, "I found it in the dictionary. It's a deep blue, a root—real earthy."

INTERPOL When the band formed in New York City in 1997, lead guitarist Daniel Kessler recalls, the band experimented with several names, including Las Armas (Spanish for "The Weapons") and the French Letters: "We had played shows with no name and then I got

"We had played shows with no name and like, 'Guys, we're getting decent crowds, so no one knows who to go see again.'"

to the point where I was like, 'Guys, we're getting decent crowds, but, like . . . we don't have a name, so no one knows who to go see again.'" Lead singer Paul Banks thought of the name Interpol, after a friend's pronunciation of his first name as "Pole" instead of "Pawl." Interpol is the International Criminal Police Organization, founded in 1923 to foster cooperation between law enforcement agencies around the world. Kessler noted, "Paul's the one who found the name, but it immediately stuck with us. The idea sort of matched us, and it sounded good and simple." Some members of the public have confused Interpol the band with Interpol the organization. Kessler explained: "We've had some really weird emails. I mean, I've received some serious emails about people that were lost, that other people were trying to find, or emails about scams people had fallen into, like in the Philippines and Afghanistan, some crazy stuff. Some were really bad, like really important, and I wrote back, 'We're just a rock band called Interpol— sorry for the confusion.' Some people would attach documents. I just don't know what they're thinking when they see the website, you know what I mean? Wouldn't you think the email address would be some- thing a little more credible, or a bit more governmental?"

INXS Regarding its origins in Sydney, Australia, in 1979, drummer Jon Farriss recalled: "We would like to say that INXS thought of its own name. But we didn't. In fact, a roadie who was working with us

> then I got to the point where I was but, like . . . we don't have a name,
> —DANIEL KESSLER, INTERPOL

"Good consists of being heavy, tight—together, not only musically, but as people. It also means being light, dynamic, versatile, and original. I added all those qualities together and it boiled down to heavy and pretty."
—DOUG INGLE, IRON BUTTERFLY

for a short while during a tour of Australia in 1979 came up with the idea. One of our first managers suggested that we use it and adopt a mysterious 'inaccessible' type of image. We played behind a wall of lights in Devo-style clothing without saying anything except 'ours' before playing one of our own songs. Cool idea and it worked for a while, but we outgrew it pretty quickly. 'Inaccessible' and 'in excess' was a mild contradiction of terms, as well as the fact that we didn't enjoy being inaccessible! Excessiveness, well, we preferred that. We chose the name INXS simply because we loved it. It had an interesting twist, four letters, (an) in-your-face type of attraction to it."

IRON BUTTERFLY Iron Butterfly formed in San Diego in 1966. Their biggest hit, 1968's "In-a-Gadda-Da-Vida"—an edited version of the seventeen-minute album track that featured a two-and-a-half-minute drum solo—was allegedly a play on the phrase "in the Garden of Eden." Lead singer and keyboard player Doug Ingle explained, "I wanted a name we could live up to. We wanted to be good. Good consists of being heavy, tight—together, not only musically, but as people. It also means being light, dynamic, versatile, and original. I added all those qualities together and it boiled down to heavy and pretty. At the time, insect names seemed to be the big thing, so we became Iron Butterfly."

IRON MAIDEN Bassist Steve Harris launched Iron Maiden in 1976 in London, naming the band after a medieval torture device referred to in *The Man in the Iron Mask*.

THE JAM The band took shape in 1975 in Woking, England, where singer and bassist Paul Weller and drummer Rick Buckler began jamming together during lunch hour in their school music room. These jams inspired the band's name, not a favorite breakfast jelly, as sometimes reported.

JAMIROQUAI The name of the British group is a hybrid of the words "jam"—as in a musical jam—and "Iroquai," a variation of "Iroquois," the name of the Native American tribe with whom front man Jason Kay was enamored.

JANE'S ADDICTION Perry Farrell started Jane's Addiction in Los Angeles in 1986, following the breakup of his first band, Psi Com, which he started in 1981. Farrell explained, "Jane's Addiction came about through . . . well, my friend Jane, who was my roommate. We lived in a house that was very busy, socially, a lot of musicians living there. And Jane was like this femme fatale that I loved very much, and I named it in her honor." When asked what the addiction was, Farrell demurred, "Well, the addiction. Let's keep the addiction broad. Addiction is addiction in every case. It's the same thing, just with a different format. You know what I mean. It doesn't matter if it's coffee. It doesn't matter if it's drugs. It doesn't matter if it's religion. It doesn't matter. You know what I mean. It doesn't matter if it's lifting weights. Addiction is addiction." Farrell said there's no truth to the rumor that the name is in reference to the Velvet Underground song "Sweet Jane," nor was Jane a hooker through whom the band met. "We had a woman that was a prostitute who was managing us," Ferrell said, "but that was not Jane."

JEFFERSON AIRPLANE Jefferson Airplane was formed in San Francisco in 1965 by singer Marty Balin, whose first recruit was guitarist Paul Kantner. Kantner recalled, "We just had a lot of boring names swirling about. Jorma (Kaukonen, guitarist) brought the name to us, actually. He was hanging out with a lot of white blues players, white college kids who learned blues licks, some of them real good. They would immerse themselves in the blues legend, somewhat sarcastically—not disrespectfully, but just in sort of an educated-white-boy snide way, pleasant, fun. One of the blues players had this dog that was called Blind Thomas Jefferson Airplane, sort of like Blind Lemon Jefferson with a twist. And Jorma suggested the Jefferson Airplane; the name surfaced somehow. So we took that name as sort of our temporary name—just a name we could use until we chose a real name, a respectable name that looked like it could be on the charts or something. Actually, we weren't thinking of charts in those days, but we were thinking of a respectable name. By the time our band opened, which was on Friday the thirteenth in 1965 in August, nobody had thought of a better name, so we had to sort of go with that, and it worked out OK." Balin confirmed, "Jorma came up with it, our guitar player. He had a friend who had a little dog named Thomas Jefferson Airplane. One day we were trying to think of a name and he said, 'Why don't we call ourselves Jefferson Airplane?' We all laughed and thought it was pretty funny and didn't take it seriously, but we tried all these names out on our friends and they didn't like any of them, but when we said 'Jefferson Airplane' they all laughed and cracked up. So when we got back together, we all said, 'Y'know, all my friends, they kind of liked that Jefferson Airplane.' Everybody had the same reaction, so we said, 'Yeah, let's call ourselves that,' because that's the reaction that we were trying to get from people. That was the spirit of the band, and so we kept that name." In 1974, Jefferson Airplane officially became Jefferson Starship. Kantner explained the name change: "Jefferson Starship—that's when the band went their separate directions. Jorma and Jack (Casady) went off into Hot Tuna, and I, being a science-fiction freak, took that particular bent of just going one step up the evolutionary ladder, as it were, from airplane to starship. It's just a science-fiction thrust, and remains so to this day." It has been reported that the band was named after a kind of roach clip made by splitting a paper match at one end. Kantner explains: "It was the other way around. That came around in the early seventies, if I'm not mistaken. It's something we used, we just never called it a Jefferson Airplane." Balin concurred: "That came after our name. They named that after us. It was kind of a thing that we used to crack up at, y'know. It was kind of nice that people named their roach clip after us."

"...we tried all these names out on our friends and they didn't like any of them, but when we said 'Jefferson Airplane' they all laughed and cracked up. So when we got back together, we all said, 'Y'know, all my friends, they kind of liked that Jefferson Airplane.'"
—MARTY BALIN, JEFFERSON AIRPLANE

THE JESUS AND MARY CHAIN Brothers William and Jim Reid formed the band in 1983, performing their first gig in Glasgow, Scotland, the following year. When asked how they chose their distinctive name, William Reid explained, "I just made it up one day. The

> "I've always thought it was a brilliant name. The only regret really is that the world is so conservative, and I think it's probably done our career damage having that name. To me it doesn't have any blasphemous connotations at all. It just states the Jesus and Mary Chain. It doesn't say that Jesus is a junkie or whatever." —WILLIAM REID, THE JESUS AND MARY CHAIN

circumstances were that we had a gig coming up, our very first gig, and we needed a name, within two weeks basically. So I made up the name, there and then. I'd always liked the word 'Jesus,' and I had an idea that when we needed a name that I would somehow get Jesus into it, but then I just said Jesus and Mary Chain, and Douglas and Jim, who are in the band, said, 'Yeah, that's good enough, that'll do.' And that was it. Over the years people have asked me, 'How did you get the name?' and I've told people countless lies. Like I told people that I got it from a Bing Crosby film, and I told other people that I got it on the back of a cornflakes packet, just to make it sound interesting. But let's face it—the real story is pretty mundane, really." When asked if he had any regrets, Reid said, "I've always thought it was a brilliant name. The only regret really is that the world is so conservative, and I think it's probably done our career damage having that name. To me it doesn't have any blasphemous connotations at all. It just states the Jesus and Mary Chain. It doesn't say that Jesus is a junkie or whatever. There's no disrespect to anybody in the name. I think the names Jesus and Mary are sacred and a lot of people don't allow you to use them. I know it's harmed our career. I know that in the States lots of radio stations don't play our records because of the name. I know that if U2 were called the Jesus and Mary Chain, they wouldn't be playing stadiums because they wouldn't have got past a certain level that we find hard to get past. AOR radio stations are kind of nervous about the name. Some of them, when they do play our records, they don't say 'the Jesus and Mary Chain,' they just say 'the Mary Chain.' It's kind of annoying—it's not what we're called." When asked if there is such a thing as a Jesus and Mary chain, in the Bible or elsewhere, Reid said, "I don't think so. I don't think I've ever heard that. The words just popped into my head. They sounded good, and we needed a name for the band quick, and that was that. And what happened over the years is that people in interviews have asked me about it, and you tend to try to have a theory, you force yourself to have a theory, and I don't think it works. I always disappoint people when they ask. That's why the cornflakes and Bing Crosby things came about. I disavowed the Bing Crosby thing because it got on my nerves. People were asking, 'Well, what was the name of that Bing Crosby film?' And I was saying, 'It doesn't exist.'"

JESUS JONES The English band, best known for the hit "Right Here, Right Now," began in 1988. Louise Allen, a spokesperson at their management company in London, explained: "Jesus Jones started out inauspiciously on a beach in Spain. Originally they got together in the summer of 1988. Mike (Edwards), Jerry (De Burg), and Gen were on holiday, just sitting on a beach. They were all in bands that weren't getting anywhere, and they just decided to come back and try something else. The three of them were sitting on this beach surrounded by all these Spanish people, most of whom seemed to be called Jesus. The name Jesus Jones just seemed like a nice juxtaposition."

JET The band, which formed in Melbourne, Australia, in 2001, took the name Jet from the Paul McCartney and Wings song "Jet," which was released in 1974. The title of that song was named for McCartney's dog Jet, a jet-black Labrador.

JETHRO TULL In 1963 Ian Anderson, Jeffrey Hammond, and John Evans played their first gig as the Blades, named after the club in the James Bond books. By 1966, however, they had changed their name to the John Evan Smash and finally the John Evan Band, Evans taking the S off his last name because Hammond thought it sounded better. After two years of struggling, the seven-piece soul revue was whittled down to a blues quartet, and for the next couple of months they played under a variety of names: Navy Blue, Bag of Blues, Ian Henderson's Bag of Blues, the frequent name changes reportedly the only way they could play a club a second time. Eventually the band joined forces with producer Derek Lawrence, who wanted to call the group Candy Coloured Rain. Instead, a booker at the Chrysalis booking agency who had studied history suggested Jethro Tull, the name of an eighteenth-century agriculturalist who invented something called the seed drill. The band's first single was accidentally credited to Jethro Toe.

JIMMY EAT WORLD Jimmy Eat World formed in Mesa, Arizona, in 1993. According to Tom Linton, the band's rhythm guitarist, the name came from a crayon drawing made after his younger brothers Jim and Ed had a fight when they were kids: "It's a picture that my little brother drew. . . . My brother Jim beat up my younger brother

"It's a picture that my little brother drew. . . . Ed, and Jim ran into his room and locked 'Jimmy Eat World,' and it was a picture of

Ed, and Jim ran into his room and locked his door, and Ed drew this picture that said, 'Jimmy Eat World,' and it was a picture of him eating the world. My brother Jim is kind of a big guy. A stupid name." Some fans erroneously assumed the name references singer and guitarist Jim Adkins and the TV sitcom *Boy Meets World*, which premiered on ABC in 1993. When the band chose the name, they say they were unaware it formed the acronym JEW and would end up in headlines like "JEW Uses Live Set to Keep Fans Enlivened."

ELTON JOHN Born in London in 1947, Reginald Kenneth Dwight joined the local soul band Bluesology when he was fourteen. In 1966, Bluesology became the backing band for blues singer Long John Baldry and they were rechristened the John Baldry Show. The following year, Reg Dwight changed his name to Elton John, borrowing the first names of Baldry and saxophonist Elton Dean.

JOURNEY Journey began as the Golden Gate Rhythm Section in San Francisco in 1973, after Santana's production manager Walter "Herbie" Herbert encouraged Santana guitarist Neal Schon to form his own band. Herbert, who became the band's manager, explained: "The name Journey was created by a gentleman named John Villanueva, who worked with me during the Santana days, was actually with

> **My brother Jim beat up my younger brother his door, and Ed drew this picture that said, him eating the world."** —TOM LINTON, JIMMY EAT WORLD

Santana before I got there, and helped put together Journey in the first place. We had this contest that we ran on KSAN Radio to name the band and got all these lame suggestions. He came up with the name Journey, we all liked it, and then we said, 'Jeez, he's part of the organization—that kind of screws up our contest. We're going to have to say that someone else actually came up with the name Journey.' And so we said at the time that it was a gentleman named Toby Pratt (who won the contest) and that he got a lifetime pass to Journey shows. Then years and years later we admitted that there was no such person as Toby Pratt, that it was really John Villanueva who named the band." Herbert said of the radio contest, "There were lots and lots of postcards, maybe a couple thousand. It was a mail-in thing." The suggested names included "Rumpled Foreskin, Peter Beater and the Mound Pounders, just stuff like that. A lot of wiseass stuff. Some of it was OK, but it was John who came up with Journey."

JOY DIVISION The band, which formed in Salford, Greater Manchester, England, in 1976, was originally called Warsaw, after the David Bowie song "Warszawa." They had to change their name in 1978 after discovering there was a London-based punk band called Warsaw Pakt. The name Joy Division came from the 1955 novella *House of Dolls*, which described Nazi concentration camp brothels used by the guards that were known as "Joy Divisions." Guitarist and keyboard player Bernard Sumner recalled, "I was reading a book, *House of Dolls*, and I showed it to Ian (Curtis, lead singer), and I honestly don't know who came up with it, but we just thought it was a great pair of words, really. Regardless of the content. You do know of course that we are not Nazis? Of course we're not, and we never were." According to bassist Peter Hook, the name "was about being shocking, not about ideology. We didn't have a political bone in our bodies—none of us did, not even Ian. Arty stuff was what he liked, not political. Yes, we were naïve and stupid and probably trying too hard to get up the noses of the older generation, but we weren't Nazis. Never have been and never will be."

JUDAS PRIEST Judas Priest formed in Birmingham, England, in 1969. While it has been reported that the name came from the Bob Dylan song "The Ballad of Frankie Lee and Judas Priest," founding bassist Ian Hill recalls: "There was another band called Judas Priest, which had disbanded before the one started by K.K. (Downing, the original guitarist) and myself back in 1969–1970. The vocalist from that band, Alan Atkins, joined with K.K., myself, and John Ellis, our drummer at the time, after seeing us rehearse. We tried to think of a name for our new band but drew a blank. It may have been K.K. who suggested that we use the name Judas Priest. In any case, we all thought it was an excellent idea, as the name seemed to fit perfectly, and the original band already had a good following locally before they split. Aside from these considerations, the phrase 'Judas Priest' was also familiar to Americans, as it was used as a substitute for the exclamation 'Jesus Christ' in early, overcensored movies. So, after phone calls had been made to the other members of the original band, the name was officially used by us. Who in the first band thought up Judas Priest, why, and where it came from, I don't know. We probably never will."

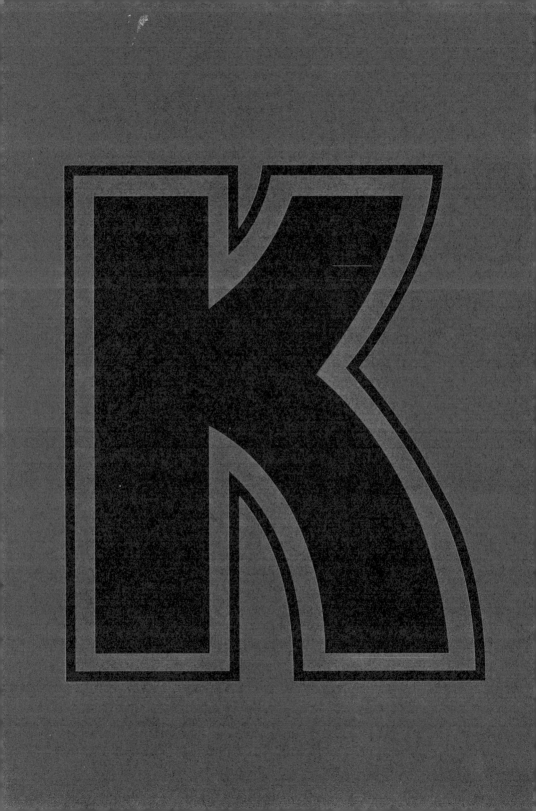

KAJAGOOGOO Originally called Art Nouveau and later the Handstands, the synth-pop band got their start in Leighton Buzzard, England, in the early eighties and had a hit with "Too Shy" in 1983. As for their name, bassist Nick Beggs said, "It's like something a child would say. When people say it they can't quite pronounce it, but once they know it they can never forget it."

KANSAS Kansas evolved from a band formed in 1970 by guitarist Kerry Livgren, bassist Dave Hope, and drummer Phil Ehart, all native Kansans and classmates at West Topeka High School. In 1972, the band changed its name from White Clover to Kansas at Livgren's suggestion.

KID ROCK Kid Rock was born Robert James Ritchie. He reportedly earned his stage name as a teenager when working as a DJ at parties and clubs with predominantly black crowds, where it was said "that white kid rock." "It's the worst name in the world. The only person that had a dumber name than me was the Fresh Prince. Hey, it sounded like a cool rap name when I was sixteen. But it stuck, and now it's me. I'll be an eighty-year-old man: 'Call me the Kid.'"

THE KILLERS The band, which formed in Las Vegas in 2001, took their name from a fictional band featured in the music video for the

New Order song "Crystal." Lead singer Brandon Flowers was a big New Order fan. In the "Crystal" video, the band is replaced by a group of teenagers. The name "The Killers" is visible on the drum kit.

KILLING JOKE Killing Joke formed in 1978 in London. They took their name from a British expression that refers to an ironic situation. Lead singer and keyboard player Jaz Coleman explained, "The killing joke is like when people watch something like Monty Python on the television and laugh, when really they're laughing at themselves."

KING CRIMSON King Crimson was formed as Giles, Giles & Fripp in Bournemouth, England, in 1967, by Giles brothers Pete (bass) and Mike (drums and vocals), and guitarist Robert Fripp. After some personnel changes, the band became King Crimson in 1969, the name suggested by Peter Sinfield, the group's lyricist. Fripp noted, "The name King Crimson is a synonym for Beelzebub, which is an anglicized form of the Arabic phrase *B'il Sabah*. This means 'the man with an aim' and is the recognizable quality of King Crimson."

THE KINGSMEN The band, best known for the 1963 hit "Louie Louie," began in Portland, Oregon, in 1958. That year, the parents of saxophonist Lynn Easton arranged for the acquisition of the name the Kingsmen from another local band that had recently broken up.

KINGS OF LEON Brothers Caleb, Nathan, and Jared Followill, who are the sons of a United Pentecostal Church preacher, formed the band with cousin Matthew Followill in Nashville, Tennessee, in 1999. Veteran Nashville songwriter and producer Angelo Petraglia helped them come up with their name. Jared remembered, "Angelo was playing on the religious thing, saying, 'Why don't you guys be called the Kings of Zion?' (Zion is sometimes used as a synonym for Jerusalem,

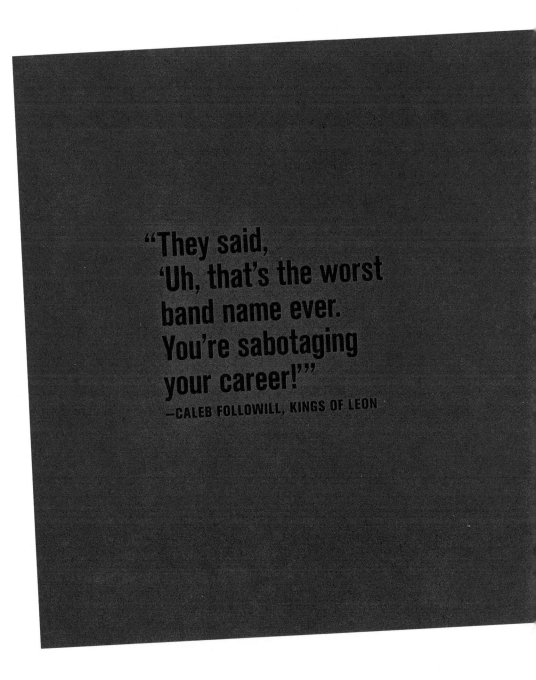

"They said,
'Uh, that's the worst
band name ever.
You're sabotaging
your career!'"
—CALEB FOLLOWILL, KINGS OF LEON

as well as for the biblical Land of Israel as a whole.) Then Caleb said, 'What about Kings of Leon?' Because our grandfather Leon is the closest relative to all four of us. We all laughed, but then we agreed it was kinda cool, like a street gang." When they landed a record deal, the label initially balked at the name. Caleb remembered, "We said we were going to be Kings of Leon, and they said, 'Uh, that's the worst band name ever. You're sabotaging your career!'" The name has no connection to the Kingdom of León, which existed from 910 to 1230 AD on the Iberian Peninsula in Europe in what is now the Kingdom of Spain.

THE KINKS The Kinks began in London in 1963 as the Ravens, a band that was formed by Dave Davies and then joined by his older brother Ray. They were renamed by manager Larry Page. "Kinky" was a word in vogue in London at the time and was applied to everything from sex to fashion.

KISS Kiss was formed in New York City in 1972. Singer and guitarist Paul Stanley recalled: "We were at the point where we were already rehearsing songs, and very clear on what the band was about and who we were. That's the point where you have to come up with a name to kind of reflect that. I was driving my '63 Plymouth Grand Fury on the Long Island Expressway, and the name suddenly came to me. I remember thinking to myself, 'God, I know this is the right name,

"I think KISS just conjured up so many different images. It's a word that I felt, no matter where you went in the world, people were going to recognize it. It's just a universal word, even where, obviously, they don't speak the language. It's also short, and it looks great, and not much more than that. It can be a kiss of death, or it can be real soft." —PAUL STANLEY, KISS

I hope I don't get any grief from the other guys.' I told them I thought the band should be called KISS and I held my breath, waiting for some sort of response, and everybody went, 'Yeah, that sounds pretty good.' So there you have it." When asked what inspired the name, Stanley said, "I think KISS just conjured up so many different images. It's a word that I felt, no matter where you went in the world, people were going to recognize it. It's just a universal word, even where, obviously, they don't speak the language. It's also short, and it looks great, and not much more than that. It can be a kiss of death, or it can be real soft. In that way, without having the kind of contrast, it has the same stuff to me as Led Zeppelin, Iron Butterfly, those kind of things, where it's light and heavy, or dark and light, but it's all in one word. Kiss has all those connotations." Stanley acknowledged the many rumors that have circulated about the name over the years: "There was Knights in Satan's Service, or Keep It Simple Stupid. Then somebody was saying that we were thinking of calling ourselves Fuck—it just never happened. It's kind of an honor and a compliment to have rumors and myths written and spoken about you, 'cause I guess it means in some way you have some sort of importance. But none of those stories are really true."

KMFDM This German industrial group's name stands for *Kein Mehrheit Für Die Mitleid*, which roughly translates to "No pity for the majority," not "Kill Mother Fucking Depeche Mode," as has been rumored.

THE KNACK The Knack formed in Los Angeles in 1978 and had a huge hit the following year with the single "My Sharona" and the album *Get the Knack*. Singer and guitarist Doug Fieger explained: "We were originally called 20/20. I had sent a demo tape to this guy named Ken Barnes, who had a local magazine called *Bomp*—he was the editor—hoping to get some publicity for the band. We didn't hear anything from him, and about two, maybe three months later I was looking through the new copy of that magazine and I saw an article about a band named 20/20—and it wasn't us. And as it turned out, he managed this band, so I always suspected that he got our tape and photo, liked the name of the band, and took it. I don't know that for sure, but that was my suspicion. It forced us to come up with another name. The day I discovered this picture in that magazine I started looking through the dictionary, and when I got to 'knack' in the K section, I stopped. It was short, it was to the point, it had a neat sound, it started and ended with a K, which I thought was nice—it kind of reminded me of the Kinks. It had a meaning that could be applied to a band—having the knack, having a special ability, which is what the dictionary definition is. More than anything, though, it was short. I didn't want to have one of those long, descriptive names, with some fruit or color in it. The funny thing is, there was a band called the Knack in the sixties. They were a local Los Angeles band and were also on Capitol Records, coincidentally. They put out a single, which I think is the only record they ever released, and it wasn't a hit. I grew up in Detroit, so I had never even heard of them. And (guitarist) Berton (Averre), who grew up out here (in L.A.), had never heard of them. When we got signed to Capitol, nobody who was there had been around back in the sixties. But somebody in the art department was going through the art archives and came up with the picture sleeve of the single cover, which they used to do pretty regularly back in the sixties. He brought it in and said, 'Did you know that there was a band on the label called Knack?' and nobody did. As a matter of fact, I heard some rumor at the time—it might not have been a rumor, it might have been real—that these people were contemplating suing us. I had done a trademark search on the name and there had been nothing with that name, so we didn't have any problem there."

THE KNICKERBOCKERS Originally called the Castle Kings, the Knickerbockers had a hit in 1966 with the Beatles-esque rave-up "Lies." They took their name from Knickerbocker Avenue in their hometown of Bergenfield, New Jersey, where they got their start in 1964.

KRAFTWERK The synthesizer band Kraftwerk was formed in Düsseldorf, Germany, in 1970 by keyboard players Ralf Hütter and Florian Schneider-Esleben. Hutter explained: "Kraftwerk basically means 'power plant.' We plug our machines into the electrical system and create transformed energy. The Human Machine (*Die Mensche Machine* in German—one of the group's nicknames for itself, another being *Klangchemiker*, or Sound Chemists) means that we plug ourselves into the machines also. We play with our brains, our hands, our mouths, our feet, and sometimes we use contact microphones, which pick up the sounds of the clothes we are wearing or how much my beard is growing that day. We play the machines, but the machines also play us. This we don't deny like they do in conventional music. There the man is always considered superior to his machine, but this is not so. The machine should not do only slave work. We try to treat them as colleagues so they exchange energies with us."

L7 The mostly female band formed in Los Angeles in the late eighties. Guitarist Suzi Gardner explained: "We didn't really want a gender reference in our name, and so we were just coming up with words or phrases. Nobody liked anybody else's suggestions, so I just said, 'Well, what about L7?' I wasn't crazy about it, thinking nobody else would be either, but when I threw it out, everybody went, 'That's OK.' They didn't jump up and down or anything. They just went, 'Ah, it's all right, it's OK. We've got a show coming up—we need a name. We agree.'" When asked if everyone knew it was an expression from the fifties that meant "square" or "uncool," Gardner said, "I thought it was common knowledge what that meant. I learned it from *The Flintstones*. On one show, Fred became a rock star, and Wilma was trying to blow his cover by spreading the rumor that he was 'L7' to all the kids because she wanted him at home. That's how I heard about it. It's also in 'Wooly Bully,' and it's in a Sex Pistols song. People weren't saying it around my neighborhood or anything, but it's something that I grew up with. We lie to the press all the time. If they don't know what it means, we assume they are L7, and we bullshit them. We say it's Lesbian Seven. We say it's a level of consciousness that you attain when you get to level seven in meditation. We say it's lubrication, a love jelly called L7. There's actually a guitar amp called L7, made by someone like Ampeg—some weird, offbeat company. There's also a panty size L7—large seven—very apropos for this band. We really just wanted a name that was easy to remember, that was brief like Black Flag. We didn't want a long name, like Men Without Hats. We wanted a short, to-the-point name, 'cause really, after your band gets going, it doesn't matter what the fuck your name is. The Pixies don't sound anything like the name the Pixies, and Nirvana sounds like they'd be a hippie band, like Jethro Tull, but Nirvana kicks ass. It doesn't really matter what your name is." When asked what other names were considered, she remembered, "I wanted to call us Keg o' Slaw. At Long John Silver's, that's what they call their coleslaw, 'keg o' slaw.' I just loved that name. Everybody went, 'Beep! Next.' Nobody else liked it. I also suggested Captain's Log."

LADY GAGA Stefani Joanne Angelina Germanotta's stage name was inspired by the song "Radio Ga Ga," released by Queen in 1984. It was music producer Rob Fusari, whom she began working with in 2006 and eventually dated, who first made the reference. She recalled, "I was playing a record for him one day in the studio called 'Again Again,' which is . . . like this super-Beatles/Queen theatrical ballad. He said, 'God, you're so "Radio Ga Ga,"' and I thought that was funny. And every time I'd come into the studio he'd say, 'Gaga is here, Gaga is here! Gaga, Gaga!' So it sort of stuck, and I tacked on the 'Lady' as a sort of ironic contrast to the crazy of the Gaga." In a 2010 lawsuit, Fusari claimed, among other things, that he was solely responsible for creating "the name 'Lady Gaga' for his protégé." The legal filing asserted that Fusari had played the Queen song whenever she arrived at his studio, and "one day when Fusari addressed a text to Germanotta under the moniker 'Radio Ga Ga' his cell phone's spell check converted 'Radio' to 'Lady.' Germanotta loved it and 'Lady Gaga' was born." The lawsuit was eventually dropped. Queen's "Radio Ga Ga," written by drummer Roger Taylor, was a critique of radio's decline in the age of television and was originally called "Radio Ca Ca," inspired by a phrase uttered by Taylor's toddler son.

LANA DEL REY Born Elizabeth Woolridge Grant, she used several different stage names, including Mary Jailer and Sparkle Jump Rope Queen, before settling on Lana Del Rey. She explained, "When I was young I often asked myself if I would one day have the courage to change my name and become the creative director of my own life." She decided she wanted a name that "I could shape the music towards. I was going to Miami quite a lot at the time, speaking a lot of Spanish with my friends from Cuba. Lana Del Rey reminded us of the glamour of the seaside. It sounded gorgeous coming off the tip of the tongue." She recalled, "I knew that I wanted a name that sounded sort of exotic and reminded me of the seaside on the Floridian coast. Lana Del Rey sounded beautiful."

Inspiration may have come from Delray Beach, a coastal city in Palm Beach County, Florida, but the name does not come from the Los Angeles neighborhood of Del Rey or the Ford Del Rey, as has been reported. The latter was a car designed exclusively for the Brazilian market in the 1980s, but was also sold in Chile, Venezuela, Uruguay, and Paraguay. Where that rumor began is unclear.

LED ZEPPELIN Guitarist Jimmy Page formed Led Zeppelin after the breakup of the Yardbirds in 1968 and originally called the band the New Yardbirds. Although Keith Moon, the drummer for the Who, is usually credited with suggesting the name, Richard Cole, Led Zeppelin's longtime tour manager, shed some new light on the matter: "What happened was Keith Moon, John Entwistle, and I were in New York at a club called the Salvation. At the time I was with the Yardbirds, so that would have been around May of '68. Now Keith and John were always going through things about leaving the Who, and they were talking about forming a new band. They were gonna try to get Jimmy Page on guitar, Stevie Winwood on vocals, and then they came up with this name in the club. I have a feeling it was Entwistle—I'm not sure, most people say it was Moon—and he said, 'Oh, that's good, I've got the name for it—we'll call it Lead Zeppelin, 'cause it will go down like a lead balloon.' So that's where it came from. It originally started out as a new name for Keith and John." Page misspelled "lead" as "led" so Americans wouldn't mispronounce it as "leed."

THE LEMONHEADS "A lemonhead is a Midwestern candy—yellow spheres that are sweet on the outside and really sour on the inside," band founder Evan Dando reported. When asked if the name was a musical metaphor, he replied: "I'm not quite sure. Our friend Ivan suggested the name when we were in high school. We had pages and pages of really bad names, but we decided we'd rather pick someone else's bad name than one of our own."

LEVEL 42 The band formed in London in 1980 and took its name from the novel *The Hitchhiker's Guide to the Galaxy* by Douglas Adams, in which "42" is the answer to the question "What is the meaning of life?"

THE LIGHTNING SEEDS Ian Broudie—a veteran of the Liverpool music scene of the early eighties and an original member of Big in Japan, a band that included Holly Johnson, later of Frankie Goes to Hollywood, and Budgie, future drummer of Siouxsie and the Banshees—explained, "Prince sang this line, 'The thunder drowns out what the lightning sees, but I heard it as 'the lightning seeds,' and it seemed like a good image."

LINKIN PARK The band had its origins in Xero, a group started in 1996 by Mike Shinoda, Rob Bourdon, and Brad Delson, who had been classmates at Agoura High School in Agoura Hills, California, a suburb of Los Angeles. After Chester Bennington joined the band on vocals in 1999, they changed their name to Hybrid Theory. After they discovered there was another band called Hybrid, they agreed to change their name to Lincoln Park, at Bennington's suggestion. Bennington would often drive past the park, which was located in Santa Monica, California, on the way to meet the other members of the band. By that point the park had been formally renamed Christine Emerson Reed Park in 1998 to honor the former mayor and councilwoman who had died in 1996. Reed had helped lead an effort to renovate the park, which by the mid–nineties had become notorious for its homeless population and drug dealing activity. When the band attempted to register the domain name lincolnpark.com, they discovered it was already taken but could be purchased for over $10,000. Instead of attempting to buy the domain, they changed Lincoln to Linkin and successfully registered linkinpark.com. The band soon discovered there were places called Lincoln Park all across the country. Lead guitarist Brad Delson recalled, "We went on tour right after we changed the name, and we pretty quickly realized there was a Lincoln Park in every town. Kids would come up to us and go, 'Dude! You're from Lincoln Park too? What side?' The joke, basically, is that everywhere we go, people think we're local. So in that aspect, it's a really cool name."

LIPPS, INC. Multi-instrumentalist Steven Greenberg and vocalist Cynthia Johnson came together in Minneapolis and had a number-one hit in 1980 with "Funkytown." The name is a pun on "lip-synch."

LITTLE FEAT Little Feat was formed by singer and guitarist Lowell George after leaving Frank Zappa's Mothers of Invention. The name was inspired by Mothers drummer Jimmy Carl Black, who used to tease George about his "little feet."

THE LITTLE RIVER BAND The band began in Melbourne, Australia, in 1975, having evolved from a London- based band called Mississippi. Criticized for using an American name, they rechristened themselves the Little River Band after a resort town near Melbourne.

LIVING COLOUR Vernon Reid formed Living Colour in New York City in 1984. He said of the name: "It was inspired by the intro to the old Walt Disney show. ("*Walt Disney's Wonderful World of Color*" ran from 1961 to 1969.) Why the British spelling? "I thought the word 'colour' was more interesting to look at when spelled with a U. I briefly considered two other names: Point of View and Dangerous Vision."

LORDE Ella Yelich-O'Connor chose her stage name somewhat impulsively when she was sixteen. She explained, "I basically chose Lorde because I wanted a name that was really strong and had this grandeur to it. I didn't feel that my birth name was anything special. I always liked the idea of having, like, a one-named alias." She recalled, "It was actually a really quick decision. Which is quite funny, because I'm like, 'Wow, if I'd known I would be having that name for the rest of my life, I probably would have spent more than two days on it. It was a good spontaneous choice, I think. I'm quite proud of my sixteen-year-old self for not messing that one up, 'cause if I'd given myself a cool, weird, hip name I hated now, that would be super annoying. Again, it's that nobility, aristocracy obsession that I had. I hit upon 'Lord' and loved the way it sounded, and then I was like, 'It would be quite cool to add an E to feminize it.'" Nonetheless, she insists, "I much prefer being called Ella."

LOVE The band, best known for their 1967 album Forever Changes, formed in Los Angeles in 1965. The group had been called the Grass Roots but was forced to change their name when another band called

The Grass Roots released a single. Guitarist Johnny Echols recalled, "Arthur (Lee, lead singer) had worked at a place called Luv Brassieres, it was spelled L.U.V., where he was in the packing department. Bryan (MacLean, guitarist) and I were driving past with Arthur one time and we saw the billboard and I said, 'You know, Arthur used to work there.' And of course everybody started laughing and then Bryan said, 'That would be a great name for a group.' I said, 'Yeah, but we should do L.o.v.e. rather than L.u.v.' And so basically that's how we got the name."

LOVE AND ROCKETS Following the breakup of Bauhaus in 1983, and after a brief incarnation as Tones on Tail, guitarist Daniel Ash, bassist David J, and drummer Kevin Haskins formed Love and Rockets. They named themselves after the underground comic book by the Hernandez Brothers.

LOVERBOY Loverboy formed in Calgary, Canada, in 1979. Lead guitarist Paul Dean explains: "I was in a band before Loverboy called Streetheart. And the one thing that I liked about the name was that it had some irony to it. It showed some toughness and some vulnerability. So I was on a name-finding mission for the band, and I was looking through my girlfriend's magazines—*Cosmo* and all these girl magazines. And I just happened to notice that all the covers had cover girls on them. So I figured, 'Coverboy—now there's a pretty good irony to that.' I don't know how I figured it at the time, but that was my thinking: Coverboy. Then the next logical step was Loverboy, and I just went, 'Hmm, this is going to get a reaction.' Mike (Reno, the band's lead singer), and I were going to call it the Mike Reno-Paul Dean Project or something. People asked me, 'So what are you doing? What's the name of your band going to be?' and I'd tell them, 'The Paul Dean Band.' They'd go, 'Yeah . . . OK.' So I figured with a name like Loverboy, at least we're going to get a reaction. Whether good or bad, these people are going to notice it—it's going to stand out, y'know? So we tried it, and we got a lot of name-calling from it, but we said what the hell, we're going to go with it anyway because at least it creates some kind of shit in the industry, not just another bland name. I think the second week we were called homos or something, and people in Japan and Germany really had a problem with the name. They couldn't figure it out—they figured it was a gearbox name. You get the idea of what I'm saying." When asked if he's glad they went with the name, he said, "Not really. It's a pretty hard thing to live up to when you're forty-six."

THE LUMINEERS Lead singer and guitarist Wesley Schultz and drummer and percussionist Jeremiah Fraites started the band in 2005 in the New York City suburb of Ramsey, New Jersey. They experimented with a number of different names before a case of mistaken identity one fateful night at the Lucky Seven Tavern, a small New Jersey nightspot across the Hudson River from Manhattan. Schultz remembered, "We got it by accident. We were playing a gig in Jersey City and there was a guy announcing each band, which is strange in and of itself because that never really happens. He was an MC of sorts, and we went by a different name, but he read the wrong sheet. I guess there was going to be a band called the Lumineers in the same time slot the following week. We thought it was a good name, so we looked the other Lumineers up and they didn't seem particularly active . . . so we just hoped for the best. We had really struggled with a lot of bad names in the past so it was kind of great. Sometimes it's easier when someone just tells you what you're called. Like when your parents give you your name. Imagine trying to name yourself as a baby. This worked out so much better." Schultz explained, "As a joke, our first band name was Free Beer, because we figured someone would see that and come out to see us. Then we called ourselves

Sixcheek, because there was this band out there called Sevendust, and that was what we based it on. We figured that there were three of us, which makes six butt cheeks. It was a terrible idea. Then we went by Wesley Jeremiah, because we had lost a third member so often that it was usually just Jeremiah and me, but then people thought we were a singer-songwriter and it got really confusing for the venues. Then the Lumineers name came along and we got stuck with it." What the band didn't realize initially was that Lumineers is a brand name for a dental product. "Yeah, it's a dental veneer," Schultz acknowledged. "I know . . . that they're paying pretty big bucks to get ahead of us in the search engine world. It would be a weird thing to be looking for a band and then land on that site (www.lumineers.com) and suddenly realize, 'Hey, I could do with some new teeth,' wouldn't it?"

"As a joke, our first band name was Free Beer, because we figured someone would see that and come out to see us."
—WESLEY SCHULTZ, THE LUMINEERS

LUSCIOUS JACKSON The band named themselves after basketball player Lucious Jackson, whose name was misspelled in a sports record book.

LYNYRD SKYNYRD The band formed in high school in Jacksonville, Florida, in 1965 as the Backyard, later changing their name to Lynyrd Skynyrd after Leonard Skinner, a gym teacher known for his hostility toward long-haired students. Later on, when the band had become famous and Skinner was working in real estate, everyone let bygones be bygones and Skinner introduced the group at a hometown concert.

M Under the name M, Paris-based British pop musician Robin Scott topped the charts in 1979 with the song "Pop Muzik." Scott recalled, "At the time when I was putting the (record) sleeve together in Paris, I was thinking that I really needed a pseudonym which would create sufficient interest. I was looking out of the window and I saw this large M, which you see all around Paris for the Metro, and I thought, ' Perfect. I'll take that. And the more people read into it, so much the better.' I should have never told anybody who I was."

MADNESS The band formed in London in 1976 as the Invaders. In 1979, they changed their name to Madness after the 1963 ska hit by Prince Buster, the Jamaican recording star who was one of their major influences.

MANCHESTER ORCHESTRA The indie rock band began in Atlanta in 2004. Front man Andy Hull recalled: "I was in high school and had gone through a summer of listening to nothing but the Smiths. And when I really get into a band I like to involve myself completely with what their story is and where they're from and how it happened and why are they called this, and so I thought the name the Smiths was such a cool name. These normal, regular guys creating this politically charged music and this heartbreaking literature and songs that will tear you apart. I always felt I was a lot like that. I mean, just looking at our band, we're not a 'rock star'–looking band. I guess the idea of Morrissey being from Manchester was really cool for me, though I've only been there once and I'm not sure I would still call it cool, but all I knew of it was that this hero of mine was from there. He's from this place that I associated with down-to-earth working-class heroes, these underdogs in a sense. That's sort of how I figured me and whoever was in my band would be, these normal guys. The orchestra was the counterpart to that. At the time I didn't want to be in a band and figured I'd just have all my friends come and be a part of it and form an orchestra. So that's the name."

THE MANHATTANS Formed in Jersey City, New Jersey, in the early sixties as the Dulcets, they had a number-one hit in 1976 with "Kiss and Say Goodbye." Bass vocalist Winfred "Blue" Lovett explained why they changed their name: "It didn't sound that exciting. 'Dulcets' means 'melodic tones,' but how could you explain that to the public? We needed a catchy name that would last. So, with the cocktail theme in mind—not the borough of Manhattan—we picked the name Manhattans."

THE MARCELS Formed in Pittsburgh in 1960, the multiracial vocal group took their name from the wavy "marcelled" hairstyle worn by several members. They had a big hit in 1961 with "Blue Moon."

MARCY PLAYGROUND Lead singer John Wozniak named the band, which formed in New York City in 1994, after the playground at Marcy Open School, a public elementary school in Minneapolis, Minnesota, that he attended as a child. "There were no grades and good vibes," he recalled. "You called your teachers by their first names." The band is not named for Marcy Playground in Brooklyn, New York, near the Marcy Projects, the housing project where rapper

Jay-Z grew up. Both places were named for William Learned Marcy (1786–1857), an American politician best remembered for saying, "To the victor belong the spoils of the enemy" in 1832, which has been changed over time to "To the victor go the spoils."

MARILYN MANSON Brian Warner placed himself firmly in rock 'n' roll tradition when he chose his yin-yang stage name, which combines the glamour of Marilyn Monroe with the horror of Charles Manson, and neatly evokes his musical sensibility and carefully crafted image. Many of his bandmates had similar stage names, including Twiggy Ramirez, named for the sixties British fashion model Twiggy, and the California serial killer Richard Ramirez.

MAROON 5 Maroon 5 has its origins in the band Kara's Flowers, which was formed in 1994 when Adam Levine, Jesse Carmichael, Mickey Madden, and Ryan Dusick were students at Brentwood School, a private school in Los Angeles. That band was named for a girl the guys had a "collective crush" on and delivered flowers to for her birthday. "That name," said Madden, "was a serious albatross and we always hated it, almost since we had it. But we couldn't come up with a name we agreed on." Kara's Flowers put out an album on Reprise Records in 1997, but the only single, "Soap Disco," was a commercial failure and the band broke up. After Levine and Carmichael briefly attended Five Towns College on New York's Long Island, they returned to Los Angeles, got back together with Madden and Dusick, and recorded a demo, which found its way into the hands of Ben Berkman at Octone Records. Berkman, who was EVP/head of promotion at the label, suggested they add a fifth member, so James Valentine joined the band in 2001. The band was first named Maroon, but then changed to Maroon 5. The band refuses to say why they chose the name. "It was my idea never to tell anybody," said Levine. "The origin of the name is so bad. It's such a horrendous story that we decided that shrouding it in mystery will make it a better story than the actual story."

BRUNO MARS Born in Hawaii as Peter Gene Hernandez to a Puerto Rican–Jewish father from Brooklyn and a Filipino mother, Mars explained, "Bruno is after Bruno Sammartino, who was this big fat wrestler. I guess I was this chunky little baby, so my dad used to call me that as a nickname. The Mars came up just because I felt like I didn't have no pizzazz, and a lot of girls say I'm out of this world, so I was like, I guess I'm from Mars." Mars said that early in his career, before he changed his name, people would say things like, "Your last name's Hernandez, maybe you should do this Latin music, this Spanish music. . . . Enrique (Iglesias)'s so hot right now." He said he didn't want to be pigeonholed musically because of his heritage, but he stresses that "I never once said I changed my last name to hide the fact that I'm Puerto Rican. My last name is Hernandez . . . There's no denying that." Mars met Sammartino in person for the first time in August 2017 on a concert tour stop in Pittsburgh, Pennsylvania, where

> "Bruno is after Bruno Sammartino, who was chunky little baby, so my dad used to call me up just because I felt like I didn't have no world, so I was like, I guess I'm from Mars."

the pro wrestling legend lived. Sammartino said, "I hope he's like that in everyday life. He was the most humble, nicest guy. He couldn't have been more respectful. He told me, 'You know, I called my dad and told him I was going to meet with you today, and he was so excited.'" Sammartino, who is considered one of the greatest pro wrestlers of all time, died eight months later.

THE MARSHALL TUCKER BAND There was nobody named Marshall Tucker in the Marshall Tucker Band, which formed in Spartanburg, South Carolina, in 1971 and sold more than ten million records between 1973 and 1984. Originally called the Toy Factory after founder Toy Caldwell, the band changed their name to the Marshall Tucker Band, after the blind piano tuner who had previously used their rehearsal space to restore and tune old pianos. According to the most frequently told story, one of the band members found an old key ring with Tucker's name on it on the floor. "Some people have said it was a business card," Tucker told the *Spartanburg Herald-Journal*, "others said a sign over the door, and others have told the story of the key ring. Choose the one you like best." The band never met Tucker and once, when they appeared on *The Merv Griffin Show*, said that they believed he was dead. The comment triggered a torrent of calls to

this big fat wrestler. I guess I was this
that as a nickname. The Mars came
pizzazz, and a lot of girls say I'm out of this
—BRUNO MARS

the Tucker residence from concerned friends and relatives. "I had my nephew, who is a lawyer, write them a letter," Tucker recalled, and for the next several weeks the credits at the end of *The Merv Griffin Show* included the line "Marshall Tucker is alive." "It never bothered me that they used my name," he noted. "I never made one penny off it, but I'm not bitter about it. I didn't want any. I'm just glad they made good."

MARTHA AND THE VANDELLAS The Detroit vocal trio of Martha Reeves, Annette Beard, and Rosalind Ashford were signed to Motown Records in 1962. Reeves changed their name from the Del-Phis to Martha and the Vandellas, inspired by Detroit's Van Dyke Street and Della Reese, her favorite singer.

MASSIVE ATTACK The group formed in Bristol, England, in 1988. Founding member Robert "3D" Del Naja noted that the name is ironic, given their pacifist leanings: "It's amusing, and perhaps a little unfortunate, but Massive Attack derives from a groovy warehouse party in Bristol of which we were quite fond." In 1991, during the Gulf War, the band name was briefly shortened to Massive at the advice of their manager, who was concerned that the name Massive Attack was too controversial to be mentioned on the radio.

MATCHBOX 20 "People would ask, 'What's the name of your band?,'" recalled Rob Thomas, "and I'd say 'Larry.' We went through entire books of names." After burning through a variety of short-lived monikers, including Big Shoe Spider, Tindersockets, and Joanie Loves Chachi, the Florida-based band took their name from the number "20" and a patch that read "Matchbox" on a softball jersey. "The two parts weren't even related," Thomas recalled. "Matchbox 20 was the stupidest name we had ever heard. But a couple months later, it was the only name that stuck in our heads."

MC5 Formed in 1967, the highly political MC5 were originally called the Motor City Five, after their hometown of Detroit.

THE MCCOYS Best known for the 1965 number-one hit "Hang on Sloopy," the band was formed by high school classmates in Union City, Indiana, in 1962. They took their name from the Ventures' instrumental "The McCoy," the B side to the 1960 hit "Walk Don't Run."

MEAT LOAF The singer, born Marvin Lee Aday, has been called Meat Loaf for most of his life. It was a nickname that referenced his bulky frame, given to him not by his high school football coach, as many reports have stated, but by his father. He explained, "This is what people don't understand. Anybody in their right mind would not have chosen that, OK? My father started calling me that when I was a kid. When I went to the first grade, my teacher said, 'Meat, sit down.' I would go to church and the minister would say, 'Meat, we're glad to see you here.' I can't win. But I don't think it's any funnier than other people's names. Start saying 'Bruce Springsteen' over and over again. Everybody's name is weird."

> "My father started calling me that when I was a kid. When I went to the first grade, my teacher said, 'Meat, sit down.'"
> —MEAT LOAF

MEAT PUPPETS Meat Puppets formed in Phoenix in the early eighties. The band's name was inspired by their sense that sometimes the music seemed to play them, not the other way around. The music becomes the master and they are but mere puppets. Singer and guitarist Curt Kirkwood explained: "After careful and prolonged deliberation, we chose that one because we had a song that was named 'Meat Puppets,' and it was named after our style that we were pursuing, which was more or less the reason that we got together and have stayed together this long. It related to whenever the three of us played together, it would be like there was something else—the actual thing that was being created by the three parts, the whole of it not only seemed greater, it actually seemed to reverse roles. It seemed to be responsible for us rather than vice versa, and that's how we got it."

MEGADETH Guitarist Dave Mustaine formed Megadeth after he was kicked out of Metallica in 1983. "The band's name means the act of dying," he explained, "but like really mega! To be more specific, one million deaths, or the hypothetical body count of a nuclear fallout."

THE MEKONS The Mekons formed in Leeds, England, in the late seventies. Founding guitarist John Langford explained: "A Mekon was a tyrannical space alien that terrorized earth in a 1950s English comic called *Dan Dare*."

THE MELVINS The band formed in 1983 after meeting at Montesano Junior-Senior High School in Montesano, Washington. According to lead singer and guitarist Buzz "King Buzzo" Osborne, the band was named after a supervisor at a Thriftway supermarket where he worked who was disliked by the other employees. The band members thought the Melvins was a suitably ridiculous name. Osborne noted, "We wanted a name that didn't sound like anything, sort of like the Ramones."

MEN AT WORK The band formed in Melbourne, Australia, in 1979. Singer Colin Hay recalled: "I was driving in the country in Australia years ago with my girlfriend, and at that time there were all these signs everywhere saying 'Men at Work,' and we drove past one of them and there were about ten guys digging a trench. One was actually digging the trench and the other nine were watching, as is usually the case. That struck me as being amusing, and kind of humorous. My girlfriend and I both kind of looked at each other and she said, 'That'd be a great name for a band.' And I said, 'Yes, it would.' I suggested it to the other guys in the band, and we already had a lot of different names that'd been come up with and everyone went, 'Yeah, y'know, well, kind of.' Then we had to start playing at this hotel, but we hadn't settled on a name. The owner of the hotel finally called up and said, 'Look, we've got to put something at the front telling people who you are.' So the guitarist, Ron Strykert, came in and he said, 'I think we should go with Men at Work.' So we did that. And they used to have this blackboard outside this pub where we played that had 'Men at Work' on it every Thursday night, and it was funny because a lot of people used to go in and apply for jobs. They used to drive past and think, 'Oh, they need people to work.' There was something underdoggy about the name as well that I quite liked. It kind of always struck me as coming up from underneath or something." When asked if he was glad they chose the name, he said, "Absolutely! It was great because, you see it everywhere on the side of the road."

METALLICA Metallica formed in Los Angeles in 1981. According to lead singer and guitarist James Hetfield, "Lars (Ulrich, the drummer) stole it from a friend of ours, Ron Quintana. Quintana shared a list of potential names for a fanzine he was starting and Metallica was one of them." Other options included "Ripshifta with a T-A, not a T-E-R. It was either that or Blitzer. The other one that wouldn't quite have made it was Thunderfuck." Quintana decided to go with Metal Mania for his fanzine, and the band took the name Metallica.

MFSB The name of the group, a rotating crew of more than thirty studio musicians who played on the majority of the records released by Philadelphia International Records in the early seventies, has been

"We'd play shows, but usually our shows were just the two of us singing along with an iPod. We weren't playing instruments. It was more of a spectacle than an actual live concert."
—BEN GOLDWASSER, MGMT

widely reported to stand for "Mothers, Fathers, Sisters, Brothers." But according to *The Billboard Book of One-Hit Wonders*, MFSB stood for "Mother Fuckin' Son of a Bitch," adding that "if you asked any one of the group's members what the initials stood for, he or she would look you straight in the eye and reply "Mothers, Fathers, Sisters, Brothers."

MGMT Andrew VanWyngarden and Ben Goldwasser met as undergrads at Wesleyan University in Middletown, Connecticut. When they began performing together, they didn't set out to become rock stars. Their first gig was a campus party at which they performed the theme song from the movie *Ghostbusters* over and over again. "It started out as a complete joke," Goldwasser confessed. "We'd play shows, but usually our shows were just the two of us singing along with an iPod. We weren't playing instruments. It was more of a spectacle than an actual live concert. People didn't know whether to take it as a complete joke or not. It was kind of funny seeing how other people would try and gauge their reactions by us. Like, they seemed like they were trying to work out whether we took ourselves seriously or not. It left people feeling very confused. That's something that we've always enjoyed doing: confusing people." They would sign emails to each other as "the Management," which, VanWyngarden said, was meant "as a jokey, corporate-sounding thing." Eventually they began performing under the name the Management until they discovered that another band was already using the name. They then adopted the name MGMT, an abbreviation for "management" that is pronounced as a series of individual letters.

MINISTRY Singer Al Jourgensen formed Ministry in Chicago in the early eighties. He explained: "I was at home writing my first song on a four-track. I had no name for my band or the song, and as I finished the song, I looked up at the TV screen; there was a movie on called *Ministry of Fear*, with Ray Milland. I thought, 'Wow, groovy name for a band.' After that, it was changed to Ministry of Truth, then we changed it to Ministry of Canned Peaches, then finally Ministry."

THE MISFITS Marilyn Monroe's final film before her death in 1962, *The Misfits*, is often cited as the inspiration for the band's name, but according to Glenn Danzig, who formed the band in Lodi, New Jersey, in 1977, that's only part of the story. "It was just the impetus for it," he explained. "Really the reason for the Misfits was that I never felt like I fit. I used to wear an old punk-rock shirt that said 'Social Misfit' on it."

MOBY GRAPE Moby Grape formed in San Francisco in 1966. Guitarist Jerry Miller recalled, "We were all hanging out in the studio in San Francisco, and (bassist) Bob Mosley and Skippy (Alexander Spence, lead singer and guitarist) went out to have a little lunch, and they came back laughing like crazy with a name for the band. They were thinking of this joke, y'know: 'What's purple and swims in the ocean?' So they came back in and said, 'Moby Grape, we'll just be Moby Grape.' So that's how it happened. We all laughed, and whatever makes you laugh is good." When asked if there were other names in contention, Miller reported: "There was one that our manager wanted—he liked Bentley Escort. It kind of related to Jefferson Airplane, Strawberry Alarm Clock—y'know, that kind of thinking. But we hated that one. So Moby Grape sounded good, and it was made up by the band, so we liked that much better."

THE MODERN LOVERS Jonathan Richman formed the Modern Lovers in Boston in the early seventies. Richman explained, in characteristic fashion: "The Modern Lovers name came to be the day after Jonathan Richman decided to form a band. Jonathan wanted a name to describe the kind of love songs he was going to make. He figured they would be modern ones."

MODEST MOUSE The name of the band, which formed in 1992 in Issaquah, Washington, a Seattle suburb, is not a reference to a mouse, at least not directly. It comes from a line in a story by British author Virginia Woolf. Singer and guitarist Isaac Brock explained: "It was required reading in some class I was taking at the time. It was from a Virginia Woolf book where she referred to people who were working the grind as 'modest mouse-like people.' I wanted to originally name the band Modest Mouse-like People, but that seemed a little long. I regretted the name for some time because it sounds so cutesy. I got really sick of seeing posters with Mighty Mouse on them. I don't even remember which story. I just remember that part." The exact reference is to "modest mouse-coloured people" in Woolf's first published story, "The Mark on the Wall," from 1917: "I wish I could hit upon a pleasant track of thought, a track indirectly reflecting credit upon myself, for those are the pleasantest thoughts, and very frequent even in the minds of modest mouse-coloured people, who believe genuinely that they dislike to hear their own praises."

MOLLY HATCHET The band began in Jacksonville, Florida, in 1975 and took their name from Hatchet Molly, a legendary, perhaps mythical, Southern prostitute who lured men to her home, where she castrated and mutilated them.

THE MONKEES The name was coined by producers Bob Rafelson and Bert Schneider in 1965 in imitation of the Beatles, whose 1964 film, *A Hard Day's Night*, was the inspiration for their TV series.

THE MOODY BLUES The Moody Blues began as the M&B Five in Birmingham, England, in 1964. Guitarist Justin Hayward joined the band in 1966 and became their lead vocalist and chief lyricist. Hayward remembered: "In Birmingham where we used to work, all of the major gigs were in the back of pubs. The pubs were very, very large in Birmingham, still are, and they'd have a sort of big room at the back where they'd have dances. One of the major breweries in Birmingham was called Mitchell & Butler. The group had a deal working for them, with Mitchell & Butler sponsoring the group some equipment because they were working a lot of the time in their pubs. All pubs in England are owned by breweries, and Miller & Butler owned lots of them in the Midlands. So that's why the original group was called the M&B Five. Associating yourselves with a brewery meant you had gigs made for you, really—it gave you one step up on everybody else. Then, when it proved to be a rather sort of nothing name, Mike Pinder, our original keyboard player, thought of the name Moody Blues. We dropped the 'Five' and then became the Moody Blues, but it was really the initials that came first." When asked why Pinder chose Moody and Blues, Hayward explained, "The whole image of the group was kind of dark. The 'Moody' came from the fact that we never smiled in photographs, and they were very dark. If you look at all the early photographs, we're all wearing sort of these dark blue suits, what they call reefer jackets, done up, always done up, with dark shirts underneath. The whole thing was rather sinister. We were a rhythm and blues band, so that's where the 'Blues' came from. And then I wrote 'Nights in White Satin' and it all changed. It was completely different then. The fact that we did a great big left turn was really just to try and find ourselves and discover our own personalities and how to express ourselves before we went completely broke. At that point we'd gone as far as we could go singing about people's problems in the Deep South of America without knowing anything about it, and at the same time worrying about our image and how our hair looked, y'know. It was completely incongruous. And although we loved rhythm and blues, and we were good at it, it just wasn't expressing our own personalities. The songs that I was writing just didn't fit in with the rhythm and blues thing. So that was the big change, when we decided one day in the van coming home from a gig, we thought, 'Oh, sod it, let's forget all that rhythm and blues stuff; let's just do our own songs and see what happens.' Because the alternative was just to split up, really, and go and get another job." Despite the change in musical direction, the band decided to stick with the name Moody Blues. "I've often thought about that," Hayward admitted, "whether at that particular point, whether we should've changed the name as well. In the end I don't think it actually would have made any difference."

THE MOTHERS OF INVENTION The Mothers of Invention began as the Soul Giants, a band Frank Zappa discovered playing soul and R&B covers at a Pomona, California, bar in 1963. Zappa joined the band, convinced them to play original material—"I talked them into getting weird"—and changed their name to Captain Glasspack and the Magic Mufflers. After getting tossed out of numerous area bars, they changed their name to the Muthers. "It just happened to be Mother's Day (1964)," Zappa recalled, "although we weren't aware of it at the time. When you are nearly starving to death, you don't keep track of holidays." The following year they changed their name to the Mothers, and they were signed by Verve, MGM's jazz/R&B label, in 1966. Zappa remembered: "We were then informed that they (MGM Records) couldn't release the record—MGM executives had convinced themselves that no DJ would ever play a record on the air by a group called

'The Mothers' (as if our name was going to be the Big Problem). They insisted that we change it, and so the stock line is 'Out of necessity, we became the Mothers of Invention.'"

MÖTLEY CRÜE Mötley Crüe formed in Los Angeles in 1981, but the band's name dates back to 1973 when guitarist Mick Mars was still called Bob Deal and was working as a roadie for a group in San Diego called Mottley Croo. "We were a bar band, rude and nasty," drummer Jack Valentine explained. "There was one showcase club in town that brought in L.A. bands." In order to play there, Mottley Croo changed its name to Whitehorse and claimed to come from Los Angeles. "Then we got such a big following that we kept the name Whitehorse." After Whitehorse's guitar player left the band, Deal took his place. "Deal was the most destitute being I'd ever met," said Valentine. "The guy was just so poor. He didn't have a car, he didn't have a guitar that was worth beans. He had one set of clothes." Deal eventually moved to L.A. and hooked up with bassist Nikki Sixx (Frank Carlton Serafino Feranna Jr.), drummer Tommy Lee (Thomas Lee Bass), and singer Vince Neil (Vincent Neil Wharton) after running an ad that read, in part, "Loud, rude, aggressive guitarist available." Nikki Sixx explained why they added umlauts to the name: "We didn't think about its proper use. We just wanted to do something to be weird, and the umlaut is very visual. It's German and strong, and that Nazi Germany mentality—'the future belongs to us'—intrigued me." The band's improperly used umlauts did lead to some confusion. During their first tour of Germany, Sixx admitted that "all the kids were going, 'Mutley Cruh!' and we were going, 'Huh?'"

MOTT THE HOOPLE The band began as the Shakedown Sound in Hereford, England, in 1968, then changed its name to Silence. Guy Stevens at Island Records took over as manager and producer in 1969 after they sent him a demo tape. He recruited Ian Hunter to replace the lead singer and renamed them Mott the Hoople after an obscure book he had recently read by Willard Manus.

MUDHONEY Grunge pioneers Mudhoney came together in Seattle in 1988 and took their name from the classic Russ Meyer sexploitation film.

MUMFORD & SONS When Marcus Mumford, Ben Lovett, Winston Marshall, and Ted Dwane formed the group in London in 2007, they called themselves Mumford & Sons because, Lovett noted, "the band name kind of made sense as an antiquated family business name." He joked that they didn't call it Lovett & Sons because "it would have just sounded like (American country musician) Lyle Lovett's side project. No, honestly, when we put the band together Marcus was the one making the phone calls and getting the gigs. We never thought anyone outside of London was going to see us." Mumford himself regrets the name: "It's so . . . it's rubbish. It's a rubbish name. Your name, you never really think about it when you're in the pub. You've done your first rehearsal, you've written your first song, and someone's like, 'You need a band name now.' And we're all, you know, young guns and didn't really think about it very much. And then of course your band name eventually starts preceding you." In retrospect, Mumford noted: "If I'd known it was going to go this way, I would have wanted to call it anything other than my last name. It's a ball-ache. We thought about changing it, but it's a bit late now."

MUNGO JERRY Mungo Jerry, best known for their 1970 hit "In the Summertime," formed in London in 1969 as the Good Earth. They renamed themselves Mungo Jerry after the mischievous cat Mungojerrie in *Old Possum's Book of Practical Cats* by T.S. Eliot, which would later inspire the Broadway musical *Cats*.

MUSE The band came together in the seaside town of Teignmouth, England, in 1994. Drummer Dominic Howard recalls, "We didn't know what the word meant at the time, but when the band formed, I used to hang 'round with this group of girls that were doing sort of strange, improvised, witchcraft music, or something along those lines. And this old man, Richard, some old sort of posh geezer who was really into classical music, said it was like a muse had come across the town and caused everyone to try and get into something a bit more creative. And I think that we just took that name 'cause I thought it sounded like a good name."

MY CHEMICAL ROMANCE The band was formed in Newark, New Jersey, in 2001 by singer Gerard Way and drummer Matt Pelissier. The name was first suggested by Way's younger brother Mikey, who would eventually join the band on bass. Mikey was working at a Barnes & Noble bookstore, where he saw the book *Ecstasy: Three Tales of Chemical Romance*, a collection of novellas by Irvine Welsh, the Scottish author of *Trainspotting*. When Mikey mentioned the name Chemical Romance to his brother, Gerard changed it to My Chemical Romance as a reference to his own use of antidepressants. Gerard noted at the time, "On a personal level, for me, it's about antidepressants. I was, like, so depressed and I just wanted to cut my fuckin' face off. It's also like a reference to Irvine Welsh and his books.... (But) it really means for me antidepressants."

MY MORNING JACKET Singer and guitarist Jim James began writing songs for what would become My Morning Jacket while an art student at the University of Kentucky in Lexington in 1998. He recalled, "I began the My Morning Jacket project in my dorm room at Holmes Hall at UK on my buddy Todd's four-track." James has been famously coy about where the name came from. He told

CNN it was inspired by a jacket with the initials MMJ on the back that he found in a burned-out bar near campus: "It was Boot's Bar. . . . It didn't burn down, but the inside of it burned. The outside was still there, and we went in one night and they were carrying everything out. Down in the bottom of the bar was, like, the strippers' area, I guess. It used to be a strip club and there was, like, a pole and the stage was there and the whole bar was burned and everything was decimated, but the stage lights were still on and in the dressing room next to the strippers' stage was a closet and in that closet was a jacket with the initials MMJ stenciled on the jacket." But James also told another interviewer: "I was just lying on my bed, writing songs in a notebook, and I put 'my morning jacket' at the top of the page. It doesn't mean anything. A lot of things happen for me that way. Things pop into my head when I'm riding down the highway or at inopportune moments, like when I'm falling off to sleep."

"It used to be a strip club and there was, like, a pole and the stage was there and the whole bar was burned and everything was decimated, but the stage lights were still on and in the dressing room next to the strippers' stage was a closet and in that closet was a jacket with the initials MMJ stenciled on the jacket."
—JIM JAMES, MY MORNING JACKET

THE NATIONAL The group formed in New York City in 1999. Singer Matt Berninger recalled: "We were trying to find a name that didn't mean anything, that was sort of devoid of any kind of interpretation and wasn't overly clever. And that was the simplest thing we could think of. You can't walk down the street without seeing the words 'The National something or other' somewhere. So it was benign and meaningless. That's kind of why we picked it. Although that backfired a little bit because we went to Europe—we probably should have thought of this ahead of time—but nationalism has a very right-wing connotation, especially in Germany, France and . . . the Nationalists and the National Front and all that kind of stuff. So in Germany we actually had some shows boycotted because they thought we were in some way affiliated with the right-wing conservative neo-Nazi party. We had to do some press to make sure people realized that we were not associated with the Nazis. The band name, it's kind of funny, when we started out, we would probably name it something else, but we're stuck with it, and I'm happy with it."

NAZARETH The band got their start in Dunfermline, Scotland, in 1969 and took their name from the first line of the Band's "The Weight": "I pulled into Nazareth . . ."

NEON TREES The band formed in Provo, Utah, in 2005 and took their name from the neon palm trees on a sign at an In-N-Out Burger restaurant near where lead singer Tyler Glenn and guitarist Chris Allen grew up in Murrieta, California. "It's a nostalgic name," Glenn explained. "My friends hung out at a restaurant in high school, and they had neon palm tree lights there, and we were obsessed with Echo & the Bunnymen and Bauhaus and Flock of Seagulls, and we thought it sounded like a cool eighties band name. This was years and years before we started Neon Trees, and when we did the name for our band, I was like, 'Neon Trees is cool,' and we kind of stuck with it. It sort of started to fit the aesthetic that we were gunning for." In a strange coincidence, the band later learned that bassist Branden Campbell's father, Steve, installed the neon trees at the very same In-N-Out location that inspired the name while working for a Las Vegas-based sign company. In addition to the neon signs, most In-N-Out locations have a pair of real palm trees that have been planted so they form an X. Company founder Harry Snyder got the idea from the 1963 movie *It's a Mad, Mad, Mad, Mad World*, a madcap comedy in which a star-studded cast races to find $350,000 in stolen cash buried under four crossed palm trees.

NEW FOUND GLORY According to singer Jordan Pundik, the name was created when he and guitarist Stephen Klein were both working at a Red Lobster restaurant in Coral Springs, Florida, in 1997. "I'm, like, scrambling, looking through books and things like that," Pundik remembered. "Somehow in the conversation the Get Up Kids came up and we're all big fans of the Get Up Kids. They have a song called 'A New Found Interest in Massachusetts.' For some reason that kind of turned a lightbulb on. Then I drew, like, a flag burning on the piece of paper with, like, an anarchy sign. This was before the band was what we are. When we were trying to find out who we were. And then I wrote 'A New Found Glory' and it just stuck."

NEW ORDER After the death of singer Ian Curtis, the remaining members of Joy Division formed New Order in Manchester in 1980. The band's manager Rob Gretton suggested the name after seeing the phrase in the book *Leaving the 20th Century: The Incomplete Work of the Situationist International*. He recalled, "A passage about a new order of architecture stuck in my mind. At the time, I thought it was a very neutral name." While some assumed the name referred to the band's new beginning, others concluded it was, like Joy Division, a Nazi reference. The New Order was the system of government that the Nazis wanted to impose on the conquered areas of Europe under their control. The band disavowed any connection to fascism, but the mischievous Gretton later muddied the waters by claiming the reference was actually to the genocidal Cambodian Khmer Rouge's The People's New Order of Kampuchea, which he had read about in the newspaper *The Guardian*.

> "The truth of it is, I've always liked the Japanese movie *The Pornographers*. It's a mid-sixties movie. I was so fascinated by the word 'pornographer.'"
> —A.C. NEWMAN, THE NEW PORNOGRAPHERS

THE NEW PORNOGRAPHERS The band formed in Vancouver, British Columbia, in 1997, and for years it was rumored that the name came from a statement made by TV evangelist Jimmy Swaggart in a televised speech on June 1, 1986, that various rock groups and music publications were "the new pornography." He later elaborated that he regarded rock as "pornography and degenerative filth, which denigrates all the values we hold sacred and is destructive to youth." The band played along with this rumor for a while but eventually set the record straight. The name was chosen by band member A.C. Newman, who admitted, "The truth of it is, I've always liked the Japanese movie *The*

Pornographers. It's a mid-sixties movie. I was so fascinated by the word 'pornographer.' It just seemed like a weird word to me. It seemed like such a clinical word to describe what it is. I also always loved the name the New Seekers. I always thought it was a ridiculous name. There were the original Seekers and then a few years later a completely different band showed up and they called themselves the New Seekers. I really liked the 'New.' Somehow, in my head one night, it just became the New Pornographers. Before we'd written any songs—before we were a band—I thought, 'We're going to be a band, and we're going to be called the New Pornographers.' So the name came first."

THE NEW YORK DOLLS The New York Dolls, who often performed in drag, formed in New York City in 1971. Guitarist Sylvain Sylvain (born Sylvain Mizrahi) recalled: "The name, which I kind of came up with, was actually put together before the Dolls ever played together as a whole band with (singer) David Johansen, and even with (guitarist) Johnny Thunders. The original drummer, Billy Murcia—he passed away on our first English tour, and we got Jerry Nolan to replace him—we had a group, me and Billy, called the Pox. When it broke up after one of the guitar players left, we were sort of drawing up ideas for names and stuff. Usually, y'know, you come up with a name from either television or maybe a newspaper, or like a current event that's going on maybe, just basically anything that hits you. I saw the movie *Beyond the Valley of the Dolls*, the Russ Meyer film, which was sort of a parody of *The Valley of the Dolls*, and I said, 'Hmm, Dolls.' And of course they used to call pills 'dolls,' especially in the movie: 'Oh, what happened to her?' 'Oh, she took all these dolls.' So I said to Billy, 'Wow, that could be a cool name for a band, just the Dolls, y'know?' When we met David, he said, 'Hmm, the Dolls, yeah, but how about the New York Dolls?' New York really made a lot of sense to us because obviously that's where we came from, and that's where we put the band together. There was a lot of art and all kinds of groovy stuff being stirred up in those days, as New York was basically like your international center. The Dolls by itself meant different things to different people. When most people saw us, they said, 'Wow, the Dolls,' and they never really associated the movie, or the fact that it meant drugs, until later on."

NICKELBACK The band formed in Hanna, Alberta, in 1995. The name was suggested by bass player Mike Kroeger, who was working at a coffee shop at the time. He recalled: "I really liked working at the coffee shop, especially the social aspect of a coffee shop community. People would come in, talk, and share ideas, and I found that a cool environment to be placed in for work. I generally wouldn't go to that kind of thing, to just go and socialize while sipping coffee. But work placed me in those situations and forced me to be a more social creature than I am. We were struggling to find a name for the band, and a lot of people would come into the coffee shop to purchase a coffee that was for $1.45 and would give me $1.50 and very frequently I would find myself saying, 'Here's your nickel back.' After saying it probably hundreds of times, it occurred to me that it sounded interesting as one word. I stopped work in the middle of the morning rush and called the guys to ask them if they thought it was a good band name. Thankfully it wasn't one we didn't completely hate, so we decided to give it a shot and it all just took off."

NIGHT RANGER The band formed in San Francisco in the early eighties and by the middle of the decade had a handful of hits, including "Sister Christian." Drummer and vocalist Kelly Keagy explained the origins of their name: "It's about a guy named Eddie, who was a homeless man in San Francisco that used to hang out around the clubs we played. Eddie was homeless, but he took care of other homeless people. He proved he could have dignity and strength—he fed off the spirit of the streets. Everyone called him the Night Ranger, and when we met him and got to know him and what he was about, he was really an inspiration to us."

NINE INCH NAILS Trent Reznor formed Nine Inch Nails in Cleveland in 1987, as a one-man industrial-rock band. The name has been rumored to represent all sorts of things: the stakes that were used to crucify Christ, the standard size of nails used to seal coffins, and what you'll find on the tips of the Statue of Liberty's fingers. Reznor's explanation is a bit more mundane: "I don't know if you've ever tried to think of band names, but usually you think you have a great one and you look at it the next day and it's stupid. I had about a hundred of those. Nine Inch Nails lasted the two-week test, looked great in print, and could be abbreviated easily. It really doesn't have any literal meaning. It seemed kind of frightening. It's a curse trying to come up with band names."

THE 1975 The band got its start in Manchester, England, in 2002. Lead singer and rhythm guitarist Matty Healy recalled: "When I was about nineteen I went to Majorca and I came across a beautiful Spanish villa which seemed to have all of its furniture outside. I sparked up a conversation with the artist who lived there and ended up staying all day. His house was like some kind of 1960s bazaar: original Beatles records, signed Elvis stuff, a photo of him with Hendrix. . . . He gave me a whole load of beat generation stuff. I found a mental page of scribblings. It was so mad I couldn't figure out whether it was suicidal or totally life affirming. What stuck with me was that the page was dated '1st June. The 1975.'" Healy decided, "It was the perfect band name."

NIRVANA The band was formed by singer and guitarist Kurt Cobain and bassist Krist Novoselic, who met in high school in Aberdeen,

Washington, in 1987. Early names included Fecal Matter, Skid Row, and Ted Ed Fred. They ultimately settled on Nirvana because, Cobain explained, they "wanted a name that was kind of beautiful or nice and pretty instead of a mean, raunchy punk name like the Angry Samoans." The term "nirvana" is most commonly associated with Buddhism and refers to the ultimate state of relief and freedom from the cycle of rebirths. "Punk is musical freedom," Cobain said. "It's saying, doing, and playing what you want. In Webster's terms, 'nirvana' means freedom from pain, suffering, and the external world, and that's pretty close to a definition of punk rock." A British psychedelic band called Nirvana that formed in London in 1965 filed a lawsuit in California over use of the name in 1992. The case was settled out of court for undisclosed terms that apparently allowed both bands to continue using the name and put out new music without any disclaimers to distinguish one band from another. It was reported that Cobain's label, Geffen Records, paid $100,000 to the original Nirvana to allow Cobain's band continued use of the name. The British Nirvana had been planning to record an album of cover songs called *Nirvana Sings Nirvana* but shelved the project when Cobain died in 1994.

NO DOUBT Named after a catchphrase used by original member John Spence, who shared lead vocals with Gwen Stefani. He committed suicide in 1987.

OASIS The band had its origins in another Manchester group called the Rain. When Liam Gallagher joined the band in 1991, he suggested they change their name to Oasis, inspired by the Oasis Leisure Centre, an entertainment and sports complex in the town of Swindon. He saw the venue listed on a tour poster for the band Inspiral Carpets, for whom his brother Noel worked as a roadie. Noel eventually joined his brother in Oasis, despite his opinion that "Oasis was a shit name for a band." Oasis never played the Swindon Oasis before breaking up in 2009.

THE OFFSPRING The band, which formed in Orange County, California, in the late eighties, were so named because they considered themselves the second generation of California punk rockers.

OINGO BOINGO Oingo Boingo began not as a band but as a satirical stage act called the Mystic Knights of the Oingo Boingo that built a cult following in Los Angeles in the mid-seventies. The show gradually incorporated musical elements until it evolved at the end of the decade into a band with the shortened name of Oingo Boingo. Founding member Danny Elfman went on to become an award-winning film and TV score composer, notable for his longtime collaborative relationship with director Tim Burton.

THE O'JAYS They started as the Triumphs at McKinley High School in Canton, Ohio, in 1958, but later called themselves the Mascots, and eventually changed their name for the last time in 1961 in honor of Eddie O'Jay, a Cleveland disc jockey who served as their mentor.

ONEREPUBLIC Lead vocalist Ryan Tedder and guitarist Zach Filkins became friends during their senior year at Colorado Springs Christian High School in 1996 and formed a band called This Beautiful Mess, named after the second album by the group Sixpence None the Richer. After parting ways at the end of senior year, Tedder and Filkins reunited in Los Angeles in 2002 and formed a new band called Republic. In less than a year they were signed to Interscope Records, which persuaded them to change their name to avoid potential legal action from similarly named groups, so Republic became OneRepublic. Drummer Eddie Fisher explained, "Ryan came up with the name Republic originally. He wanted something strong. He wanted something unifying. Something that would translate in all languages as Republic." Some fans have assumed that "OneRepublic" is a reference to the Pledge of Allegiance, but the pledge goes "to the republic, for which it stands, one nation under God," not "one republic. . . . " Fisher admitted, "There was a rumor that it was, and we kind of went with it," but that wasn't the original intent.

ORCHESTRAL MANOEUVRES IN THE DARK [OMD] The band was formed in Liverpool, England, in 1978 by synthesizer players Andy McCluskey and Paul Humphreys. McCluskey recalled: "When I was an aspiring musician, before I was even in bands—when I was fifteen or sixteen—I used to write on my bedroom wall, much to my mother's annoyance, just names—song titles, bands, just anything that came into my head. I had a fairly bizarre collection of them up there. When Paul Humphreys and I decided to just be a two-piece, using a tape recorder and playing songs that really all our best friends thought were absolute crap, we figured we needed a name that was going to tell people that we were not a punk band, we were not a rock band or a typical pop band, we were something different. So quite simply I just went to my bedroom wall and started looking down the list of all the names and things. Orchestral Manoeuvres in the Dark had, in fact, been a title of a song which we had intended to do but never did, which just featured recorded war noises and some very, very distorted guitar. We just figured it was such a literally off-the-wall name that people would know that this was a different type of band. We actually only got together as the two of us to do one gig. We dared ourselves to go into this punk club and do our synth songs the way we wanted to, instead of having bloody lead guitarists and drummers messing them up for us, as had been happening in the previous bands. So that was how we got the name. It doesn't have any deep meaning as such. It was really just a name to set the band aside as being something different from all the very short punk band names that were around at the time." When asked if he ever regretted choosing the name, he admitted, "Oh, yeah. I mean, it's such a hell of a mouthful, although I do prefer it to being shortened to OMD. It makes it much more convenient for DJs—by the time they've actually told you the name of the band, the track is half over on the radio. But right from the very start people had trouble with it, not least because 'manoeuvres' is spelled differently in America to how it is in England. In all the various European territories, because it's a collection of words, they would actually put it into their own language. I've seen posters in Spain that say OMD and posters that say MOD, because converted to Spanish, the M comes before the O." When asked if the name was inspired by Electric Light Orchestra in any way, he said, "It had nothing to do with it. In fact, when we started, we were influenced by German electronic music. I always thought ELO were pretty passé even by then, in the seventies. So the fact that it got shorted to OMD, that was one of the first of three-letter abbreviations. I mean, now there's a million and one three-letter bands around."

PANIC! AT THE DISCO The group began as a blink-182 cover band in 2004 when the members were high school students in the Las Vegas suburb of Summerlin. Their name came from the lyrics to the song "Panic" by the band Name Taken: "Panic at the disco/ Sat back and took it so slow." (Name Taken was a rock band from Orange, California, that was originally called All That's Left until they discovered that the name was already taken—hence the name Name Taken.) The band also considered the name Burn Down the Disco, from the song "Panic" by the Smiths: "Burn down the disco/ Hang the blessed DJ." Recalled bassist Brent Wilson, "At the time we were trying to think of a name, it was between Panic at the Disco and Burn Down the Disco. It's a weird coincidence that both the songs were called 'Panic.'" The addition of the exclamation point put their own stamp on the name, but they dropped it for their second studio album *Pretty. Odd.* in 2008 because the band members said they had grown tired of it. Explained lead singer Brendon Urie, "We wrote it that way once, when we first started the band, and then people kept writing it that way. I mean, every time I write (our name), I never put an exclamation point in there." The band restored the exclamation point the following year after growing tired of being asked why it was dropped. "It's amazing because we never necessarily got asked about it that much when it was *in* there," said drummer Spencer Smith. "And then all of a sudden, we decided to take it away for *Pretty. Odd.* and we were asked about that in, I think, every interview."

PANTERA The heavy metal band formed in Arlington, Texas, in 1981 when the members were in high school. The band was originally called Gemini, and then became Eternity. At the time, lead guitarist Dimebag Darrell Abbott was called Diamond Darrell. Darrell's brother, drummer Vinnie Paul, explained how they ended up with the name Pantera: "The first name that me and Dime ever came up with for the band was Gemini, following in the footsteps of bands like Journey, Heart, stuff like that. Then it elevated from Gemini to Eternity, which was much cooler. And then one day in high school, when I was in the (school marching band) drumline, a guy suggested to me, 'Man, you oughta call your band Pantera. And I said, 'What the hell is "pantera"?' and he said, 'Oh, man, it's the coolest race car there is.' I started investigating and found out that it meant 'panther' in Spanish—and it just had a really nice ring to it—and brought it to the band. I brought a logo in that had a cat's head on it—it was the very first logo we ever had—and everybody loved it, so we became Pantera from that point on."

PAPA ROACH The band formed in Vacaville in Northern California in 1993. Their name was inspired by the nickname of lead singer Jacoby Shaddix's step-grandfather, Howard William Roatch. Shaddix recalled, "We came up with the name back in 1993 when we were, like, sixteen years old—young and dumb. At the time we were listening to lots of bands with funky names—stuff like Mr. Bungle, Primus, and the Red Hot Chili Peppers. We were also playing weird spastic funk-punk like they were, so we thought we should have a name that fit in with that vibe. At first we wanted to name the band Papa Gato after (a nickname for) Poncho Sanchez, the Latin percussionist.

But then I thought, what if we named it after my grandfather—his last name is Roatch. The other guys were like, 'You mean roach like as in weed?' But I also thought Papa Roach had a dirty, grimy sense of longevity that really represented where we were as people at the time. Roaches last, you know?" When asked what other names they considered, Shaddix said, "Other than Papa Gato? Nude was one of 'em. The Groove Merchants was another. We were goofy-ass kids."

PARAMORE The band formed in Franklin, Tennessee, in 2004. According to lead singer Hayley Williams, "Our friend's mom, her maiden name was Paramore. We thought it sounded really cool. After juggling around fifteen names, we said, 'Let's check out what 'paramour' means.' We knew it was spelled differently. The real spelling means a lot of things—real love, secret love. It felt like it was something cool that we could stand for, and we liked the way it sounded." The surname Paramore is derived from *par amour* in French, meaning "with love" or "with lover."

PARLIAMENT-FUNKADELIC As a teenager in Plainfield, New Jersey, in the fifties, George Clinton formed a vocal group called the Parliaments that, according to his manager Archie Bell, he named after Parliament cigarettes. In 1967, the Parliaments had a major hit with "(I Wanna) Testify," a straightforward love song. By then, Clinton had begun to rethink the Parliaments' sound after spending time in Detroit listening to psychedelic music, the Stooges, and the MC5. That year, after he was prevented from using the Parliaments name due to a legal battle with the owner of the group's record label, Clinton formed Funkadelic. He coined the name by crossing "funk" and "psychedelic," a combination that reflected the group's new musical direction. Eventually Clinton won the right to use the Parliaments name, which he did, after dropping the S and merging it with Funkadelic.

"When Paul signed the contract, he signed his legal name, Paul Revere Dick. And the guy looked at it and said, 'Paul Revere, that's great! You gotta use this name."

—MARK LINDSAY, PAUL REVERE & THE RAIDERS

PARQUET COURTS The indie rock band formed in Denton, Texas, in 2010 and then moved to New York City. Lead vocalist and guitarist Andrew Savage, who suggested the name, explained, "Parquet is a geometric arrangement of wooden panels, most popularly in a hatched checker pattern of opposing directions of the panels, you know what I'm talking about? It's also the material that's used for basketball courts, probably most famously the Boston Garden, and Sean (Yeaton, bassist) is from Boston, so it's kind of a geographic link for him. Also, I like that it's kind of a distinct name, and there's no other band name I can think of with 'courts' or 'parquet' in the name. It also allows you to have fun with some spelling variants and homophones." The band sometimes records and performs under the name Parkay Quarts. Parkay is a brand of margarine.

PAUL REVERE & THE RAIDERS Paul Revere & the Raiders began in 1959 in Caldwell, Idaho. Singer and saxophone player Mark Lindsay recalled: "We were a group playing around the Boise Valley area with no name. There was only one other group in that area, called Dick Cates and the Chessmen, and we were just 'the other group.' We played for a bit and then we began to realize, when we started drawing crowds, that we had to have some kind of nomenclature to identify ourselves. (Organist) Paul Revere's name was Paul Revere Dick. His folks were of German stock. They were second-generation immigrants, and they thought, I suppose, it would be great to name their son after a great American hero. Even though Paul Revere never made the ride. Samuel Prescott, a doctor, actually made that ride, but it didn't rhyme: 'Listen my children and you will hear of the midnight ride of Samuel Prescott.' Eventually, we cut our first tape under the name the Downbeats, vying for a record contract, in Idaho. And Paul took it down to Los Angeles, La-La Land, to try to get us a deal. He went around everywhere and no one would even arrest us. But he went out to Gardena, where a guy named John Guss had a pressing plant and two labels, Apex Records and Gardena Records. And Gardena, I guess, was more or less of a tax write-off label. He said, 'Sure, I'll put you guys on there,' and we signed for a nickel a record. When Paul signed the contract, he signed his legal name, Paul Revere Dick. And the guy looked at it and said, 'Paul Revere, that's great! You gotta use this name. How 'bout calling yourselves Paul Revere & the Nightriders?' So Paul came back and said, 'He wants to call us Paul Revere & the Nightriders.' I thought about it for a couple of days and said, 'You know, that sounds like cowboys. What if we called ourselves Raiders? Paul Revere & the Raiders. It sounds more like pirates or something from that era.' He said, 'Yeah, that sounds good.'"

PEARL JAM When the band came together in Seattle in 1990, they first called themselves Mookie Blaylock after the professional basketball player who was then on the New Jersey Nets. After landing a record deal, they changed their name but decided to call the debut album Ten after Blaylock's jersey number. In an early interview, front man Eddie Vedder claimed the name Pearl Jam was a reference to his great-grandmother Pearl, who made a peyote-infused jam. He later admitted the story was "total bullshit" although he actually had a great-grandmother named Pearl. Bassist Jeff Ament is credited with coming up with the name Pearl, although the exact reason why remains shrouded in mystery. Jam was reportedly inspired by seeing Neil Young jamming live in concert.

PERE UBU Singer and lyricist Dave Thomas formed Pere Ubu in Cleveland in 1975, naming the band after the hero of *Ubu Roi*, a play by French absurdist Alfred Jarry. Thomas explained why he chose the name: "Well, the glib remark would be that all the good names were taken already. At the time, Pere Ubu was quite clearly a good name because it met the prime requisites: that it had three syllables, that it didn't mean anything particularly—I mean, obviously it does, but to an audience in the American Midwest, which was where we were, one could be assured that it really wouldn't mean anything—that it seemed to mean something at the same time, that it looked good and sounded good. Those are just about all the things that you need in a band's name. Also, it had another sublevel of groovy art factors attached to it. I liked Jarry's production methods, and the way he required the audience to become involved in the production, and engaged the imagination of the audience with suggestion, and all that stuff. Mainly, it looked good and sounded good and didn't mean anything and had three syllables. A band's name is always one of the critical things to me. If you pick a stupid name, it indicates that you haven't thought too much about the whole thing, and it's a clear indication of where you hold yourself and what you're doing in your own mind. If you give your band a stupid, trivial name, then it indicates that you consider what you do stupid and trivial. Obviously, the inverse is true, or the obverse, or whatever it is, that if you give yourself a stupid, pretentious name. . . . We can only hope that Pere Ubu is on the good side of all those equations."

"If you give your band a stupid, trivial name, then it indicates that you consider what you do stupid and trivial."
—DAVE THOMAS, PERE UBU

PET SHOP BOYS Neil Tennant and Chris Lowe met at an electronics store on London's Kings Road in 1981. Discovering that they shared a love of dance music, they became friends and formed a band called West End. Later, they switched to Pet Shop Boys, after two friends of Lowe's who owned a pet shop in the Ealing district. They said they liked the name because they "thought it sounded like an English rap group."

PHISH The band formed in 1983 at the University of Vermont. In the June 1998 issue of *Döniac Schvice*, the band's official newsletter, bassist Mike Gordon explained, "Our drummer's name is Jon Fishman. His peers have favored the nickname Fish—it's the first part. So if I had to guess, I would think that someone, maybe me, maybe who knows, said, 'Let's call the band Phish.' The Ph, of course, was a marketing ploy that, by the way, has worked. Of course, if you ask Fish himself, he'll say, 'We liked the Phhhh sound that an airplane makes during takeoff.' But that's a pile of crap."

PHOENIX Indie pop band Phoenix formed in Versailles, France, in 1997. When asked how the band chose the name, lead singer Thomas Mars said, "Honestly, we can't remember. We lied so much about this, we lost the truth . . ." It's been speculated that the band named themselves after the instrumental song "Phoenix" by Daft Punk, whose members Thomas Bangalter and Guy-Manuel de Homem-Christo were formerly in the band called Darlin' with Phoenix guitarist Laurent Brancowitz. It's also been rumored that the band named themselves after actor Joaquin Phoenix, who, like Brancowitz and his older brother and bandmate Laurent Brancowitz, has a scar from surgery to correct a cleft palate as a child. (Joaquin Phoenix was actually born with the scar and did not have corrective surgery. He has what's known as a microform cleft, a mild form of cleft lip.)

P!NK P!nk was born Alecia Beth Moore in 1979, in Doylestown, Pennsylvania, and adopted her stage name Pink around the time she began performing at Philadelphia clubs when she was about fourteen years old. She recalls, "The name came from a lot of different places. It's been following me my whole life. The first time was actually not very nice. This kid I had a crush on, Devin—I went to the YMCA summer camp, 'cause it was the cheapest one—and this kid pulled my pants down in front of everybody at this auditorium. 'Cause we'd gone swimming and I swam in my underwear 'cause I didn't have a bathing suit, and then it's like, 'Oh, there's only one thing left in the day, I just won't put my underwear back on.' And then he pulled my pants down in front of everybody and I totally blushed and my butt cheeks were pink. And he was like, 'Yeah, pink!' and everyone made fun of me and I ran home crying. And I lived it down. That was when I was about eight. And I lived it down and then, when the *Reservoir Dogs* movie came out, (from director) Quentin Tarantino, Mr. Pink is, like, the smart, sassy, smartass kind of guy with the attitude, and me and all my friends are sitting around, we all kind of just dubbed each other, and they picked me for Mr. Pink. And then I told them the story, and they were like, 'Ah, you see you are Pink.' And that was basically it." Her name is often stylized as P!nk.

PINK FLOYD The band formed in London in 1965 to play a mix of R&B and blues. They were named the Pink Floyd Sound by singer and guitarist Syd Barrett, after two Georgia bluesmen, Pink Anderson and Floyd Council. As the band's sound changed, so did its name, first shortened to the Pink Floyd, and finally just Pink Floyd.

GLADYS KNIGHT AND THE PIPS At a birthday party for her ten-year-old brother Merald in 1952, Gladys Knight formed a quintet with Merald, their sister Brenda, and their cousins William and Eleanor Guest. They made such an impression that cousin James Woods urged them to turn professional and offered to manage them. They agreed and called themselves the Pips after Woods' nickname, Pip.

THE PIXIES The band formed in Boston in 1986. The name was chosen by lead guitarist Joey Santiago after flipping through a dictionary, and it was approved by the rest of the band because they liked the fact that it didn't have any real relevance to their sound. About his own name, vocalist and guitarist Black Francis, born Charles Michael Kittridge Thompson IV, told *Rolling Stone* in March 1989: "I always liked the sort of funny, corny, pompous stage names, like Iggy Pop and Billy Idol, so I wanted one. My father suggested Black Francis. It's an old family name."

THE PLATTERS The vocal group formed in Los Angeles in 1953. Bass vocalist Herbert Reed recalled, "I remember coming out of one of the fellas' houses thinking to myself, 'On the radio they always say, "Here's the latest platter by so-and-so." And every time I put a nickel in the jukebox, I'd see another platter come down.' It seemed the right name for a group."

PLAYER Formed in Los Angeles in the mid-seventies, the group topped the charts in 1978 with "Baby Come Back." Lead vocalist and guitarist John Crowley explained: "We saw the word on television when the players from the show were listed. We knocked off the S and went with it. I think the word holds a certain ambiguity."

> "It doesn't have any bad meaning, any meaning other than 'small,' and people will just think it's a typographical error."
> —RUSTY YOUNG, POCO

POCO The country-rock band Poco began in Los Angeles in 1968, after guitarists Richie Furay and Jim Messina left Buffalo Springfield. Guitarist Rusty Young remembered: "I was just looking at a book on the Beatles that a friend of mine had, and we're in there. It says that John Lennon actually gave us the name Poco—that we had to change our name from Pogo to Poco, and that John Lennon was the one who came up with it—which couldn't be further from the truth. I have no idea where they came up with that. Lennon was around, but I don't think he really was until after we started playing as Poco. Harrison was there in the beginning and we even auditioned for him, but at any rate, it didn't happen like that at all. We started off in L.A. playing this hip club called the Troubadour. On Monday nights, a band could come and play for free, and if they really liked you then they'd book you to be one of the opening acts for a headliner. We didn't have a name, and there were a bunch of ideas going around. Jimmy wanted to name the band Flintlock Pepperbox. Richie's choice was Buttermilk. Popcorn was another idea. Every week there were your joke suggestions for names. We'd throw them all in a hat, and the manager would pull one out, and that would be it. Our manager, Dickie Davis, had a favorite comic character called Pogo, and he actually looked like him. He put that name in the hat, and as it turns out, we drew it one day. We were always auditioning for labels, and the Troubadour was a club where labels would come looking for new talent as well. So that particular night, when we were playing as Pogo, Epic/CBS came down to see us, and they liked us, and they started talking about a deal. We kept the name Pogo because we couldn't change our name or they wouldn't know who we were. I don't think anyone was really crazy about it, but we kept it. So we were playing some shows, and we got the chance to open for Canned Heat. We were onstage getting ready to play, during sound check, and we were served with papers. Walt Kelly, the comic's creator, sued us, so we had to stop using the name Pogo. We'd only been using the name three months at the most, but he'd got wind of it. We started going, 'Oh, my goodness, everyone knows us now as Pogo. What are we going to do?' And actually I suggested, from my high school Spanish, 'Why don't was just call ourselves Poco?' It doesn't mean anything, really. We thought, 'It doesn't have any bad meaning, any meaning other than "small," and people will just think it's a typographical error.' So that's what we did. We called ourselves Poco, and everyone seemed to like it."

THE POGUES The Irish band came together in 1981 in London, where they performed punkified versions of traditional Irish folk songs. They began as Pogue Mahone, which is Gaelic for "kiss my arse."

POI DOG PONDERING The band was formed in 1985 in Hawaii, where "poi dog" is slang for a mutt or mongrel. The name was chosen by the band because their music was a mix of different styles. Singer Frank Orrall says he added the "pondering" because he "liked the way it rolled, or stumbled, off the tongue."

BUSTER POINDEXTER In 1984, former New York Dolls front man David Johansen took on the persona of an ultrasmooth lounge singer and changed his name to Buster Poindexter, derived from a nickname he earned growing up as an intellectual thug on Staten Island in New York City.

POISON The pop-metal band got its start in Harrisburg, Pennsylvania, in 1983. Bassist Bobby Dall takes credit for the name and explained that "people were always saying that rock 'n' roll poisons the youth of America, so rather than dispute it, we called ourselves that."

THE POLICE The Police were named by drummer Stewart Copeland in 1977 as an ironic reference to his father, who served as chief of the CIA's Political Action Staff—the agency's dirty tricks department—in the fifties and later left to form his own "private CIA." Copeland's father boasted to *Rolling Stone* that his organization was the largest private security service operating in Africa and the Middle East, and that "nobody knows more about changing governments, by force or otherwise, than me."

PORTISHEAD The group was formed in Bristol, England, in 1991 by Geoff Barrow and Beth Gibbons, and is named with irony after

Barrow's hometown. "It's a place where the local newspaper headline is 'Vera's Birthday' or 'The Flower Show.' It looks pretty and twee, but it's actually quite horrible."

PORTUGAL. THE MAN The band formed in Wasilla, Alaska, in 2004, before relocating to Portland, Oregon. The group originally started as a side project for lead singer John Gourley when he was in the band Anatomy of a Ghost with Zach Carothers, a high school class-mate and a future member of Portugal. The Man. Gourley explained how they chose the name: "The name is an alter ego. I don't know if that's obvious by "The Man"? We all love David Bowie, and James Brown, and Elvis, things like that, and we wanted to create this alter ego, much like Ziggy Stardust or Sgt. Pepper. And in doing that we wanted to find something that was representative of our band, and our group. We just were talking about it at the time; we said, you know, a country is an individual within the world that is a group of people with its own voice. And I think it just came down to Portugal being the guy's name. The period is there, so that's the name. And 'the Man' . . . just lets you know he's the man. Keeps it cool."

PREFAB SPROUT Singer and guitarist Paddy McAloon formed Prefab Sprout in Consett, England, in 1982, choosing a name he said he'd wanted to use for a band since he was a child and misheard the words "pepper sprout" in a Nancy Sinatra song.

PRETENDERS Singer and guitarist Chrissie Hynde, a native of Akron, Ohio, launched the Pretenders in London in 1978. She explained: "I was hanging out with this guy who was in a motorcycle club. One day while visiting their 'clubhouse,' he took me into his room and bolted the door shut. He wanted to play me his favorite record, but he didn't want any of the 'brothers' to hear it—probably because it wasn't off *Live at Altamont*.

It was Sam Cooke singing 'The Great Pretender.' I looked at this white supremacist lowlife, with his hand on his heart and his eyes shut, swaying to that clear black voice, and I thought, 'I'll have some of that!'"

THE PRETTY THINGS After leaving an early version of the Rolling Stones in 1962, guitarist Dick Taylor named his new band after the song "Pretty Thing" by Bo Diddley, whose music he sought to emulate.

PROCOL HARUM Procol Harum formed in London in 1967 and are most famous for the hit "A Whiter Shade of Pale." Lyricist Keith Reid, who was always listed as a full-fledged member of the group on their albums, recalled, "It's the name of a cat, a Siamese cat. It's the pedigree name, and it belonged to a friend of ours, just somebody that we used to hang out with when we were forming the band. One day, somebody pulled out the cat's birth certificate and said, 'Have a look at this,' and the name of the cat was Procol Harum. And somebody else, in fact a chap called Guy Stevens who was quite instrumental in Gary (Brooker, the singer and pianist) and myself getting together in the first place, said, 'Oh, you must call the group Procol Harum.' And we just accepted that. We never even questioned it, never even thought if it was a good name. We just went ahead with that suggestion. Once we put the record out, people started to say, 'Oh, it's Latin, and it means 'beyond these things.' But, in fact, we had spelled it incorrectly. It should have been P-R-U-C-U-L, I think, or P-R-U-C-O-L H-A-R-U-N. I believe that's right, anyway. If we'd spelled it correctly, it would have meant 'beyond these things.' But somehow it seemed quite apt. That was it really. It was the suggestion of a friend and we just stuck with it." When asked if he was glad they chose it, he said, "No. I think it was silly—a silly name. And the trouble with it is that people have a great deal of difficulty under-standing what it is. One of our favorites is Broken Arm. Broken Arm, Purple Horrors . . . It's very difficult for people to get the hang of."

What became of the cat? "The cat would now be more than twenty-five years old, so I would guess that it's no longer of this world." And who owned this cat? "It belonged to our dealer. We used to score off of him."

THE PRODIGY Band founder Liam Howlett came up with the name to describe himself in 1987 before meeting the other members of the group. At the time, he was spinning records at local raves in his hometown of Braintree in Essex, England. He says the name did not come from a Moog Prodigy synthesizer, as has been reported. "It was B-boy largeness," he explained. "Like Grandmaster Flash had a grand name, larging himself up with his name. When I first thought up the name, obviously I didn't consider it would be four people. It was just me, faceless in my bedroom, writing music: 'the prodigy.'"

PRONG The metal band formed in New York City in 1986. Guitarist Tommy Victor explained, "We wanted a name that didn't have 'dark' or 'death' or 'youth' or 'big' or 'black' in it. I tried to think of an object that was industrial sounding. Being a three-piece, I thought of a three-prong plug."

THE PSYCHEDELIC FURS The Furs formed in London in 1979. Singer Richard Butler recalled, "It was weird—we never thought of ourselves as a particularly psychedelic band. It's just that all the other bands around England at that time were all called the Sex Pistols and the Clash and names like that, and we wanted a name that sort of made it obvious that we were different from that. We weren't like a punk band. We were like the first of the bands that came after punk. I listened to a lot of sixties music, whether it was psychedelic or not, like Bob Dylan and the Velvet Underground, which I would really describe as psychedelic." When asked where "Furs" came from, he explained, "It simply sounded good. We thought of Psychedelic Shirts, Shoes, you name it—everything. sychedelic Furs just rang nicely. We thought of calling ourselves RKO for a while, which was Howard Hughes's old picture company. I liked the mystery of him." When asked if he came up with the name, Butler said, "Yeah, it was me. Me drunk. I think I was sitting in a pub, and I was with the rest of the band, and I was musing over all these different names and then came up with it."

PUBLIC IMAGE LTD. Soon after the Sex Pistols broke up in 1978, Johnny Rotten reverted to his given name, John Lydon, and formed Public Image Ltd., which is frequently referenced as PiL. The name Public Image came from the 1968 novel *The Public Image* by Scottish author Muriel Spark. Lydon recalled, "It was just a cheap little small book. But it's just, to my mind, a very well-told story about corruption and how industry can rot your brain if you're not careful. It's a good reminder. I got a good sense of grounding from it, and I also got the name for the band. Success! And I don't think that book cost me more than a pound in a junk store." The "Ltd." was not initially part of the name.

PULP In 1979, the teenaged Jarvis Cocker formed the band Arabicus Pulp in his hometown of Intake, a suburb of Sheffield, England. The name is a coffee bean commodity that he heard about in an economics class, but it was soon shortened to Pulp.

PUSSY GALORE Formed in the mid-eighties and fronted by Jon Spencer, the Washington, D.C.-based noise-rock band took their name from Honor Blackman's character in the James Bond movie *Goldfinger*.

PYLON Pylon formed in the late seventies and was part of the same music scene in Athens, Georgia, that spawned the B-52s and R.E.M. The band took their name from a novel by William Faulkner.

"It was just a cheap little small book. But it's just, to my mind, a very well-told story about corruption and how industry can rot your brain if you're not careful. It's a good reminder. I got a good sense of grounding from it, and I also got the name for the band. Success! And I don't think that book cost me more than a pound in a junk store."

—JOHNNY ROTTEN, PUBLIC IMAGE LTD.

QUEEN Queen formed in London in 1970, when singer Freddie Mercury joined guitarist Brian May and drummer Roger Taylor, who had played together in the band Smile. Mercury, who named the band, explained: "I'd had the idea of calling a group Queen for a long time. It was a very strong name, very universal and very immediate; it had a lot of visual potential and was open to all sorts of interpretations. I was certainly aware of the gay connotations, but that was just one facet of it."

QUEENS OF THE STONE AGE After his previous group Kyuss broke up in 1995, the following year singer and guitarist Josh Homme formed the band Gamma Ray. In 1997, Gamma Ray was forced to change their name when a German metal band by the same name threatened to sue. Queens of the Stone Age was an irreverent nickname given to Kyuss by their producer Chris Goss. Homme explained, "I liked the idea of something that was fifty percent stupid and fifty percent gay." He noted that the name "worked on so many levels. We're almost trying to eliminate the pissed-off angry dudes who want to hurt everyone at the show. We want it to be guys and girls partying and being mellow. It's supposed to be fun—not 'Why do I have a bloody fuckin' nose?'"

QUEENSRŸCHE The metal band formed in Bellevue, Washington, in 1981 and were originally called the Mob until it was discovered

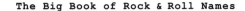

"[The name] worked on so many levels. We're almost trying to eliminate the pissed-off angry dudes who want to hurt everyone at the show. We want it to be guys and girls partying and being mellow. It's supposed to be fun—not 'Why do I have a bloody fuckin' nose?'"

—JOSH HOMME, QUEENS OF THE STONE AGE

the name was already taken. The name Queensrÿche, pronounced "kweenz-rike," came from the title track of their demo called "Queen of the Reich." Drummer Scott Rockenfield recalled, "We started as a covers band playing Judas Priest, Iron Maiden, all the fun stuff. We were called the Mob, but that didn't last long . . . so someone suggested we combine the words from our tune 'Queen of the Reich,' and that was it. It sounded powerful and fitted with the direction we wanted to head." *Reich* is German for "realm" and is commonly associated with the Nazi Party in Germany. The band changed the spelling to Queensrÿche to avoid being viewed as Nazi sympathizers. It is the only known use of the letter Y with an umlaut in English.

? [QUESTION MARK] AND THE MYSTERIANS The garage rock band, which had a hit with "96 Tears" in 1966, formed in Bay City and Saginaw, Michigan, in 1962. The founding members were children of Mexican migrant workers, including lead singer Rudy Martinez, who was never photographed without sunglasses and had his name legally changed to "?" They took their name from a low-budget Japanese sci-fi movie called *The Mysterians* that was released in the US in 1959. The *New York Times* called the film "an ear-splitting Japanese-made fantasy, photographed in runny color and dubbed English . . . crammed with routine footage of death rays and scrambling civilians, not one of whom can act."

QUICKSILVER MESSENGER SERVICE An early version of the Quicksilver Messenger Service formed in San Francisco in 1964. Bassist David Freiberg remembered, "Originally there were four Virgos in the band and one Gemini. Of the four Virgos, there were only two birthdays: John (Cipollina, guitarist) and I were born on August 24, and Gary (Duncan, guitarist) and Greg (Elmore, drummer) were born on September 4. We were looking for a name, and the ruling planet for Virgo in astrology is Mercury, and it is for Gemini also. So in searching for a name, we said, 'Well, let's see—mercury's the same as quicksilver, right? Mercury's the messenger god? Quicksilver Messenger Service.'" When asked who came up with the name, Freiberg said, "Well, of course I think it was mine, and Jim Murray thought it was his, but we were talking together when we came up with it, so I assume it's probably both of ours. Although I'm sure that I was the one who thought of it. As I'm sure he probably is, you know? It seemed like too long and complicated a name, so we kept trying to call it something else, and every time we did, our equipment would blow up or something, so we just said OK. And everybody was using fairly complicated names anyway—Jefferson Airplane, Big Brother and the Holding Company. It seemed to fit the time. I don't think it'd work anymore, but one never knows."

> "I told him I was forming a band. He asked what it was called, and I said Little Women. He said that if he had a band, he'd call it Quite Right. I said, 'Why would you want to call a band Quite Right?' And he said, 'I'll say it with your accent—Quiet Riot.'" —KEVIN DUBROW, QUIET RIOT

QUIET RIOT Heavy metal band Quiet Riot formed in Los Angeles in the early eighties. Singer Kevin DuBrow explained, "Originally it was Little Women, but we didn't even do one show under that name. It was really Jerry Shirley, the drummer of Humble Pie, who had a band called Little Women, and we thought it would be funny to have a heavy rock band with such a light name. I was friends with Richard Parfitt, the guitar player of Status Quo, and we were hanging out one day, and I told him I was forming a band. He asked what it was called, and I said Little Women. He said that if he had a band, he'd call it Quite Right. I said, 'Why would you want to call a band Quite Right?' And he said, 'I'll say it with your accent—Quiet Riot.' And I go, 'Really? Wow.' And he said, 'Yeah, we were going to call one of the Status Quo records by that name, but we decided not to,' and he told me that we should use the name for our band. It's so hard to come up with a good name for a band, and the thing that we loved about the name is that it's one of the few names, like Bad Company or Led Zeppelin, that actually says something about the music the band plays and the people that play it. Few of them are like that." When asked if there were any other names they considered, DuBrow said, "No, once we got that, that was it. All the band members thought it was great. It was immediate. It sounded like the name of a big band."

RADIOHEAD The band members met in Abingdon School, in Abingdon, Oxfordshire, England, in 1985. They originally called the band On a Friday, named for the day they rehearsed in the school's music room. When they signed to Parlophone Records in 1991, they were given two weeks to come up with a new name. At the last minute they chose Radiohead after "Radio Head," a track on Talking Heads' 1986 album *True Stories*, which they were listening to at the time.

RAGE AGAINST THE MACHINE The band formed in Los Angeles in 1991. Their name came from the title of an unreleased song that singer Zack de la Rocha wrote for an earlier band he was in called Inside Out. He explained, "I just felt it applied in the kind of message we were trying to put at the forefront of our music. I wanted to think of something metaphorically that would describe my frustrations toward America, toward this capitalist system and how it has enslaved and exploited and created a very unjust situation for a lot of people."

RAINBOW Guitarist Ritchie Blackmore formed Rainbow in 1975 in Hertford, Hertfordshire, England, after leaving Deep Purple. He named the band after the Rainbow Bar & Grill, a legendary rock 'n' roll hangout on the Sunset Strip in Los Angeles.

THE RAMONES The Ramones formed in New York City in 1974. The original lineup, after some minor adjustments, included singer Joey Ramone (Jeffrey Hyman), guitarist Johnny Ramone (John Cummings), bassist Dee Dee Ramone (Douglas Colvin), and drummer Tommy Ramone (Thomas Erdelyi). The surname Ramone was modeled after Paul Ramon, the alias Paul McCartney used for a two-week tour of Scotland in 1960, when his band was still calling itself The Silver Beatles. Joey Ramone recalled: "When we met Dee Dee, he was callin' himself Dee Dee Ramone and he was a big fan of Paul McCartney. Paul used to check into hotel rooms under the alias of, like, Paul Ramon. So Dee Dee kind of adapted it from there. When we met Dee Dee, the name Ramone was, like, kind of a cool-sounding name—it had a nice ring to it, y'know? When we were thinking of a name—it's really hard to think of a name—we just liked the name Ramone because it was different. It was distinct and unique and the whole bit. So we kind of adapted it as our surname to create a sense of unity. Then everyone could have their unique personality within their own thing, almost like the Beatles kind of did to some degree. Y'know, everybody is a distinct and unique multitalented individual in this band, but the Ramone surname defines us as a unit, a team." Joey admitted, "I once told this writer a story, about how I met the guys in an elevator and found out that we all had the same last name so we decided to form a band. One time I said I had an Uncle Pedro Ramone and we took it from him. You have to keep yourself amused or else it's boring. Gotta make it fun for yourself. A lot of people didn't know what to make of the Ramones at the beginning. They thought we were a mariachi band, or they thought we were some kind of Spanish or Mexican group, y'know what I mean?" Paul McCartney said he can't remember why he chose the name Ramon: "I must have heard it somewhere. I thought it sounded really glamorous." As for the reason why he was using an alias when the band was relatively unknown, he explained: "It was exciting changing your name. It made it seem all real and professional. It sort of proved you did a real act if you had a stage name."

BRUCE HORNSBY AND THE RANGE Bruce Hornsby formed the band in Los Angeles in 1984. Hornsby explained: "Originally our band was just called the Range. But the record company, after we finished the record, they wanted it to just be Bruce Hornsby, so we compromised on a rather unwieldy, lengthy name, Bruce Hornsby and the Range. The reason we thought of the Range was that it sounded vaguely sort of folksy and rural, and my music was a bit in that vein then, with the accordions and mandolins and more acoustic instruments. But we used to joke it was 'cause we were into cooking and golf."

RATT Ratt formed in Los Angeles in 1981. Guitarist Robbin Crosby recalled: "The band initially called itself Mickey Rat, after a character in a comic book. But the cartoon writer objected, so we just changed it to Ratt. We thought about changing (that) too, but once we got a big following that didn't make sense. We couldn't see using a name with the words 'Formerly Ratt' in parentheses."

THE RAVENS The Ravens, considered the first of the R&B vocal groups, formed in New York City in 1946. Their name is said to have been inspired by the fact that everyone was "ravin'" about their sound.

REAL ESTATE The indie band got their start in the New York City suburb of Ridgewood, New Jersey, in 2009 and chose the name Real Estate because singer and guitarist Martin Courtney was studying for his real estate license at the time. His parents, who ran a real estate agency and in whose home the band often practiced, encouraged him and the rest of the band to get real estate licenses in case their careers in music didn't pan out.

RED HOT CHILI PEPPERS The band formed in Los Angeles in 1983 when the members were students at Fairfax High School. Singer Anthony Kiedis recalled: "I guess it was in 1983, the first gig we ever played, and we were called Tony Flow and the Miraculously Majestic Masters of Mayhem. Then after the show we said, 'That name sucks.' Next, it was about a week-long process of trying to find a name, and we went through about a thousand." Kiedis said bassist Flea and former saxophonist Keith "Tree" Barry both claimed they came up with Red Hot Chili Peppers: "It's a derivation of a classic old-school American blues or jazz name. There was Louis Armstrong with his Hot Five, and also other bands that had 'Red Hot' this or 'Chili' that. But no one had ever been the Red Hot Chili Peppers, a name that would forever be a blessing and a curse. If you think of Red Hot Chili Peppers in terms of a feeling, a sensation, or an energy, it makes perfect sense for our band, but if you think of it in terms of a vegetable, it takes on all these hokey connotations. There's a restaurant chain named after the vegetable (Chili's), and chili peppers have been merchandised in everything from home-decoration hangings to Christmas-tree ornaments. Suffice to say that we were weirded out when people started bringing chili peppers to our shows as some kind of offering." It's worth noting that Chilli Willi and the Red Hot Peppers was one of the leading British pub-rock groups in the early seventies.

R.E.M. The band formed in Athens, Georgia, in 1980, choosing the name from a list of ideas written in chalk on the walls of the converted church where they lived and rehearsed. Among the names passed over were Twisted Kites and Cans of Piss. Although the term R.E.M. usually refers to "rapid eye movement," the stage of the sleep cycle when dreaming occurs, the band picked the name because they claimed it could ultimately stand for anything and was therefore appropriately ambiguous.

REO SPEEDWAGON REO Speedwagon formed in Champaign, Illinois, in 1968, adopting the name of a fire engine designed by Ransom Eli Olds, father of the Oldsmobile. Guitarist and chief lyricist Gary Richrath recalled: "Neil (Doughty, the keyboard player) thought it up while he was going to college there (in Champaign). REO was the first fire truck, built somewhere around 1918–1920 by Ransom E. Olds, who was like a renegade against GM and other big companies. So the symbolism seemed good, and it also was a nice catchy name for a rock band. We also stuck with the name because, when it was put on a marquee with other band names, those capital letters stood out."

THE REPLACEMENTS The Replacements formed in Minneapolis in 1979. Peter Jesperson, who managed and produced the group for the first six years, recalled: "They were originally called the Impediments, which was a dumb name, so I'm glad they changed it. They were playing at a chemical-free coffeehouse in South Minneapolis and showed up intoxicated. They were thrown out by the manager before they had a chance to play—the manager or who-ever the camp counselor was at this coffeehouse said, 'I'll make sure you never play this town again,' so the next day they changed their name to the Replacements. They were replacing themselves. The only other time I heard Paul (Westerberg, the vocalist and rhythm guitarist) specifically refer to it, someone said, 'Well, if you are the Replacements, who are you replacing?' and he said, 'Everyone.' But that was just a glib answer for some reporter. It was a good name because it had a slightly cheeky air to it and they were a slightly cheeky band. They weren't really a punk-rock band, but they had a lot of punky attitude."

THE RESIDENTS The mysterious Residents, who materialized in San Francisco in 1974, have never identified themselves by name or appeared onstage or in photographs without some kind of mask. Hardy Fox, one of the band's managers, explained: "The first audition tape that the Residents ever sent to a record company was to Warner Brothers, and they didn't have a name. They didn't use a name; they didn't even believe in names. So they sent it in, and when it was returned as a rejection, it was just addressed to 'The Residents' at that address, so they said, 'It must be us,' and it has been ever since."

THE RIGHTEOUS BROTHERS The Righteous Brothers, Bill Medley and Bobby Hatfield, began performing together in 1962. The name came from the reaction to their shows at black clubs in Southern California, where they were told, "That's righteous, brother."

"I mean, suddenly here it is, we didn't have Muddy Waters's *The Best of Muddy Waters* track list, you know. The first song is 'Rollin'

RIGHT SAID FRED Brothers Fred and Richard Fairbrass formed the group in London in 1989 and had a number-one hit in 1992 with "I'm Too Sexy." Their name was suggested by a friend who had heard the 1962 British novelty song "Right Said Fred" by Bernard Cribbins. Richard remembered, "I think we went for it because we knew it was stupid. It had a good eccentric English sound to it."

THE ROLLING STONES Formed in London in 1962, the band was originally called Rollin' Stones, named by lead guitarist Brian Jones after a song by Muddy Waters, whose style of music he wanted to emulate. The following year they added a G to their name at the insistence of their new management and became the Rolling Stones. According to Keith Richards, they picked their name by "sheer accident." He recalled: "We finally got a gig, all right? This is, like, 1962. We were rehearsing for like a month, and we'd done a few interval shows, and you know we were pretty good, and people were digging it. But finally we got our own night in a pub in London, you know? So we said, 'Great, call them up, let out the news. How much money have we got? Call up the local magazine, *What's On*, or whatever, and put an ad in. You do it. How much a word?' Brian's doing the business on that. And,

a name. And just lying on the floor was album, face-side down with the Stone Blues.'''—KEITH RICHARDS, THE ROLLING STONES like, 'Fine, OK, who's appearing?'—this is the chick on the other end, you know what I mean? I mean, suddenly here it is, we didn't have a name. And just lying on the floor was Muddy Waters's *The Best of Muddy Waters* album, face-side down with the track list, you know. The first song is 'Rollin' Stone Blues.' So right off the top of his head, Brian went, 'Well . . . ' 'What's the name? This phone call's costing money, man, you know? I mean, man, what's the name of the band?' And he looked and went 'Rollin' Stones.' OK. Boom. That's the way it happened. I mean, there's no thought behind it. That's the way the Stones operate, man. It's always been. Still the same. Things just fall together at the right time."

THE RONETTES Sisters Veronica (aka Ronnie) and Estelle Bennett and cousin Nedra Talley began their career in 1961 in New York City when they recorded their first single as Ronnie and the Relatives while also performing as dancers at the Peppermint Lounge. Ronnie recalled: "After we started dancing at the Peppermint Lounge, we decided it was time to change our name again. With all the exposure we were getting, we knew it was just a matter of time before people in New York started talking about us. And when they did, we didn't want them talking about a group called Ronnie and the Relatives. It just didn't have that magic. My aunts and uncles were tossing names around one night when my mother pointed out that the Bobbettes and the Marvelettes had both had hits recently. 'There seemed to be a whole lot of '-ettes' going around,' Mom said. 'Why don't we call them the Rondettes?' Everyone in the room suddenly sat up. 'Yeah,' said Nedra's mother, my aunt Susu, 'that's a good one. It's got a little piece of all three girls' names in it.' We dropped the D and shortened it to Ronettes soon after that—no one seems to remember why—and that was the name that stuck."

ROXY MUSIC Bryan Ferry formed the band in London in 1971, originally calling it Roxy, after a local movie theater. "Music" was added to distinguish them from a US band called Roxy.

> "There was a column called Ask Rufus. That's where it came from. It was out of nowhere and made no sense at all—that's why he thought it was cool. Everybody ended up loving it."
> —PAULETTE MCWILLIAMS, RUFUS

RUFUS The funk band, best known for launching the career of lead vocalist Chaka Khan, got its start in Chicago in 1969. The group had its origins in the band the American Breed, best known for the classic rock hit "Bend Me, Shape Me." After some lineup changes, members of that band re-formed as a group called Smoke. Vocalist Paulette McWilliams, who eventually left the group and suggested Kahn as her replacement, recalled, "We had the name Smoke for about three weeks. Then we found out that there was some group who had the name already. We were really pissed because we loved the name Smoke. Then we were in Minnesota somewhere. (Singer) Jimmy Stella was reading *Popular Mechanics*. He said, 'I know what our name should be. Ask Rufus!' We looked at each other like, 'What?' There was a column called Ask Rufus. That's where it came from. It was out of nowhere and made no sense at all—that's why he thought it was cool. Everybody ended up loving it." The column actually appeared in *Mechanix Illustrated*, a *Popular Mechanics* competitor.

THE RUNAWAYS The Runaways formed in Los Angeles in 1975. Guitarist Joan Jett left the band in 1979 to form her own band, the Blackhearts. She explained how both bands got their names: "With the Runaways, that was it. It was the Runaways. It was just one of those names. I said it and that became the name. There really wasn't an anecdote, unfortunately. It wasn't one of those things where we sat down and brainstormed. I just thought, 'The Runaways.' All girls. It sounded good. That was it." When asked why the name appealed to her, Jett said, "Rebellion—just kind of like the normal thing that a fifteen-year-old girl would be doing, leaving for Hollywood and playing in a rock 'n' roll band. When we started, we were a three-piece, so I didn't have to run it by that many people." When asked why she chose the name the Blackhearts, she noted, "Because—and this is a really dumb reason—you're on the road and you stop at gas stations and you have to go to the bathroom, and you go in there and everybody writes on the walls. I just thought that the Blackhearts would make a really cool, easy logo to leave on a bathroom wall. You just get a Sharpie and draw a black heart and color it in, and it's a Blackheart. For some reason that was important at the time. But also, to be someone who's a blackhearted person means to be a loner. I think it's a nautical term or something, nautical slang. I think it might also be a reggae thing too. It was very generic. It wasn't flashy. It was simple and to the point. I do remember writing it in many bathrooms in gas stations in the Northeast, because when we first started, we were based in New York and we did a lot of traveling in Connecticut, Massachusetts, Pennsylvania, and Maryland. So it's probably in countless bathrooms."

RUSH The band started in the Willowdale neighborhood of Toronto, Canada, in 1968 when the members were still in high school. Guitarist Alex Lifeson remembered, "It was cool to be young and be in 'a band.' I had a friend named John Rutsey who played drums, and we had a little basement band called the Projection. The guy that lived next door to me, Gary Cooper, was the bass player. He was older than us, and he was the only one who had a car. That was a very important friend to have. That band never really gigged. We just played at a party maybe once every six weeks during the summer. It was mostly about getting together and playing the three or four songs that we knew. And Gary Cooper didn't stick around for long. But out of the Projection came the first gig as Rush. John's brother Bill had said, 'You need a better name for the band—how about Rush?' And we liked it." As Bill Rutsey remembers it, he was trying to watch TV at home when he heard his younger brother John and his friends down in the basement arguing loudly about what to call their band, so he went downstairs and said, "You should just call yourselves 'Rush' in an effort to end the argument and get them to quiet down. He acknowledged it was a drug reference—the rush one feels when taking a drug—but said the band liked it primarily because it was short and sounded cool. They were not named Rush because they were in a rush to find a name, as has been rumored. Nor is the name a reference to a brand of amyl nitrate, an inhalant used to get a "head rush."

SAVAGE GARDEN One in a long line of bands whose names are contradictions in terms, the Brisbane, Australia-based duo took theirs from novelist Anne Rice's description of the lush yet brutal world of a vampire. "It's talking about the duality," singer Darren Hayes explained. "A vampire is someone who is immortal (and) beautiful, yet the harsh reality is they kill to survive, just like a beast in the jungle." Part of the name's appeal, Hayes noted, was its identification with the lord of darkness: "It's not necessarily the obvious, tacky vampire themes. It's a lot about relationships and desires, and in a lot of ways I do feel like a vampire. I think a lot of performers do."

SAVAGES The post-punk group formed in London in 2011. The band's guitarist, Gemma Thompson, explained, "No matter how evolved human beings become, there's a primal instinct there. We wanted to convey that." She said this notion of underlying savagery was inspired by books she read when she was growing up, like *Lord of the Flies*: "I remember sitting on a train and realizing that if it was suddenly the end of the world, we'd take on animal instincts again. I had an apocalyptic vision of everyone tearing each other apart."

THE SCREAMING TREES The band formed in Ellensburg, Washington, in 1985, and were part of the grunge scene in the early

1990s. The band was named for a guitar distortion pedal, the Electro Harmonix Screaming Tree Treble Booster.

SCRITTI POLITTI A post-punk band with Marxist leanings that turned pop, Scritti Politti began in Leeds, England, in 1977 and took their name from an Italian phrase meaning "political texts."

THE SEARCHERS The Searchers started out in Liverpool, England, in 1961, their name taken from the 1956 John Ford Western starring John Wayne and Natalie Wood. A catchphrase from the film inspired the title of Buddy Holly's 1957 number-one hit, "That'll Be the Day."

SEPULTURA The metal band was formed in Belo Horizonte, the sixth largest city in Brazil, in 1984 by brothers Max and Igor Cavalera. The name Sepultura, the Portuguese word for "grave," came from Max's translation of the lyrics of the Motörhead song "Dancing on Your Grave." In Portuguese, the song is "Dançando na sua Sepultura."

"The name meant for me all sorts of things. It came about by the idea of a pistol, a pinup, a young thing, a better-looking assassin, a Sex Pistol." —MALCOLM MCLAREN, THE SEX PISTOLS

THE SEX PISTOLS Guitarist Steve Jones, bassist Glen Matlock, and drummer Paul Cook were calling themselves the Swankers when vocalist Johnny Rotten, born John Lydon, joined the band. It was manager Malcolm McLaren who suggested the name the Sex Pistols, which was partly inspired by his clothing shop, SEX. He explained: "The name meant for me all sorts of things. It came about by the idea of a pistol, a pinup, a young thing, a better-looking assassin, a Sex Pistol."

THE SHINS The indie rock band was formed by singer and guitarist James Mercer in Albuquerque, New Mexico, in 1996 as a side project to another band, Flake Music. The name was inspired by the Shinns, a family in the 1962 movie adaptation of the Broadway musical *The Music Man*, which was a favorite of Mercer's father's. Mercer explained, "There are scenes where people are like, 'Are the Shinns home? Are the Shinns here?' Stuff like that. It sounded kind of weird to me—a bit strange and cool." He said of the musical, "The songs are incredible. The Beatles covered one of the songs on one of their records. I got it from that. I just changed the spelling. Outwardly, it's totally meaningless. And we sort of wanted that too. Something that wouldn't point you in any direction." Mercer said that when picking the name, he had one of his favorite bands, My Bloody Valentine, on his mind: "I remember thinking it was the dumbest name. It seemed so silly. Then they were this terrific band. I wanted to avoid that, and have something that was nonsensical and abstract. And, of course, the side effect is some people hate the name because it doesn't bring anything to mind, it just sounds absurd. And eventually My Bloody Valentine meant 'that band I love' and has no other context for me."

THE SHIRELLES In 1961, the Shirelles became the first girl group to have a number-one single with "Will You Still Love Me Tomorrow?" The four women met in junior high school in Passaic, New Jersey, in 1958 and formed a group called the Poquellos, Spanish for "little birds." They were signed to Tiara Records, a small label owned by Florence Greenberg, a classmate's mother. She asked them to come up with a new name and suggested the Honeytones, but they wanted something similar to their favorite group, the Chantels, and considered calling themselves the Chanels. Ultimately they chose the Shirelles, although there is some dispute over whether they named themselves specifically after member Shirley Owens, who was not the lead singer at that point.

SHOES The power-pop group, which got their start in Zion, Illinois, in 1974, took their name from a wisecrack made by John Lennon, who, when asked about the name the Beatles, looked down at his feet and said, "Well, we could just as well named ourselves the Shoes." They were one of the first bands to be played on MTV when the channel launched in 1981.

TOMMY JAMES AND THE SHONDELLS Tommy James, born Thomas Gregory Jackson, formed the Shondells in 1960 in Niles, Michigan, when he was twelve years old. In 1962, they recorded "Hanky Panky," a song that would hit number one and sell a million copies four years later. Between 1966 and 1970, the group had over a dozen hits, including "I Think We're Alone Now," "Mony, Mony," and "Crimson and Clover." When asked how he chose his group's name, James explained: "I wish there was a more dramatic story to tell. The name Shondells was simply two syllables that sounded very musical to me as I was searching for a name to call my band, on an otherwise boring day in seventh-grade study hall in the spring of 1960."

SIGUR RÓS Originally from Reykjavík, Iceland, Sigur Rós's name was inspired by the sister of lead singer Jón Þór "Jónsi" Birgisson, Sigurrós Elín, who was born a few days before the band was formed in 1984. Sigur Rós translates to "victory rose" in Icelandic and is a fairly common female name in the country.

SILVERSUN PICKUPS The band originally kicked off in the Silver Lake neighborhood of Los Angeles in 2000 and is named for Silversun Liquor, a liquor store in the area. Guitarist Brian Aubert explained, "It's homage to our neighborhood in L.A. called Silver Lake. Nikki (Monninger, bassist) and I lived in this house for quite a while, and there was a liquor store there that everyone would go to, and we just named the band in homage to that. But now, every time I go into that liquor store, the guy says I need to talk about it more in interviews. I said, 'Man, you are doing fine. You are a liquor store.'" When asked if he gets a discount, he said, "No, I think he charges more." The rumor that the band was originally named A Couple of Couples, because the original lineup was made up of a pair of romantically involved couples, is not true.

SIMPLE MINDS The band was formed in Glasgow, Scotland, in 1978 by former members of the punk group Johnny and the Self-Abusers. Singer Jim Kerr explained: "The origin of our name comes from a David Bowie song. Bowie had a song called 'Jean Genie' and there was a line in it, which I can't remember the full line—but it was 'He's so simpleminded he can't find . . . whatever.' And I'm pretty sure that the origin comes from that song." The exact lyrics from "The Jean Genie" are: "He's so simpleminded, he can't drive his module/He bites on the neon and sleeps in a capsule."

SIMPLE PLAN The band began in Montreal, Canada, in 1999 and took their name from the 1998 movie thriller *A Simple Plan*. Guitarist Sébastien Lefebvre explained, "It's not a very exciting story. We were making demos with a producer called Graham and we were in his studio, and then one day he came in and said, 'Hey, I just saw this movie called *A Simple Plan*, and it was really good. You guys should watch it,' and we're just like, 'Aw, you know what, that would be a decent band name. We'll drop the A, we'll just say Simple Plan!' Because we had a show coming up and we needed a name, and we're like, 'We'll change it later,' you know? And then maybe, like, thirty people came to the show, so we definitely could not change the name later because, you know, those thirty people, they would have got confused and forgot about us, so we had to keep the name. Later on we just figured what it meant for us to be called Simple Plan was that it was our plan to not have a nine-to-five job and to not have a regular type of life. We just wanted something more, so that was the plan."

SIMPLY RED Vocalist Mick Hucknall formed Simply Red in Manchester, England, in 1984. According to a publicist at Elektra Records, the story goes like this: "Hucknall decided to try singing one night at the nightclub where he was working as a disc jockey. When the manager asked how he wanted to be billed, he replied, 'Just "Red,"' a nickname given to him as a child because of his bright red hair. 'What was that?' the manager asked. 'Simply "Red,"' he replied, and the rest is history."

SIOUXSIE AND THE BANSHEES Siouxsie and the Banshees started off in 1976 and played their first gigs as part of the 100 Club Punk Festival in London. Singer Siouxsie Sioux was born Susan Ballion. Bassist Steven Severin, who was then calling himself Steve Havoc, recalled: "Of course once we had insinuated our way onto the bill of the 100 Club Punk Festival, the most important thing was a brilliant name. With a mere week of preparation, how to sing, how to play, where to plug in, and other such trifles were secondary to the correct 'nom de noise.' Halfway through that week, ITV had shown the film *Cry of the Banshee*, starring Vincent Price, and as is the way of these things, some kind of synchronicity occurred (cue light bulbs over Siouxsie and Severin's heads): 'The Banshees—what a great name.' 'No,' I said, 'how about Susy and the Banshees?' Hence began the great misspelling saga. Two days later, Siouxsie said, 'I hate cowboys,' and Souxie . . . Siouxie . . . no, Siouxsie and the Banshees were born. As a postscript, I would just like to say that there were no other names or suggestions. No skeletons in our closet like the Nosebleeds or the Bottom Burps or even Johnny and the Self-Abusers (see Simple Minds). How vulgar!"

SIR DOUGLAS QUINTET San Antonio-born Doug Sahm formed the Sir Douglas Quintet in California in 1964, the name an attempt to pass the group off as a British Invasion band. Their hits included "She's About a Mover" in 1965 and "Mendocino" in 1969.

THE SISTERS OF MERCY Originally from Leeds, the English goth rockers Sisters of Mercy took their name in 1980 from a song by Canadian folk singer Leonard Cohen. Singer Andrew Eldritch observed: "Whenever you get in a taxi, the driver says, 'What's the name of your band then?' It is at that point that I think the name of my band is so embarrassing. The Sisters of Mercy is an actual order of nuns, but I took the name from a Leonard Cohen song, which is about prostitutes. I thought that the juxtaposition between nuns and prostitutes was very appropriate for a rock band, still do. But it's very hard to explain that to a taxi driver."

SKINNY PUPPY Skinny Puppy was formed in Vancouver, British Columbia, in 1983 by Nivek Ogre and cEvin Key. Their ugly vision of the world, they explain, is one seen through the eyes of a starving mongrel dog. Notes keyboardist Dwayne Goettel, who joined the band in 1986: "It all goes back to the image that cEvin and Ogre created of Skinny Puppy being this little, scrawny, abused animal that didn't say very much. Every once in a while the dog would have to scream out or somebody would step on its tail. When it did make a noise, it was something you could understand or feel too."

SLADE The band formed in Wolverhampton, England, and were called the 'N Betweens when they were signed to Fontana Records in 1968, under the condition they change their name. The band reluctantly agreed and suggested Knicky Knacky Noo, after a phrase uttered by another musician. ("It's the best thing since the knicky knacky noo.") That was vetoed by label exec Jack Baverstock, who instead suggested Ambrose Slade. Drummer Don Powell recalled, "He had this secretary who used to name all of her things, like her pens and shoes and handbags. One of her things was called Ambrose and another Slade. Jack Baverstock put the names together and said, 'You're gonna be called Ambrose Slade.'" The band acquiesced, but weren't exactly happy about it. Powell said, "The 'N Betweens was bad enough, but Ambrose Slade? It was always misspelled, as people couldn't figure it out. We were billed as Ambush Shake, Arnold Shed, Amboy Spade—it was horrible." They eventually dropped Ambrose and simply became Slade.

SLEATER-KINNEY The band formed in Olympia, Washington, in 1994 and took their name from Sleater Kinney Road in Lacey, Washington, where they had an early practice space.

SLIPKNOT The metal band formed in Des Moines, Iowa, in 1995. According to bassist Paul Gray, "We had a show booked and we had a song called 'Slipknot.' It was the first song we had written full-on. . . . We all thought the name Slipknot rolled off the tongue pretty easy, and we needed a name so we could play the show. We did one other show before that and we were called Meld, but we didn't like that at all. So we went with Slipknot. And that show, people just tripped out. They'd never seen anything like it. After that, we couldn't really change the name."

THE SMALL FACES The band was formed in London in 1965 and chose the name because they were indeed small—they were all under five feet six inches—and they considered themselves "faces," mod lingo for cool guys, as in "I'm the Face," which the Who recorded in 1964 when they were still called the High Numbers. After guitarist Steve Marriott left in 1969 to form Humble Pie with Peter Frampton, and Rod Stewart and Ron Wood joined the band, they were no longer small and re-launched as the Faces.

> "My line on it now is that it's God's cruel joke on me. On the other hand, in some weird way it separates us from your typical band name. And it's ambiguous enough to not hold us down musically, like Metallica, or some metally kind of name. And, conversely, in some strange way it kind of describes us."
> —BILLY CORGAN, SMASHING PUMPKINS

SMASHING PUMPKINS Smashing Pumpkins formed in Chicago in 1989. Singer and guitarist Billy Corgan explained: "The name of the band existed before there was a band. I was in somebody's kitchen and we were sitting around talking about something and somebody said something about smashing pumpkins and I thought, 'Oh, that's a pretty good mythical band name, ha-ha.' I thought of smashing more in terms of glorious or something, not as the physical act. So I began telling people that I was forming a band called the Smashing Pumpkins, as a joke. When I actually formed a band, I said, 'Well, I've got this name, but I think it's kind of stupid.' But everyone remembered the name, and that was it. It just stuck. And once you play one show with it, then you go: 'Well, gee, we shouldn't change it 'cause the people who went to the first show . . .' Didn't give it a lot of thought. It was just one of those things. It could have been the Amazing Tomatoes. It just struck some weird chord in me for some ungodly reason. Some dumb joke—that's it. My line on it now is that it's God's cruel joke on me. On the other hand, in some weird way it separates us from your typical band name. And it's ambiguous enough to not hold us down musically, like Metallica, or some metally kind of name. And, conversely, in some strange way it kind of describes us."

SMASH MOUTH This San Jose, California, band is is best known for their late nineties hits "Walking on the Sun" and "All Star." The band's name is an American football term that refers to an offensive strategy that relies on a strong running game.

THE SMITHEREENS The Smithereens started out in 1980 in Carteret, New Jersey. Drummer Dennis Diken recalled, "We were calling ourselves What Else at the time. I was walking around with this spiral pocket notebook compiling names for bands. I probably had a couple hundred of them, actually. One that Jimmy (Babjak, guitarist) came up with was Shag Rug and the Lost Contact Lenses. A lot of stupid shit, really. Smithereens was just a word that we heard in cartoons when we were kids. You know, 'I'll blow you varmints to smithereens.' That was Yosemite Sam, from the Warner Brothers cartoons."

THE SMITHS The band from Manchester, England, chose the name the Smiths in 1982 because of its implied anonymity. According to singer Morrissey, "The most surreal, overtly artistic names were being pinned to the most pathetically dull groups, so we thought we'd latch ourselves onto the most simplistic name we could possibly think of and still produce inspiring music. Simply by having a really straightforward name, we were saying that you don't have to hide behind any veil of artistry to produce something worthwhile."

> "The most surreal, overtly artistic names were being pinned to the most pathetically dull groups, so we thought we'd latch ourselves onto the most simplistic name we could possibly think of and still produce inspiring music."
> —MORRISSEY, THE SMITHS

SNEAKER PIMPS The British trio says that they took their name from a comment made in an interview by Mike D of the Beastie Boys that his band employed a designated "sneaker pimp," someone in charge of finding them footwear. Mike D, however, said he cannot recall making the comment.

SOCIAL DISTORTION Front man Mike Ness formed the punk band in Fullerton, California, in 1978. Drummer Casey Royer recalled, "Mike was, like, fifteen, trying to play guitar, but he couldn't. Social Distortion was named for my distortion pedal, which I gave to Mike to play 'cause back then he was no good." When bassist Dennis Danell was asked about the name, he said, "Gosh, who knows? It's just something we made up and thought was cool. It kinda goes along with a lot of our songwriting—it's got a lot of connotations. We've always considered ourselves more of a social band, for the people."

SOFT MACHINE Begun in Canterbury, England, in 1966, the progressive rock band took their name from the novel *The Soft Machine* by William Burroughs.

SONIC YOUTH Sonic Youth formed in New York City in 1981. Guitarist Thurston Moore explained: "Sonic came from Fred 'Sonic' Smith, guitar player for the MC5, and Youth came from Big Youth, the reggae toaster from the mid- to late seventies. It's a name that came out of the seventies, when I was a teenager, and those were two things that I was really into: Sonic Smith—the high-energy Detroit thing—and then I was really into the reggae thing. I just sort of wanted to use both those worlds. Actually, when we first started, that was one of our concepts, to use big dub rhythms with, like, sonic guitar. Our first record comes out of that kind of concept. But then it became a total slamfest after that."

SOUL ASYLUM Originally called Loud Fast Rules, the band started out in Minneapolis in 1981. Singer and guitarist Dave Pirner explained how he came up with the name: "I had a dream, and I woke up and wrote it down. And we talked about it for a long time and couldn't come up with anything better, basically."

SOUL COUGHING Mike Doughty formed the band in New York City in 1992. According to Opus Moreschi, the band's webmaster at the time, "The name is taken from a poem Doughty once wrote about Neil Young throwing up in the back of a bus. Doughty claims the only good thing about the poem was its title, and so he used it when forming his band. When Soul Coughing performed with Neil at the 1997 HORDE Festival, neither party mentioned it."

SOUNDGARDEN The seminal 1980s grunge band is named after a sculpture on the beach by Lake Washington in their hometown of Seattle. "It looks a lot like a *Star Trek* set," singer Chris Cornell explained. "It's kind of like Stonehenge in outer space. It hums in the wind."

SOUP DRAGONS The band, which formed in Bellshill, Scotland, in 1985 and is best known for their cover of the Rolling Stones song "I'm Free," is named for a character in the British stop-motion children's TV series *Clangers* that premiered in 1969. The show was about creatures who live on a small moon-like planet, speak only in whistles, and eat green soup provided by the Soup Dragon.

SPANDAU BALLET After an earlier incarnation as the Makers, the London-based band finally came together as Spandau Ballet in 1979. A spokesperson at the band's management company related this story: "Spandau were just about to go onstage, and they still didn't have a name. Then a journalist friend of theirs, who'd just been to Berlin—his name was Robert Elms—apparently, on a toilet wall in Berlin he'd seen the name Spandau Ballet written, so he suggested it and they all said, 'Yeah.'" During the rise of the Nazi Party in Germany in the 1930s, Spandau Prison was used to hold Hitler's opponents. "Spandau ballet" refers to the method of hangings at the prison that would cause victims to drop suddenly and jerk violently.

THE SPANIELS The group, led by James "Pookie" Hudson, got together in Gary, Indiana, in 1952 and had a string of R&B hits, including "Baby, It's You" and "Goodnight, Sweetheart, Goodnight." They first considered calling themselves the Hudsonettes, until some-body pointed out that "-ettes" suggested women. They briefly called themselves Pookie Hudson and the Hudsonaires, until Faye Gregory, wife of bass vocalist Gerald Gregory, joked that they sounded like "a bunch of dogs" while rehearsing at their house. That prompted her husband to come up with several dog names, including the Cocker Spaniels. When everyone agreed that "Cocker" might leave them open to ridicule, Mrs. Gregory suggested they simply call themselves the Spaniels, because she liked the way it sounded.

SPARKS Formed by brothers Ron and Russ Mael, the band formed in California in 1967 but eventually moved to England. Russ recalled: "Originally, we were called Halfnelson when we signed with Bearsville Records to record our first album. The album didn't sell very well, and everyone looked around for the problem, and they said, 'Well, obviously the name is too obscure, that's your problem. If you would just change the name, then we could re-release the album and it will sell tens of millions of copies.' Albert Grossman, who was one of the owners of Bearsville, thought that Ron and I were just hilarious people, and he said, 'You're not the Marx Brothers—you should be the Sparks Brothers.' We thought that was really horrible, and kind of asinine. So we said, 'Well, we'll compromise and we'll keep the Sparks part of it, but absolutely not the Brothers part.' So that was the birth of Sparks."

THE SPECIALS Leaders of the British two-tone movement of the late seventies and early eighties, the Specials formed in Coventry, England, in 1977. They took their name from the "special" one-shot records made for early Jamaican mobile sound systems.

SPIRIT Spirit took off in Los Angeles in 1966 and were originally called Spirits Rebellious, the name taken from a book by poet Kahlil Gibran.

SPOON The band formed in 1993 in Austin, Texas, and took their name from the song "Spoon" by the seventies German avant-garde group Can. The song was a top-ten hit in Germany in 1972. The lyrics are as follows: "Carrying my own in the afternoon/Hiding a spoon she will be soon/Waiting fork brings a knife."

SQUEEZE Squeeze began in London in 1974. For a while the band was forced to call themselves Squeeze UK because there was an American band called Tight Squeeze; when that band split, they reverted to Squeeze. In an interview, the band's manager, John Lay, explained how they chose the name: "(Singer and guitarist) Chris Difford originally was in a band called Porky's Falling Spikes. Then they had the idea of calling the band Cum. This, you've got to bear in mind, was when they were sixteen. And then nobody could think of a proper name, so all of them got in a room and wrote their name choice on a piece of paper and put it in a hat, and Squeeze came out. It was a secret ballot, and to this day, not one of them has admitted which one of them it was." When asked about the rumor that Squeeze took their name from the Velvet Underground album *Squeeze*, Lay conceded, "There's some truth to that. My suspicion is that Chris Difford was the Squeeze donator—at that time he was massively influenced by the Velvet Underground."

STEELY DAN Singer and keyboard player Donald Fagen and bassist Walter Becker, who met as students at Bard College in 1967, founded Steely Dan in Los Angeles in 1972. They took the name from a milk-spurting dildo in the William Burroughs novel *Naked Lunch*.

STEPPENWOLF Led by singer and guitarist John Kay, who was born Joachim F. Krauledat in Tilsit, Germany, the band began as Sparrow in Toronto, Canada. After they relocated to Los Angeles in 1967 and were signed to Dunhill Records, at the suggestion of producer Gabriel Mekler, they changed their name to Steppenwolf, after Herman Hesse's classic novel.

STIFF LITTLE FINGERS They first formed in Belfast, Northern Ireland, in 1977 as a cover band called Highway Star, named after a Deep Purple song. They rechristened themselves Stiff Little Fingers from a song of the same name by the Vibrators that includes the lyrics "If it wasn't for your stiff little fingers, nobody would know you were dead."

THE STONE ROSES The band began as the Patrol in Manchester, England, in 1980, changing their name to English Rose, after a song by the Jam, in 1983. In 1985, the band combined their name with that of their idols, the Rolling Stones, to become the Stone Roses.

STONE TEMPLE PILOTS After meeting at a Black Flag concert in San Diego in 1989, singer Scott Weiland and bassist Robert DeLeo formed the band Mighty Joe Young, named after the 1949 movie about a giant gorilla. One day, inspired by the logo for STP motor oil spotted on a bumper sticker at Weiland's apartment, the band decided to change their name to three words beginning with the initials STP. Shirley Temple's Pussy eventually lost out to Stone Temple Pilots.

THE STOOGES The Stooges were formed in Ann Arbor, Michigan, in 1967, by Iggy Pop, who was born James Osterberg. He took the name Iggy from his first band, the Iguanas, and Pop from local junkie Jim Popp. Iggy recalled: "We were hanging around, stoned on acid, and had just been watching *The Three Stooges* on TV. The band didn't have a name, and (guitarist) Ron Asheton, who was a major fan of the Stooges, said, 'How 'bout the Stooges? They can be the Three Stooges and we'll be the Psychedelic Stooges!'"

THE STRANGELOVES The Strangeloves, best known for the 1965 hit "I Want Candy," were a band formed in 1964 by a New York-based songwriting production team that pretended to be from Australia. The team—Bob Feldman, Richard Gottehrer, and Jerry Goldstein—originally found success writing and producing pop songs for a variety of acts, including the Angels' "My Boyfriend's Back," but the sudden popularity of the British Invasion almost put them out of business. In response, they decided to release a single under the name of a fictitious British act. Feldman remembered, "Marty Kupersmith (aka Marty Sanders, a member of the band Jay and the Americans) stopped by our office while we were deciding what to do with this record. He was wearing these silly dark glasses and giving right-arm salutes, emulating Peter Sellers's character in *Dr. Strangelove, Or: How I Learned to Stop Worrying and Love the Bomb* (the satirical film directed by Stanley Kubrick). I took his glasses, started talking in my best British accent, and voilà! The Strangeloves were born." When Feldman's English accent proved shaky, they shifted the band's origins to

Australia—mythical Armstrong, Australia, to be exact—and became Miles, Niles, and Giles Strange, wealthy sheepherders who lived to rock.

THE STRAWBERRY ALARM CLOCK The band formed in Santa Barbara, California, in 1967 and are best remembered for the flower-power anthem "Incense and Peppermints." Bassist George Bunnell recalled: "Michael Ochs, the rock historian, has this story of how we came up with our name that's really not how it happened. The Michael Ochs story was that we took out a *Billboard* magazine and went through the top one hundred songs at the time, and hit 'Strawberry Fields Forever' and decided to call the band Strawberry Alarm Clock. He said that we wanted to call the band *something* Alarm Clock, and that that was how we got the Strawberry. Well, 'Strawberry Fields' wasn't out yet, so that puts a fork in that one. Actually, we were told to put Strawberry in our name. The band had a stupid name—it was called Three Sixpence, to be English. We wore English Beatle boots and we wore the preacher jackets with no collar. And then the record company said, 'This'll never work. This is all old, it's already all been done, you're doing stuff that you've seen.' And we thought, 'Yeah, we are.' The music was really unusual. The music wasn't anything like we looked, though we were trying to sing with English accents. That was what we were trying to do when we did 'Incense and Peppermints,' oddly enough, and it came out psychedelic. They wanted us to put strawberries in the name. Russ Regan at MCA specifically said that strawberries were like a sign of the

> "We were sitting around on the bed trying to think of different names that had strawberry in them, like Strawberry Toilet and stuff like that, and this alarm clock went off and fell on the floor and broke. We laughed and thought, 'Strawberry Alarm Clock.'"
> —GEORGE BUNNELL, THE STRAWBERRY ALARM CLOCK

time—they were like the 'peace and love fruit,' the 'fruit of love,' sort of
like an aphrodisiac." When asked if that was the going wisdom at the
time, he said, "No, actually it was to kind of try to create a new one. The
predecessor was bananas, with Donovan. 'Electrical banana.' (From
the Donovan song "Mellow Yellow": "Electrical banana/Is gonna be a
sudden craze.") So that whole thing created the fruit thing. They said,
'Put strawberry in the name,' and we thought, 'Oh, God, should we even
do this?' We decided to do it, and we sat around trying to think of names.
Mark Weitz, the keyboard player, his parents built like a guesthouse
for him to live in, and the band rehearsed in it. It was a great little setup.
And we were in there, and he had an alarm clock that sat on this table.
We were sitting around on the bed trying to think of different names that
had strawberry in them, like Strawberry Toilet and stuff like that, and
this alarm clock went off and fell on the floor and broke. We laughed
and thought, 'Strawberry Alarm Clock.' And it sounded so goofy. So
we called Russ Regan and we told him, and he said, 'That's fucking
great!' That was that. We thought, 'Oh, my God, we've created a
monster!' We couldn't even say the name. When somebody asked us,
'What's the name of your band?' we were like, 'Uhhh . . . ' We ended
up having a real hard time saying it. It became a crippling psychological problem for each one of us. We couldn't even say the word

'strawberry'—it would kind of slur. We were really kind of insecure about it, even though we came up with half of it. We thought it was a joke." He was asked if they eventually came to accept it. His answer: "Never."

THE STRAWBS The band got their start in Leicester, England, in 1967 as the Strawberry Hill Boys, named for the district where they rehearsed.

THE STRAY CATS Rockabilly revivalists the Stray Cats started out in Massapequa, New York, in 1979 with Brian Setzer on vocals and guitar, Lee Rocker (Leon Drucker) on bass, and Slim Jim Phantom (Jim McDonnell) on drums. Recalled Phantom: "When we started in New York, about 1979 I think it was, in Manhattan they wouldn't hire you every week. Like, if you played at Max's one week, they wouldn't hire you at CBGBs the next week. So we would change the name of the group all the time to get gigs, and the kids who liked us knew what it was. We were the Tom Cats, and we were the Bob Cats, and the Dead Cats. We changed the name monthly almost. 'Cats' was pretty much the key to it so that the kids who liked us could kind of read between the lines. When we moved to England about six or seven months after that, we had nowhere to live, nowhere to go, no food—we were buying a hamburger at McDonald's and splitting it three ways and sharing the last french fry. Lee kind of came up with it. He said we felt like stray cats. The name had always fit because 'cat' was kind of a groovy term in the fifties—you know, Elvis was the 'Hillbilly Cat.' So it was a term of a kind of a hipster. We found ourselves with no money, nowhere to live, nowhere to sleep, nowhere to do anything. So Lee came up with the name Stray Cats and it just kind of stuck. It suited the feeling at the time, as well as what we needed in a name. It's as simple as that."

THE STROKES The Strokes formed in New York City in 1998 and singer Julian Casablancas suggested the name. Bassist Nikolai Fraiture recalled: "We had a running joke that every time we met up we had to have a certain number of names. Some were horrible. One day Julian said, 'How about the Strokes?' and it was the one name we all didn't disagree on." Lead guitarist Nick Valensi remembered, "When it first came up, it was like, 'Oh, the Strokes, like a wank.' Then a person said, 'No, it's the Strokes like a heart attack.' Then another person said '. . . like a caress.' It rolled off the tongue really well—sort of violent and sort of sexual, and it just sounded cool to everybody." Fraiture noted: "There were so many different meanings to it, it could never pin us down. So many people have said 'stroke of luck,' 'stroke this' . . . there's never one thing they can focus on. There's when you have a stroke, cerebral congestion. There's a stroke when you play guitar. Then there's the obvious sexual undertones." Rhythm guitarist Albert Hammond Jr. noted: "We'd come in with all these bad names—the De Niros, the Rubber Bands, the Motels, Flattop Freddie and the Purple Canoes—and no one would agree. One day we're in the studio after practice and Julian said, 'The Strokes.' And everyone was like, 'That sounds great!' It was that easy. Five guys agreeing. It doesn't really mean anything. We thought it was a cool rock 'n' roll name. When I first heard it, it sounded so old, like someone would have already taken it, but no one did. Then I looked it up in the dictionary and 'a powerful blow to the face, chest, or body' was the first thing. Perfect. That's exactly what our music is. It's like a powerful blow to the face."

STRYPER The Christian heavy metal band began in Orange County, California, in 1983 as Roxx Regime, then changed their name to Stryper, after a passage in Isaiah: "With His stripes we are healed."

> "I think the Nick Cave song, which I took the name St. Vincent from, that's a hilarious song. It illustrates the squalor and the grandeur." —ST. VINCENT

ST. VINCENT Singer-songwriter Annie Clark said her stage name was inspired by lines in the song "There She Goes, My Beautiful World" by Nick Cave and the Bad Seeds—"And Dylan Thomas died drunk in/St. Vincent's hospital"—that referenced the Welsh poet's death in New York City in 1953. She said that song reflects her own dark sense of humor: "I think the Nick Cave song, which I took the name St. Vincent from, that's a hilarious song. It illustrates the squalor and the grandeur." St. Vincent's Hospital closed in 2010 and was demolished to make way for luxury condos.

STYX The band formed in Chicago in 1963. Keyboard player Dennis DeYoung explained: "It was the name no one in the band hated. At the time, we were actually called TW4. There were five of us in the band, so that shows you how stupid we were. We had been a four-piece for a long time, and we added a fifth member. We had kind of a clientele locally in Chicago—we'd developed a reputation—so we didn't want to change the name. But when we got the deal with Wooden Nickel Records, we had to come up with a new name. Every time we had a list of fifty names that one of the band members would submit, someone, as is always the case, would say, 'I hate that name.' As for the name Styx, I was a schoolteacher at the time. I was teaching music appreciation, how music and art relate to the social upheaval of the times from the Renaissance to the twentieth century, which sounds relatively boring, and it was. Anyway, Dante's *Inferno* was one of the things in the class, and that was one of the names that was mentioned—the River Styx." When it was noted that the name Styx might be fitting for a death-metal band, DeYoung observed, "The thing about the death metal, we were never that kind of a band, although in the early days we certainly were a bit more on the art rock, superpretentious side, because there seemed to be a following for that. There was a kind of heavier rock element to the music in the beginning, but really, the River Styx is not necessarily just the river that runs through hell. I guess as the story goes, according to Greek mythology, when you die you get on a boat, and there's this guy and a dog on the boat, Charon, and it circles the underworld seven times, but then it comes out into (the) Elysian Fields, which is like heaven. So it's that river that circles the underworld. I guess when you get on the boat, the worse you are, the lower it goes into the underworld, something like that. I guess if you're really bad you come out in New Jersey. But anyway, there was this feeling in the band that there was the hard rock element and then there was a softer element in our music, and there was an idea that the River Styx was kind of the bridge between those two places. People over the years have thought Styx was just another way to spell 'sticks.' You'd be surprised how few people actually know what the name refers to, so it never really played for one second into our development as a musical act. It was just 'that name.'" When asked what TW4 stood for, DeYoung said, "Well, this is pretty wacky. We were originally called the Trade Winds. Can you imagine that? We were three kids who lived on the same street, and we picked the name Trade Winds so we could paint a palm tree on the drum. And, unbelievable as it may seem, a band in New York a couple years after we chose this name had a hit record called 'New York Is a Lonely Place,' and the name of that band was Trade Winds. After that, we changed our name to TW4 because there were four guys in the band." When asked what other names they considered, DeYoung reported, "Believe it or not, one guy wanted to name it Kelp. It would've been a really seventies kind of thing. It was down to two, and the other name was Torch. It's funny to think about names. When I first heard the name the Beatles, I said—I was a real Beatle hater when they first came out—I thought it was the worst name I'd ever heard in my life. All I could think of was a bug. I didn't get the idea of it being 'the beat.'"

SUEDE Formed in London in 1989, the band took their name from the song "Suedehead," the 1988 debut single by Morrissey after he left the Smiths. Morrissey has claimed the song has nothing to do with suedeheads, an offshoot of the skinhead subculture in the UK and Ireland in the early 1970s. Suedeheads wore their hair longer and had a more formal dress code than the skinheads. Suedehead was the title of a 1971 novel by Richard Allen, a follow-up to the popular *Skinhead*. Morrissey said, "I did happen to read the book when it came out and I was quite interested in the whole Richard Allen cult. But I really just liked the word 'suedehead.'"

THE SUGARCUBES The alternative rock band orginated in Reykjavík, Iceland, in 1986. The band had its origins in an earnest post-punk group called Kukl, which Drummer Sigtryggur "Siggi" Baldursson described as "experimental and quite intense." After Kukl disbanded in 1986, the members of the group started a creative collective called Smekkleysa, which meant "bad taste" in Icelandic,

"It was like the most silly name we could think of, a bit like 'Monkeys' or something. We were just being a sort of opposite [of] the serious group we were in before."

—BJÖRK GUÐMUNDSDÓTTIR, THE SUGARCUBES

Adam Dolgins

that was inspired by Picasso's dictum that "good taste and frugality are the enemies of creativity." The goal was that members would pitch in to help each other get projects off the ground, including books and music. Siggi recalled: "We decided that it would be a good idea to have a silly pop band on that label, so we got together a name for a silly pop band called the Sugarcubes (Sykurmolarnir in Icelandic)." Lead singer Björk Guðmundsdóttir remembered, "It was like the most silly name we could think of, a bit like 'Monkeys' or something. We were just being a sort of opposite (of) the serious group we were in before. Kind of like, 'Fuck this sort of existentialism and all those -isms and art. Fuck that pretentiousness.' Like, 'Let's be happy,' you know?" Björk explained, "We just did this little record as a joke, and a year later we'd forgotten about it almost, and some English journalist found it and made it "Song of the Week" in *Melody Maker*, and then everything went berserk in England." That song was their breakout hit "Birthday." Björk said, "Of course, the most silly thing we've ever done in our lives is, ironically, the thing that's been taken most seriously by the media." The rumor that the name the Sugarcubes was a reference to a method for taking the drug LSD was false.

SUGAR RAY The band got their start in Newport Beach, California, in 1986 and were originally called Shrinky Dinks, and later Shrinky Dinx, after the children's arts and crafts kits that were baked in the oven. After they signed with Atlantic Records in 1994, under the threat of a lawsuit by Shrinky Dinks manufacturer Milton Bradley, they changed their name Sugar Ray after the boxer Sugar Ray Robinson.

SUM 41 The band formed in Ajax, Ontario, in 1996. When asked why they chose the name Sum 41, lead vocalist and rhythm guitarist Deryck Whibley said, "We started the band forty-one days into the summer, and we thought it was a good name. You know, a California thing."

SUPERTRAMP Singer and keyboard player Richard Davies started the band in London in 1969 with the backing of Dutch millionaire Stanley August Miesegaes, who spotted him playing in a band called the Joint. After rejecting the name Daddy, the band followed the suggestion of original sax player Dave Winthrop and took the name Supertramp from the book *The Autobiography of a Super-Tramp*. The book, published in 1908 by the Welsh poet and writer W. H. Davies (1871–1940), chronicles the travels of the author in the United Kingdom, Canada, and the United States in the final decade of the nineteenth century. Irish literary legend George Bernard Shaw discovered Davies and wrote the book's introduction.

> "After rejecting the name Daddy, the band followed the suggestion of original sax player Dave Winthrop and took the name Supertramp from the book *The Autobiography of a Super-Tramp*."

THE SUPREMES Diana Ross, Mary Wilson, and Florence Ballard began as the Primettes in Detroit in 1959, formed by manager Milton Jenkins to support his male group the Primes, who would later become the Temptations. In 1960, the women were signed to Motown Records by label president Berry Gordy Jr., who insisted they change their name despite their desire to remain the Primettes. Ballard picked the Supremes from a list supplied by Janie Bradford, a Motown employee. At first the women hated it, complaining that it sounded like a male group. In fact, the name was first used in 1957 by a male quartet from Columbus, Ohio, who recorded a single for Ace Records and named themselves after a bottle of Bourbon Supreme.

SWEET The band, whose hits included "Ballroom Blitz," "Fox on the Run," and "Love Is Like Oxygen," formed in London in 1968 as the Sweetshop. They eventually shortened it to the Sweet, and alternately simply Sweet. Explained guitarist Andy Scott: "The name Sweet was totally right for the band, because we certainly are not sweet in reality. So we all agreed it was appropriate."

TALKING HEADS Bassist Tina Weymouth met guitarist David Byrne and drummer (and future husband) Chris Frantz at the Rhode Island School of Design in 1970. After graduating in 1974, they moved to Manhattan together. Weymouth recalled: "We had a long list of possible band names taped to our wall at the loft on Chrystie Street where the three of us lived. Anybody who wanted to could add a name. Sometimes Chris would try one out by putting it on his kick drum. One of those names was the Vogue Dots. We were looking for a name that wouldn't specifically connote any kind of music. One day a friend from Rhode Island School of Design, Wayne Zieve, was looking through *TV Guide* and came across 'talking heads.' The *Guide* said it was TV camera jargon for a head-and-shoulders shot, such as would be used to shoot a news commentator. It further said a talking heads shot was to be distinguished from its opposite cousin, action footage, by the fact that it was 'all content, no action.' Wayne added it to the list and everyone liked it. . . . Carnivals and circuses used to often have a 'talking head' as well. When I was a little girl, I used to make my siblings and neighborhood kids put on circuses in imitation of *The Little Rascals*. One little kid would crouch inside a cardboard box and stick her stockinged head out of a hole in the top. Members of our audience would be encouraged to ask the 'talking head' questions of prophesy. When they did, she would make hilarious predictions about that person's relationships with everyone else in the neighborhood."

THE TEARDROP EXPLODES The Teardrop Explodes formed in Liverpool, England, in 1978, evolving from the band A Shallow Madness and taking its name from a caption in a Marvel comic book.

TEARS FOR FEARS Curt Smith and Roland Orzabal met at school in Bath, England, in 1974 when they were both thirteen and later played together in a band called Graduate. In 1981, the duo named themselves Tears for Fears, inspired by the book *Prisoners of Pain* by Arthur Janov, who pioneered "primal scream" therapy. Janov's theories, which endorsed the confrontation of hidden fears and the release of suppressed emotions, had a profound effect on the pair, who both had unhappy childhoods. Orzabal recalled his reaction after reading the book: "I rushed out to everybody I knew and started blubbering to them about it. Everybody thought I was a nutter. The only person who could see any sense in it was Curt." Their 1983 debut album, *The Hurting*, further reflected their debt to Janov and included such songs as "Suffer the Children," "Watch Me Bleed," "Mad World," and "Start of the Breakdown."

> "I rushed out to everybody I knew and started blubbering to them about it. Everybody thought I was a nutter."
> —ROLAND ORZABAL, TEARS FOR FEARS

TELEVISION Television began in New York City in 1973, after guitarist Richard Lloyd teamed up with vocalist and lead guitarist Tom Verlaine (born Thomas Miller), bassist Richard Hell (born Richard Meyers), and drummer Billy Ficca. Hell, who left Television in 1975, said of the name: "I contributed it. There'd been a previous incarnation of the band called the Neon Boys that existed for a few months as we searched for a second guitar player. There were only three of us, and we wanted a second guitar player (but) were never able to find anyone. When we finally found the guy who seemed like he would work, we decided to come up with a new name for ourselves, and we had a band meeting and everyone was supposed to bring suggestions. I had a list of a bunch of possibilities, and Television was among them, and I really liked the name. It had only been in the previous few months that my collaborator, my partner in crime, Verlaine, had changed his name to Verlaine, from Miller. When I recited my list of suggestions, Tom immediately jumped on Television. Pretty soon afterwards I realized that it was probably influenced by the fact that his new initials were T.V. So I regretted it slightly, once I realized that."

THE TEMPTATIONS The group was formed in Detroit in 1960 as the Elgins by members of two other groups, the Primes and the Distants. They changed their name in 1961 when they signed to Motown Records. Founding member Otis Williams recalled: "Not knowing that the name was taken, we christened ourselves the Elgins, after the watch....It was only a few days before signing when we discovered that another group was calling itself the Elgins and we'd have to change names again. Switching monikers was the last thing on our minds, but it had to be done. We first figured out what kind of name we didn't want: anything too damned long or hard to remember or meaningless or silly, like the El Domingos or the Siberians. That in mind, the five of us were standing on Hitsville's front lawn (the renovated two-story house where Motown was headquartered) with a guy who worked for Motown, Bill Mitchell. We were throwing around names when off the top of my head I blurted out, 'Temptations.' Bill said he really liked it, but when he asked the other four their opinions, we all took one look at ourselves in our raggedy, long winter coats and cracked up. We knew we weren't likely to tempt anyone or anything, but what the hell—it was as good a name as any. As was typical of Paul

(Williams, a fellow group member), he saw something else in it. 'It's just a name,' he said, 'but maybe it will give us something to live up to.'"

10CC The band started out in Stockport, England, in 1972, and were calling themselves Hotlegs when they teamed up with British music industry impresario Jonathan King, who rechristened them 10cc. He explained: "I started my own label in the early seventies called UK Records, and I picked up this master called 'Donna' by this group that was put together by a guy that I knew from Wayne Fontana and the Mindbenders a long while back (guitarist Eric Stewart). I had to give them a name there and then because I'd signed the record, and I went to sleep that night and had this dream that a band of mine on my label made number one on the album and singles charts simultaneously in America, and the band was called 10cc. So I gave them that name the next morning. Everybody then decided that this was apparently meant to be the amount of an average male ejaculation (in cubic centimeters). Which was absolutely far from the truth. It had not been a wet dream, I can promise. There's a lot of apocryphal stories about names, and unfortunately, most of them are much more amusing than the ugly reality, which in this case is that the name came to me in a dream, a bit like Joseph. I have to say, though, that one of the reasons that I like names like 10cc is you can immediately see them on the charts, and therefore you don't have to go through all the other boring names. It's short and punchy and looks different. It's all sorts of letters and small figures and things. It makes you sit up and pay attention."

10,000 MANIACS Originally from Jamestown, New York, the band took their name in 1981 from the misremembered title of the cult horror film *2,000 Maniacs*. They had previously performed as Still Life and the Burn Victims, among other names. Keyboard player Dennis Drew said they selected the name so that people would know "that we weren't going to do Led Zeppelin covers." While distinctive, the name initially alienated some radio programmers, who assumed the Maniacs were a punk band or a novelty act. The name even confused one early band member, a sax player who would take the stage wearing pink slippers and a colander on his head, explaining to his bandmates: "We're maniacs, aren't we? I thought we were supposed to be funny."

TEN YEARS AFTER The band formed in Nottingham, England, in 1966, led by singer and guitarist Alvin Lee. Their name is a reference to the birth of rock 'n' roll a decade earlier.

TESLA The hard rock band got its start in Sacramento, California, in 1981 as a garage rock group called Earth Shaker, then morphed into the blues-rock outfit City Kidd. They changed their name to Tesla in 1986 after one of their managers lent them *Tesla: Man Out of Time*, a book about inventor Nikola Tesla.

THE THE Matt Johnson formed The The in London in 1980. Johnson said the name was chosen for its ambiguity: "It doesn't suggest any particular preconceptions."

THEM Begun in Belfast, Ireland, in 1962 and originally called the Gamblers, Van Morrison's band took their name from the 1954 monster movie *Them!* about giant man-eating ants that terrorize California. The band chose the name because it suggested a sense of menace and mystery, and didn't have a "the."

THEY MIGHT BE GIANTS Guitarist John Flansburgh and accordion player John Linnell, both natives of Lincoln, Massachusetts, formed They Might Be Giants in Brooklyn, New York, in 1982. The name comes from an obscure 1972 film starring George C. Scott and Joanne

Woodward, which *Halliwell's Film Guide* once described as a "curious fantasy comedy which rather tentatively satirizes modern life and the need to retreat into unreality; mildly pleasing entertainment for intellectuals." The film's title came from a line in the novel *Don Quixote* in which the title character famously attempts to joust with windmills, thinking them to be "monstrous giants." Flansburgh recalled: "We first had a really bad name—a name so bad that John and I have made a vow that we will never tell anyone, even our children. We used it for our first show, a Sandinista rally in Central Park. We had this really terrible, terrible, embarrassing name. So we put together this long list of new names, a page of names, but none of them were that great. This long list of names included Dumptruck, and we liked that one OK. This friend of ours, Raoul Rosenberg, had this act with his dummy, Julius. He's now a political activist, but back then he was a ventriloquist. He was trying to think of a name for his act that would be something more than just 'Raoul and Julius,' and he came up with the idea of calling his act They Might Be Giants, but then decided not to use it. It was a reference to this movie that I hadn't seen at the time, this sort of second-rate seventies cult movie. We asked him if we could borrow his name, and he said yes. So we made up two posters for our next gig, and one of them was Dumptruck and one of them was They Might Be Giants, and fortunately we chose They Might Be Giants because there was a band from Boston called Dumptruck, so we would've had to become Dumptruck NYC or Brooklyn Dumptruck or something. So we named ourselves They Might Be Giants. The key ingredient to its interest to us was the fact that it was a full sentence. It wasn't so much that it had the word 'giants' in it, or that it suggested that we had some larger future. In fact, we were kind of surprised that people thought that the 'they' was referring to us. We always thought it was an outward-looking name, and that was another point of interest. You know, 'they' as opposed to 'we.' Everyone knows that bands name themselves, so why would you call your band 'they' if you meant yourselves? We just thought it was kind of an outward-looking, paranoid name, and the fact that it was a full sentence seemed kind of interesting. This was at the point where bands had just moved from the Pencils to Pencil Pencil, and there were very few bands who had any names more interesting than that. It was in the era of new wave. It was like 1983, so still, if new wave wasn't the most vital thing, it was still influential. The reference to *Don Quixote* didn't seem that important;

> "To us, it seemed obvious that we were destined for the margins of popular culture. It was just a functioning name for a bar band. It actually took us a long time to figure out that people didn't even understand the name." —JOHN FLANSBURGH, THEY MIGHT BE GIANTS

it seemed pretty obscure. I've never read the book, but I have read the passage. It wasn't that big a part of it. We didn't believe that people would catch the reference. It just seemed like a good full sentence. One of the things about our name is that people got the impression that we were ambitious because of it when nothing could have been further from the truth. To us, it seemed obvious that we were destined for the margins of popular culture. It was just a functioning name for a bar band. It actually took us a long time to figure out that people didn't even understand the name. It was so totally uncalculated. I think if we knew then what we know now, we probably would have gone for a more streamlined name. But it does look good on a marquee sometimes, filling up all the space."

THIN LIZZY The band was formed in Dublin, Ireland, in 1969 by three schoolmates: singer and bass player Phil Lynott, drummer Brian Downey, and guitarist Eric Bell. Downey recalled: "When we started off first in Dublin, we had a three-piece band—Eric Bell, Phil, and myself. We used to sort of rehearse in a place called the Countdown Club. We were sitting around trying to think of a name. We went through various names—the Mod Con (as in Modern Convenience) Cave-dwellers, and various other stupid names. We were racking our brains for days and days, maybe weeks. Eric Bell used to be a big fan of this comic here on sale, an English comic, and there's all these strange characters in it like Dennis the Menace and Mickey the Monkey and people like that. There was also a person called Tin Lizzie. This was Tin, T-I-N L-I-Z-Z-I-E. She was like a little female robot. He was a huge fan of this comic and liked Tin Lizzie. That was his favorite character in the comic. So he came up with this idea. He asked me, 'Look, seeing that we went through so many names, and we couldn't seem to figure out what we liked, why don't we call it Tin Lizzie?' We all went, 'Aw, forget it, no way, it's terrible,' you know? Phil said, 'No, absolutely no way. There's no way you could call the band Tin Lizzie.' So we sort of pondered it over for a couple of days, and Phil came back one day and said, 'Tell you what we do. Why don't we sort of stick an H in and call it Thin Lizzie—to confuse the Irish, because people in Ireland don't pronounce the H anyway—and call it Lizzy, L-I-Z-Z-Y, put a Y at the end instead of an I-E.' So he got some guy to draw up this little logo, and it looked pretty good with the H and the Y at the end. But we still weren't one-hundred-percent sure. We really weren't completely convinced that it would work, until we played the first few gigs. On the posters, the first pubs spelled it 'Tin' anyway. That created a bit of controversy, so we went back to the promoter and said, 'Look, that's the wrong way to spell Thin Lizzy,' and he said, 'But it's called "Tin Lizzie."' We said, 'No, it's T-H—it's Thin Lizzy.' That's basically how we got our name. It was very simple, but it took a while to get it together. The name of the comic was *Beano*.

Tin Lizzie was a female robot, looked sort of like a trash can. It appeared in the *Dublin Evening Herald*."

THIRD EYE BLIND Stephan Jenkins started the band in San Francisco in 1990. When asked if the name refers to the metaphysical third eye in Eastern religions, Jenkins said, "Yeah, but it's also kind of taking the piss out of that. I like names with wit and a sense of punk-rock irony. I was a big fan of Camper Van Beethoven. The name reflects a certain sense of magic and dreams—we thought that was very lacking in music when we started—music for a blind time, if you will. It also takes the piss out of that phony spiritual thing. Third Eye Blind has always been about real things."

THE 13TH FLOOR ELEVATORS Psychedelic rock pioneers the 13th Floor Elevators formed in Austin, Texas, in 1965 by guitarist and vocalist Roky Erickson, electric jug player Tommy Hall, and guitarist Stacy Sutherland. Clementine Hall, Tommy Hall's wife, recalled: "There was a lot of confusion about who actually named the group the 13th Floor Elevators, but I clearly remember how it happened. I was sitting in our bedroom with Tommy when he asked what they should call the band. I suggested the Elevators to Tommy, not only because the band was making psychedelic music, but because I thought it would sound like a black band. We would always listen to R&B groups, especially at this one place where we always ate barbecue. A day or so later Tommy came back and said that the rest of the band liked the suggestion of the Elevators, but they thought it wasn't long enough. It was then that I suggested the 13th Floor Elevators. Adding the '13th Floor' to the name provided various interpretations, the most obvious being that the thirteenth floor was usually nonexistent in the older high-rise buildings. Also, M is the thirteenth letter in the alphabet, and in street vernacular the number thirteen became associated with marijuana. It was also my lucky number."

THIRTY SECONDS TO MARS The band, often represented as 30 Seconds to Mars, was formed by actor Jared Leto and his brother Shannon in Los Angeles in 1998. Jared recalled, "It's something that was referred to in a thesis we found on the Internet, that a professor at Harvard wrote. It was a subsection in the thesis about the impending advancement of science and culture and how it's happening quicker and quicker and we're almost literally thirty seconds from Mars." He elaborated, "I think the idea is interesting. It's a metaphor for the future. It's a silly metaphor on one hand, but it's an idea that is being proven, I think, every single day. Thirty seconds to Mars—the fact that we're so close to something that's not a tangible thing/idea. Also, Mars being the god of war makes it really interesting as well. You could substitute that in there, but the thing that's nicest about the name and what's important for my brother and I when we were thinking about all of this is that it be imaginative and really represent the sound of our music in as unique a way as possible. I think that it does that. It's different . . . It was either that or 'Boiled Hard.'"

"They had their guns drawn, and they told us to walk outside, or these .38 Specials would do their talking for them. So they scared us plumb to death. That's how we really got our name."
—DONNIE VAN ZANT, .38 SPECIAL

.38 SPECIAL The Southern rock band formed in Jacksonville, Florida, in 1974. In an interview, lead singer Donnie Van Zant recalled: "I guess .38 was like most bands; when we first got together, we had a problem finding rehearsal halls. All the places that we found were in residential areas. We'd be there for like a week at a time, and before you knew it, you had the cops on you for disturbing the peace. So we had to go on the outskirts of Jacksonville. We found this place, right on the Florida-Georgia line, a place called Yulee, Florida. We found this abandoned auto warehouse, and we nicknamed it the Alamo. It was on a golf course out there, and the golf course used it to put fertilizer in it. We got this place for about sixty dollars a month. We were out there rehearsing one night—it was like no-man's-land out there—and we heard sirens, and people just ramming at the door. Before we could get our guitars off to answer the door, they'd knocked it open, and it was the cops—they called 'em the constables, that's what they called them out there. They had their .38s out, and they didn't know what was going on. We heard a couple of them reply that they thought there was an orgy or drug party going on. They had their guns drawn, and they told us to walk outside, or these .38 Specials would do their talking for them. So they scared us plumb to death. That's how we really got our name. But it's got a good ending to it. Some of them constables later on joined the Jacksonville Police Department, so when we had a successful record and were able to get another practice house in Jacksonville, they guarded our rehearsal hall there for us. We became real good friends with them." When asked about the rumor that the name came from a '38 Buick Special his parents gave him for his sixteenth birthday that he used as an equipment van for the band, Van Zant laughed and said, "No, I don't know where that one came from. You know, I don't advocate guns or anything like that, but I think the whole thing about it is that the .38 Special is pretty powerful, and we felt that we were a pretty powerful band. We had dual guitars and dual drummers and thought that was perfect for .38 Special."

THE THOMPSON TWINS The Thompson Twins began as a trio in Chesterfield, England, in 1977. Led by keyboard player Tom Bailey, they were named after a pair of hapless detectives in the *Adventures of Tintin* comic books, which are wildly popular in Europe but haven't made as much of an impact in the United States. By 1981 the lineup had expanded to include seven members, but they returned to a trio the following year comprised of Bailey, Alannah Currie (vocals, sax, and percussion), and Joe Leeway (percussion). In late 1986, Leeway left the group, leaving the Twins, at last, a duo.

THREE DOG NIGHT The band, formed in Los Angeles in 1967 by singers Danny Hutton, Cory Wells, and Chuck Negron, was briefly called Redwood. Hutton's girlfriend at the time, actress June Fairchild, (who would later gain fame as "the Ajax Lady" from the Cheech and Chong movie Up in Smoke) is most frequently credited with suggesting the name Three Dog Night, after a phrase she had read in a magazine article. Wells recalled, "She was reading in a magazine about the Aborigines in Australia. Where they end up at night, they take a dog to keep them warm. The Australians got a hold of that and said it was a 'three dog night' to describe particularly chilly weather." But composer and arranger Van Dyke Parks, who was an associate of the group, disputes that story: "I got the name Three Dog Night from an issue of *Mankind* magazine of an Aboriginal fellow with three dogs around him."

311 Pronounced "three eleven," the band formed in Omaha, Nebraska, in 1988 and took their name from the local police code for indecent exposure. The inspiration was apparently an arrest of original guitarist Jim Watson for skinny-dipping in a public pool.

'TIL TUESDAY Best known for the 1985 hit "Voices Carry," the band formed in Boston in 1983. According to drummer Michael Hausman, the name did not come from the David Bowie song "Love You till Tuesday" as had been rumored: "'Til Tuesday, the name, did not come from anywhere in particular. There's no great story. We were sitting around the rehearsal space, we were talking about names, and we got onto this thing about days of the week. And 'Til Tuesday—maybe it was the alliteration, I'm not sure what it was—but that's what just kind of popped out and that was the name. No secret meaning. Sorry."

TOAD THE WET SPROCKET The band was formed in 1987 in Santa Barbara, California, by four schoolmates and became the house band at a local bar called the Shack. Bassist Dean Dinning explained, "It's a Monty Python skit from an album called the *Contractual Obligation Album*. It's on the one called 'Rock Notes.' It starts out, 'Rex Stardust, lead electric triangle for Toad the Wet Sprocket, has had to have an elbow removed following their recent worldwide tour of Finland.'" Drummer Randy Guss recalled, "We thought it was funny. And then, when we had our first gig coming up, we had no name. We thought it was so funny that in the newspaper it said, 'At the Shack: Toad the Wet Sprocket.' Lead singer and songwriter Glen Phillips noted, "We were gonna think of something better. We were going to think of a good name, and a real name, but it just never happened."

TOM TOM CLUB Talking Heads bassist Tina Weymouth and drummer Chris Frantz, who married in 1977, formed Tom Tom Club in 1980. Weymouth remembered: "In 1980, Chris Blackwell, who owned Island Records, wanted to build an apartment building to house artists and musicians working at Compass Point Studios in the Bahamas. He wanted to create a small artistic community, which Chris Frantz and I wanted to be a part of when we weren't away working with the Talking Heads. In the Bahamas, people name their houses instead of giving them numbers. Blackwell's house is Terra Nova, and the beach house across from the studio where many bands have stayed is called Press On Regardless (but it has been called Pass Out Regardless by insiders). Since we were the first occupants of the new building, Blackwell gave us the honor of naming it. We chose Tip Top for the building, in reference to its location and view, and Tom Tom Club for our own space because it was where we played and wrote our music. We put drumsticks in the walls in the style of Shaker wall pegs. Even the toilet paper holders are drumsticks. We had many great jams and parties there with a lot of different musicians, including Ian Dury and Chas Jankel, Lee 'Scratch' Perry, Wally Badarou, 'Sticky' Thompson, Tyrone Downie, Robert Palmer, Adrian Belew, and many others who eventually played on our records. The band was just such a natural outgrowth of that creative, fun scene that we just kept the name Tom Tom Club for the record and the bands we had afterwards. I believe we were the first of the Club bands—even ahead of Culture Club—that were to follow in the eighties. Someone told us that there exists an old black-and-white film that contains scenes that take place at the Tom Tom Club. Perhaps we had seen that film and loved the name, but we can't remember. We thought we were inspired by Peanuts Taylor's Drumbeat Club in Nassau. Peanuts is a really good conga player, and tourists regularly go to see him and his fire-eating limbo dancers."

> "We need to get a name like Toto, something really simple, easy to remember, and easily identified in every language, that if you hear once, you're going to remember it."
> —STEVE LUKATHER, TOTO

TOTO Toto was created in Los Angeles in 1978 by six veteran session musicians. Lead guitarist Steve Lukather recalled, "We were doing demos for our first record in early '77, and we needed something to write on the demo tapes, because we didn't have a name for our group. So we said, 'We need to get a name like Toto, something really simple, easy to remember, and easily identified in every language, that if you hear once, you're going to remember it.' Always with the intention of finding a better name, 'cause the name doesn't fit the music at all. I think it's actually been detrimental to our career more than anything. Shit happened so fast for us, the next thing you know people said, 'You know, that's not a bad name.' I was like, 'Man, the word doesn't fit what we're doing.' It was just one of those things where we were making a record and the record was out before we even really had a chance to get deep into thought about it. Believe me, compared to a lot of other names, it's not so bad." Lead singer Bobby Kimball recalled, "(Keyboard players) Jeff Porcaro and David Paich were sitting around watching *The Wizard of Oz* one day, and they came up with the name from the movie." Kimball debunked the enduring rumor that his last name was originally Toteau: "That may have been a thing we did with *Rolling Stone* just as a joke, told them my name was Robert Toteau, T-O-T-E-A-U, and we all had a big chuckle about it. Next thing you know, I was seeing it printed everywhere that my name was Toteau." When asked if he was glad they picked the name Toto in retrospect, he said, "Oh, yeah, I thought it was great because as we went around the world, we found about seventeen different connotations. It's a betting term in Europe—Toto Lotto. There's a cartoon character in France named Toto, and I think it means 'child' in Swahili. And 'toto' means 'all-encompassing' in some language. It's pretty wild. Also, it's the name of the largest toilet manufacturer in Japan. So the first time we went to Toyko, we saw our name early every morning."

TRAFFIC Steve Winwood started Traffic in 1967 in Birmingham, England, after leaving the Spencer Davis Group. The name was suggested by drummer Jim Capaldi while standing on a corner one day waiting to cross the street.

TRAIN The band formed in 1993 in San Francisco. Lead singer Patrick Monahan recalled, "One of the guys heard an interview with Echo &

the Bunnymen, and they were claiming that there was nothing romantic about America. And we thought, 'That's not true.' The locomotive is very romantic and is an American image, hence the name Train. And it stuck because we couldn't think of anything better."

T. REX Marc Bolan formed the band as Tyrannosaurus Rex in London in 1967. Producer Tony Visconti, who worked very closely with Bolan, explained: "Marc Bolan was always impressed as a youngster by the Tyrannosaurus rex skeleton in the British Museum of Natural History. I'm sure all of us have had a similar experience. When you finally see those bones firsthand, it just knocks you away that something was actually that big, and that's what he said. He said he couldn't believe that. He said Tyrannosaurus rex was like 'the warlord of the royal crocodiles.' He said it was the most powerful beast. Of course he set it up as his idol because he was into power, and also he had a very rich imagination. He was very much into Tolkien, Middle Earth, and all that. So in some way, Tyrannosaurus rex fitted in with his whole mythology of great, wondrous beasts that lived millions of years ago. He always said when he got a band together, a band of his own, he was going to call it Tyrannosaurus Rex—which is exactly what he did. It's what he always wanted to call it. There's some references to that in some of his early lyrics, to the warlord of the royal crocodiles. He really did worship this beast. He gave him that nickname. His poetry was marvelous—what a poetic way of describing Tyrannosaurus rex." When asked how the name evolved from Tyrannosaurus Rex to T. Rex, Visconti explained, "We did four albums as Tyrannosaurus Rex. Then one day he came into my office and noticed that I had been writing 'T. Rex' in my diary. For every day of the week that I was in the studio with them, I didn't want to write out 'Tyrannosaurus Rex.' In my diary and also my wall chart. You know, every producer or A&R guy has a chart on the wall, so it actually was in public view.

And he was actually insulted by that. He said, 'It's Tyrannosaurus Rex and you shouldn't shorten it.' So I said, 'I'm sorry, but this is the way I'm going to keep doing it. I can't write that out, it's too long.' But I think the writing was on the wall, so to speak, and other people began to shorten it to T. Rex. DJs especially could not pronounce it, being the illiterate idiots that they are. They could not say the words Tyrannosaurus Rex, which limited our airplay. The British DJs would stumble on it and make jokes of it. So after this little incident when he told me off about shortening the name, the very next album was called *T. Rex*. He said, 'I'm shortening the name of the group to T. Rex.' I said, 'Why?' 'It's easier to say,' he said."

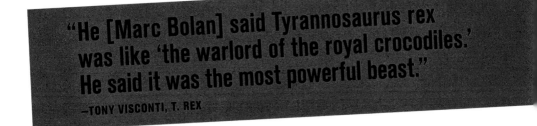

"He [Marc Bolan] said Tyrannosaurus rex was like 'the warlord of the royal crocodiles.' He said it was the most powerful beast."
—TONY VISCONTI, T. REX

THE TROGGS The Troggs began as the Troglodytes in 1964 in Andover, England, and were discovered by the Kinks' manager the following year. In 1966, the band changed their name to the Troggs, lead singer Reginald Ball changed his name to Reg Presley, and their single "Wild Thing" shot to the top of the charts. In an interview, Presley recalled: "We were looking for a sort of earthy type of name because you had your Stones, and that was a sort of hard, aggressive name in those days, and we were looking for something like that. Everybody had their own opinions on what the band should be called. We picked up a couple of student schoolteachers that were hitchhiking their way to London when we were going up there to get some new equipment, and I asked them for name suggestions. They said, 'Why don't you call yourselves the Grotty Troggs?' 'Cause we were sat in the back of an old Ford Transit van, you know. I kind of liked the name the Troggs, and then we voted for it, quite a while after that, and I picked the longest straw, so I was able to choose the band name. Grotty Trogg, you know, grotesque. I liked the name, and I got the vote, so that was it. Trogg is short for troglodyte—a mythical cave dweller, it says in the Oxford dictionary. So we thought caves, rocks, rock, roll—it sort of went in there somewhere."

> "We thought of changing it to something that included beans, like the Laserbeans or the Holy Beans, but then decided to come up with something new."
> —FEE WAYBILL, THE TUBES

THE TUBES Lead singer Fee Waybill (born John Waldo Waybill) explained: "When we first got together back in San Francisco in, like, '72, we were two different bands from Arizona that had kind of combined. We'd moved to San Francisco one after the other, and I was the roadie for the band originally called the Red White and Blues Band that had changed its name to Arizona after the move to San Francisco. The other band was called the Beans, and after the band that I was the roadie for lost its bass player, our trio decided to join their quartet and became Beanizona. I became a background singer because there were too many roadies. They said, 'Here, take this tambourine and, like, sing in the back,' and I eventually worked my way into being the lead singer. After we were Beanizona for a while and that didn't work, we changed it back to the Beans. We were playing gigs and didn't have a deal or anything when a band from the East Coast called the Beans came out with a record on United

Artists. It was a New York sitar rock band or something like that. We were freaked out and wrote a letter saying, 'We're the Beans—you can't call yourselves the Beans!' And they said, 'Well, by virtue of being published first, we own the name—not you.' So we had to change our name, although we didn't want to. We thought of changing it to something that included beans, like the Laserbeans or the Holy Beans, but then decided to come up with something new. Everyone's assignment was to come up with a full page of names. We had thousands of names. We went through tons of them. We were almost called the Gasmen and some other horrible names that I can't remember. Somebody, I think it was either Mike (Cotten, synthesizer) or Prairie (Prince, drums), was looking through a medical dictionary for names of body parts and came across tubes, rods, and bulbs—the bones inside the inner ear. We thought, 'Oh, inner ear, it's perfect for a rock group, how perfect—Tubes, Rods, and Bulbs.' And then we thought, 'No, that's too long, and it's too hard to say.' So we shortened it to TRB—another initial band, we hated that. So someone suggested, 'Why not just Tubes?' We all liked it because it had so many different connotations. You couldn't pin it down. It could be inner tubes, TV tubes, laser tubes, fallopian tubes . . . "

THE TURTLES The Turtles evolved from a high school surf band formed in Los Angeles in 1963 that was first called the Nightriders and then the Crossfires. The following year, with both the British Invasion under way and folk rock gaining in popularity, the band stopped playing surf instrumentals and began passing themselves off as an English group and played several folk gigs as the Crosswind Singers. In 1965, when local White Whale Records offered them a deal but asked them to change their name, manager Reb Foster suggested the Tyrtles, in imitation of the Byrds. The band initially balked but agreed to the conventionally spelled Turtles.

TV ON THE RADIO Indie rock band TV on the Radio came together in Brooklyn, New York, in 2001. Their name came from a tagline used by influential British radio personality Tommy Vance, who would refer to himself as "TV on the radio," a play on words that referenced his initials. Vance was one of the first radio DJs in the UK to champion hard rock and heavy metal in the early 1980s. Born Richard Anthony Crispian Francis Prew Hope-Weston, after a stint in the Merchant Navy he began his radio career in the US under the name Rick West. He adopted the name Tommy Vance at KOL Radio in Seattle from a DJ who failed to turn up after the station had paid to have jingles recorded promoting Vance. When he was asked if he would be willing to change his name, he reportedly answered, "For this money, you can change my name to Judas Iscariot!"

TWENTY ONE PILOTS Lead singer Tyler Joseph and drummer Josh Dun formed the group in Columbus, Ohio, in 2009. The name comes from the 1947 Arthur Miller play *Twenty One Pilots*, which Joseph studied in a theater class as an undergraduate at Ohio State University. The play yielded both a title and a philosophy for the band. Dun explained: "*Twenty One Pilots* is a play by Arthur Miller, who also wrote *All My Sons*. It's about a guy who's creating and developing parts for airplanes in wartime when it comes to his attention that some of these parts were faulty. He was faced with a decision: Do I send the parts out and risk people getting hurt and potentially dying, or do I recall the parts and most likely hang my name and probably end this business? That was a huge decision, and ultimately he decides to send the parts out, and as a result twenty-one pilots die. There ends up being no correlation between the deaths and the parts, but one of the pilots killed happens to be one of his sons, and his daughter blames him for his death the rest of the play. At the end, he kills himself. The way we apply that to our band is that all of us are constantly faced with decisions. It could be a moral decision or just a small decision, like, should we watch the opener play? Maybe a bigger decision, like, should we sign this publishing deal? Or which label should we sign with? It's been surprising how many times we've used that reference throughout the last couple years to help us base our decisions that we've made."

UB40 UB40 started out in Birmingham, England, in 1979, taking their name from the British unemployment benefit card. Guitarist Robin Campbell explained, "A friend said, 'You're on the dole, so why not call yourselves UB40?' We didn't realize it at the time, but it was a stroke of genius." His brother Ali, the lead singer, noted, "It meant we had three million fans automatically. But it wasn't a calculated political move. Individually, we're politically motivated, but as a band . . . we never set out to be the spokesmen for the unemployed youth of Great Britain. We set out to play reggae and make money."

UGLY KID JOE The band formed in 1990 in Isla Vista, California, and played under a variety of names, including SWAT (Suburban White Alcoholic Trash), before settling on Ugly Kid Joe. The name was inspired by Pretty Boy Floyd, an L.A.-based glam band, for whom they had been scheduled to open. Guitarist Klaus Eichstadt explained: "We'd used, like, three names in the past month, so we were like, 'What are we gonna call ourselves for this one?' I said, 'Let's go for something dumb like Ugly Kid Joe, you know, opening for Pretty Boy Floyd.' Everybody kinda chuckled and we were like, 'Yeah, it'd look funny on the marquee, and we could give, like, a dollar off for ugly chicks or something.'" As luck would have it, the show was canceled. The other band members thought it was pointless to keep the name,

> **"Let's go for something dumb like Ugly Kid Joe, you know, opening for Pretty Boy Floyd.' Everybody kinda chuckled and we were like, 'Yeah, it'd look funny on the marquee.'"** —KLAUS EICHSTADT, UGLY KID JOE

but Eichstadt had sketched a cartoon character he called Ugly Kid Joe. The cartoon was polished by a friend, Moish Brenman, who did artwork for local skateboarders. Eichstadt noted: "The design was done by Moish for, like, fourteen bucks. That was all we had. We gave him, like, a bag of Doritos, a candy bar, a Mountain Dew, and fourteen bucks. That was the coolest—to have our own logo. Then we had him do the drumhead and suddenly we knew we were a real band."

URGE OVERKILL The band came together in Chicago in 1986. Singer and guitarist Nash Kato explained that their name was "off a Parliament record. I believe it was the title track off *Funkentelechy* (1977's *Funkentelechy Vs. The Placebo System*). 'Mood control is designed to render the funkable ideas brought to you by the makers of Mr. Prolong, better known as urge overkill, the pimping of the pleasure principle'—something like that."

URIAH HEEP Uriah Heep formed in London in 1970, having evolved from a band called Spice. They named themselves after the unctuous Dickens character in *Great Expectations*.

U2 U2 evolved from a band called Feedback formed in Dublin, Ireland, in 1976 by vocalist Bono (born Paul Hewson), guitarist the Edge (David Evans), guitarist Dick Evans (the Edge's brother), bassist Adam Clayton, and drummer Larry Mullen Jr., all friends from the Mount Temple School. Later that year, Dick left to form his own band, the Virgin Prunes, and Feedback became the Hype. Clayton, acting as the band's manager, sought advice from Steve Rapid, singer for the local band the Radiators, who suggested they change their name. When Clayton agreed, expressing a desire for a name that was somewhat ambiguous, Rapid suggested U2. There was a U2 spy plane, a U2 submarine, and a U2 battery made by Eveready, in addition to the suggestion of "you too" and "you two." When Clayton suggested the name to his bandmates, they were somewhat skeptical but eventually accepted it. Bono was initially called Bonovox, after a local shop that sold hearing aids. Bono gave the Edge his name, allegedly inspired by the shape of Evans's head.

VAMPIRE WEEKEND The band started out at Columbia University in New York City in 2006. The group began with a rap collaboration between lead singer and guitarist Ezra Koenig and drummer and percussionist Chris Tomson named L'Homme Run. The name Vampire Weekend comes from the title of a short film that Koenig worked on one summer while still in college. Bassist Chris Baio explained, "Ezra (Koenig), our singer, was in between (his) freshman and sophomore years of college—he was home for the summer and had seen *The Lost Boys*. He wanted to make his own East Coast, New England version of *Lost Boys*. For two days he filmed this movie called *Vampire Weekend* about this guy named Walcott whose dad gets killed by vampires, and he travels up to Cape Cod to warn the mayor of Cape Cod that vampires are attacking the country. He only made it for two days, and then sort of forgot about it for a while. And then, two and a half years later, during his senior year, he sort of unearthed the footage for it and made it into a two-minute trailer. And that was about a month before the band got together; so when the band came together, we sort of took it and (didn't) overthink it."

VAN DER GRAAF GENERATOR Formed in Manchester, England, in 1967, the art rock band was named by drummer Chris Judge Smith after a machine that creates static electricity.

> "We were white guys doing rhythm and blues stuff, and one day this girl in this club said, 'You guys are like white soul—like vanilla fudge.'" —CARMINE APPICE, VANILLA FUDGE

VANILLA FUDGE The band originated in New York City in 1966. Drummer Carmine Appice recalled: "We were white guys doing rhythm and blues stuff, and one day this girl in this club said, 'You guys are like white soul—like vanilla fudge.' And we said, 'Yeah, that's an interesting name.' Before that we were called the Pigeons, and as we were signing to Atlantic Records, they said, 'Well, the name the Pigeons isn't really that good.' Actually, maybe it was the producer, Shadow Morton, who said change the name. It was somebody from that end of it, from the record end, who said, 'This name's no good. We need something that describes you guys better.' So when this chick came up with this Vanilla Fudge name, we went, 'Hey, that's a great idea.' It was at a place called the Page Two, in Oceanside, New York, in the beginning of '67." When asked if they were conscious of the contrasting name phenomenon that included bands like Iron Butterfly and Led Zeppelin, Appice said, "No, not really. We were just white guys doing a lot of black music in our own way—you know, like 'Hangin' On,' 'Take Me for a Little While,' 'Hold On I'm Comin'.' We did a lot of stuff like 'The Tracks of My Tears' and we rockified it, a blue-eyed soul sort of vibe. That's basically what we did, but we didn't want to call it 'white soul.' So when Vanilla Fudge came along, we thought, 'Yeah, that's pretty cool. Yeah, this might sell.'" When asked why they were originally called the Pigeons, Appice explained, "The band already had the name when I joined. It had something to do with the Byrds. We actually played a show one time with the Byrds and the Seeds—the Byrds, the Seeds, and the Pigeons."

THE VELVET UNDERGROUND An early incarnation of the Velvet Underground formed in New York City in 1964. After performing under a variety of short-lived names, including the Primitives and the Warlocks, they settled on the Velvet Underground, taken from an obscure paperback that viola and bass player John Cale's friend Tony Conrad found on the sidewalk of the Bowery in Manhattan. The book claimed to chronicle the seamy sexual underside of everyday America. Guitarist Sterling Morrison recalled: "We had a name at last! And it was adopted by us and deemed appropriate not because of the S&M theme of the book, but because the word 'underground' was suggestive of our involvement with the underground film and art scenes." Singer and guitarist Lou Reed recalled: "There was a place in Philadelphia we used to play, the Second Fret. One of the weirdest stories about that is that I had taken the name Velvet Underground from this paperback book I had seen, just this junky book with a great title. I went into the Second Fret, and this girl was there taking tickets. She said to me, 'My father just died.' 'Oh, I'm sorry to hear that.' 'He wrote that book.' Small world."

THE VENTURES The instrumental rock band began in Seattle in 1960 as the Versatones, soon changing their name to the Ventures because they were "beginning a new adventure."

VERUCA SALT The Chicago-based band formed in 1992 and named themselves after a greedy, demanding, manipulative character in Roald Dahl's children's novel *Charlie and the Chocolate Factory*.

THE VIOLENT FEMMES Guitarist Gordon Gano, bassist Brian Ritchie, and drummer Victor DeLorenzo started the Violent Femmes in Milwaukee in 1980. When asked about their name, Ritchie explained, "Well, it's a very mundane story. Everybody wants to look for some sort of social or political motivations for our name, and we've usually tried to mislead people and tell them the wrong story. I suppose since this is a real, official name encyclopedia, I'll give you the truth. There was this guy named Jerry Fortier—he's a musician and he's a photographer, he did the photography for our first album—and he started talking to me about my family. He asked me, 'What's your brother like?' and I just started to lie. I don't know why, but I just decided to lie. I said, 'Well, he's just like me. He's got the same haircut, he dresses like me, he's got a punk-rock band, and everything.' And it's not true at all. My brother's straight—he works for an insurance agent, doesn't look anything like me. So then Jerry caught me by surprise and he said, 'Well, what's the name of your brother's band?' And I said, 'Um, uh, the Violent Femmes!' It was just, you know, one of these spur-of-the-moment, flow-of-consciousness, Freudian slip–type pronouncements that I made—and he accepted that at face value. Then I went over to Victor's house, and I said, 'Hey, listen to this weird name that I just came up with today.' And I told him, 'Violent Femmes,' and Victor was quite taken with that. So originally, when we started, we were freelancing as a rhythm section. We played with Gordon Gano, and we played with a lot of other people too. So we just called our rhythm section Violent Femmes, and that's how it started. Of course, after a while we just adopted it as the name of the whole band." When asked what they called themselves before they settled on the Violent Femmes, Ritchie recalled, "Oh, we had a lot of different names: the Romboids, Hitler's Missing Teste, Nude Family Portrait . . ." When asked how they've explained the name in the past, he said, "Usually we just refused to talk about it, but then sometimes we would say that it was a schoolyard thing, like Milwaukee slang. The word 'femme' is slang for sissy. I don't know if it's slang all over America, but it was in Milwaukee in the fifties—violent obviously being the opposite of that connotation. So the name ends up having a nulled effect. I mean, it really doesn't make too much sense. Violent Femmes—it's a non sequitur. The interesting thing about the name is that we would have never chosen that name except for the fact that we didn't give a shit and we didn't expect the band to survive. We intended to just do a couple gigs and then we were going to split up and move on to other things. . . . I never appreciated Crosby, Stills & Nash until I realized how smart they were to name themselves that."

RICHARD HELL AND THE VOIDOIDS After he founded the Neon Boys with Tom Verlaine, which later became Television, and cofounded the Heartbreakers with Johnny Thunders, Richard Hell launched the Voidoids in New York City in 1976. He recalled: "I was sitting in a restaurant on Second Avenue with Tom Verlaine after a rehearsal one night, just watching the parade go by, and to amuse ourselves we began calling each other names, attaching 'oid' to different words, like, 'You're a bulboid,' 'You're a transmissionoid.' I was wracking my brain for the best 'oid' I could conceive of, and that's when I had the brilliant illumination and conceived the original Voidoid. It turned up in a novel I was working on at the time that I called *The Voidoid*. That word was used to describe a certain kind of personality. I meant it was a sort of late-twentieth-century human mutation that had taken place from the influence of all the pollution and broadcast waves filling the air." When asked if he considered any other names for the band, he said, "Oh, tons of them . . . the Beauticians, that was one of my favorites."

WALK THE MOON Lead singer Nicholas Petricca started the band in 2006, while a student at Kenyon College in Gambier, Ohio. The band's name was inspired by the song "Walking on the Moon" by the Police. Petricca explained, "The Police have always been a great influence for us. Just their attitude, and Sting's sort of impossible vocal range and delivery. The song itself, it shows this guy walking home from his friend's house, or maybe it's a girl's house or whatever, and he's got this feeling like he's on cloud nine, like he can do anything. And I love that feeling, and we love the idea, of feeling sort of super powerful, and that's I guess the vibe the song gives us."

THE WALKER BROTHERS Launched in London in 1964 by three Americans, the group consisted of nobody who was born a Walker or related in any way to a Walker. Before moving to England, guitarist John Maus and bassist Scott Engel lived in Los Angeles, where they had to use fake IDs to get in and play local clubs because they were underage. Maus's card was in the name of Walker, which he preferred to his given surname, which is German for "mouse." Because he and Engel looked alike, they jokingly adopted the name the Walker

Brothers, as did drummer Gary Leeds when he joined the band. The group had several hits in the mid-sixties, including "Make It Easy on Yourself" and "The Sun Ain't Gonna Shine (Anymore)."

WALL OF VOODOO Wall of Voodoo was a new wave group from Los Angeles best known for the 1983 hit "Mexican Radio." Front man Stan Ridgway recalled: "In 1975, I was out of work. I had been playing in a lot of Top 40 and country and western kind of bands around bars in Whittier (California) with names like the Three Little Pigs and the Come On Inn and stuff. But I really wanted to get out of that, and I had this idea to start this soundtrack company that would just service sci-fi and horror films, where we would undercut the competition because we were so cheap. We might even work for free—it didn't make much difference. But I needed a facade, so I rented an office on Hollywood Boulevard that ended up being right across the street from the Masque (the seminal L.A. punk club) when it started in '77. So a lot of characters were flying around then, and I would kind of collect them and bring them up to the office, and we'd try a lot of things out up there. The name Wall of Voodoo was actually a twist on Phil Spector's wall of sound. I had a big collection of rhythm machines, and I thought that what we were doing was not a wall of sound but really a wall of voodoo. It was a company long before it was a band, but after a while people wanted us to come out and play, and so we did."

WAR In 1969, after leaving the Animals, singer Eric Burdon met Danish harmonica player Lee Oskar and together they recruited Night Shift, an all-black band they spotted playing in an L.A. nightclub, to form War. Jerry Goldstein, the band's longtime manager and producer, explained: "We were in the middle of the peace movement, and Eric Burdon used to do a lot of weird things. We figured if we called the group War, people would notice it. At first the idea was "war is music." You wouldn't believe the outcry. People were like, 'How can you call a bunch of brothers blah, blah, blah!' We had so much static that when we did the first album, UA (United Artists Records) wanted us to make the letters mean something, like We Are Righteous. We all fuckin' laughed and said, 'We'll just make hit records.'" When asked about the name, Burdon commented: "Well, I didn't like the name at first. I thought it was capitalizing on a conflict, but I let myself get talked into it because the guys in the band thought it was aggressive and thought it was hip to 'take a negative word and turn it into something positive,' as they put it. But war spelled backwards is raw, and that's what I got—a raw deal. So, what's in a name?"

> "I think we made the right choice. I always felt, though, that it was the kind of name I could record all sorts of different music under without any sort of predictability inherent in the name . . . kind of mysterious. But you have to have the 'the' in there."
> —ADAM GRANDUCIEL, THE WAR ON DRUGS

THE WAR ON DRUGS The indie rock band formed in Philadelphia in 2003. When asked why they are called the War on Drugs, front man Adam Granduciel replied, "No real reason, really. My friend Julian and I came up with it a few years ago over a couple bottles of red wine and a few typewriters when we were living in Oakland. We were writing a lot back then, working on a dictionary, and it just came out and we were like, 'Hey, good band name,' so eventually when I moved to Philadelphia and got a band together I used it. It was either that or the Rigatoni Danzas. I think we made the right choice. I always felt, though, that it was the kind of name I could record all sorts of different music under without any sort of predictability inherent in the name . . . kind of mysterious. But you *have* to have the 'the' in there."

WAS [NOT WAS] Multi-instrumentalists Don Was (Don Fagenson) and David Was (David Weiss), who grew up together in Detroit, formed Was (Not Was) in 1979. Don explained the origins of the band's name: "Well, it's actually the living embodiment of Piaget's reversibility theory. Basically, my son was a year and a half old at the time and was starting to grasp onto the concept of opposites and found it amusing to point to something that was blue and say, 'Red,' and wait for a disapproving face and go, 'Not red.' So this motif provided the template for the name. The only thing missing was that we had to hallucinate a decent verb. Then we just took our names based on the band, figuring that it was a one-off twelve-inch. 'Hey, it's funny. You'll be David Was, I'll be Don Was, it'll be great.' Everyone said it was the stupidest possible name because people wouldn't be able to remember it, and as a result the band would be forgotten. My argument was always, 'No, it doesn't matter if you call it something very simple if you don't have records that stick with people—then they'll forget the name no matter what. But if you actually have a hit, and you're called something impossible, people are going to be forced to remember the name, and once they remember it, they'll never forget it.' We get a lot of people who say, 'Which one of you guys is Was and which one is Not Was?' Like a vaudeville team. When we got to Europe, we found that the accepted theory was that we were correcting people's pronunciation of our last name—that it's 'Vas, not Was.' The name's probably the coolest thing about the band. Someday I hope to live up to the originality of the name. It's been downhill since then."

THE WATERBOYS The band was formed in London by Scottish-born Mike Scott in 1981. He named the group after a line in the Lou Reed song "The Kids" from the album *Berlin*: "And I am the water boy/ The real game's not over here." The controversial song was reportedly inspired by Reed's wife at the time, Bettye Kronstad, who had been taken from her mother by state authorities when she was a child.

WEEN Mickey Melchiondo (Dean Ween) and Aaron Freeman (Gene Ween) began recording together in 1985, when the two were in junior high school in New Hope, Pennsylvania. Their name is a cross be- tween "wuss" and "peen," as in penis.

WEEZER The band formed in Los Angeles, California, in 1992. Some of the names the band considered included Fuzz, Hummingbird, This Niblet, and the Big Jones. Front man Rivers Cuomo suggested the name Weezer after his childhood nickname. That name was given to him not by grade school classmates because he was asthmatic, as is commonly believed, but by his father when he was a toddler after Wheezer, a character in the Our Gang shorts, which were later known as The Little Rascals. Wheezer was played by Bobby Hutchins, who reportedly earned the nickname after running around so much on his first day at the film studio that he began wheezing. Rivers is indeed Cuomo's given name. His younger brother's name is Leaves.

WET WET WET Wet Wet Wet formed in Glasgow, Scotland, in 1982 and took their name from a line in the Scritti Politti song "Getting Having and Holding": "It's tired of joking/wet, wet with tears."

WHAM! George Michael (born Georgios Panayiotou) and Andrew Ridgeley met in school and played together in a band called the Executive in 1979. When that band broke up, the duo recorded a demo tape that included a song that would become their first single, a rap parody called "Wham! Rap," from which they took their name in 1981. The song, which jokingly endorsed unemployment, was their first hit.

WHITESNAKE After leaving Deep Purple in 1976, singer David Coverdale recorded his first solo album the following year, titled *White Snake*, which featured the song "Whitesnake." That song included the lyrics: "Got a whitesnake mama/You want to shake it mama/Come and let it crawl on you/." If there was any ambiguity about what a "whitesnake" might be, when asked point blank by a fan, Coverdale said, "Whitesnake is named after my willy.... What's yours called?" In 1978, he formed the band David Coverdale's Whitesnake, which eventually became simply Whitesnake.

THE WHITE STRIPES Jack White, who was born John Anthony Gillis, took his wife Meg White's surname when they married in 1996. The following year they formed a two-person band they initially called the Red and White Stripes, reportedly after Meg's love of peppermint candy. The name was soon shortened to the White Stripes. They divorced in 2000, but stuck together as bandmates through 2011.

THE WHO Singer Roger Daltrey, guitarist Pete Townshend, and bassist John Entwistle began performing together with drummer Doug Sandom as the Detours in London in 1962. Late in 1963 they met managers Helmut Gorden and Pete Meaden, who gave them a better-dressed Mod image and renamed them the High Numbers, Mod slang for stylish. In 1964, after Sandom was replaced by Keith Moon, filmmakers Kit Lambert and Chris Stamp took over the band's management and rechristened them the Who, a name they had used previously for a short time.

WIDESPREAD PANIC The band got their start in Athens, Georgia, in 1986. Their name was inspired by guitarist Michael Houser's nickname, Panic. Bassist Dave Schools explained: "He used to believe that he suffered from anxiety disorders, panic attacks. His heart would start racing, he'd be sweating. He'd make us take him to the hospital, and they'd tell him that there's not a damn thing wrong with him. Then one day he saw a poster for this swing band called the Widespread Depression Orchestra, and he came in and flopped down on the chair and said, 'You know, guys, I don't want to be just Panic anymore. I want to be Widespread Panic.'"

WILD CHERRY Best known for the 1976 hit "Play That Funky Music," the band was formed in 1970 in Steubenville, Ohio. Lead vocalist and guitarist Rob Parissi was laid up in the hospital when inspiration struck. As his bandmates prepared to leave his room, someone mentioned that they needed a name, and Parissi, spotting a box of flavored cough drops, jokingly suggested Wild Cherry.

WINGS Following the breakup of the Beatles, Paul McCartney formed Wings in 1971. McCartney initially planned to call the band Turpentine, then the Dazzlers, before settling on Wings. The name was reportedly inspired by the difficult birth of his second child, Stella, whom he prayed would be delivered "on the wings of an angel." McCartney recalled: "It was dodgy at the time, so rather than just sitting around twiddling my thumbs, I was thinking of hopeful names for a new group, and somehow this uplifting idea of Wings came to me."

X The band formed in Los Angeles in 1977 after singer and bassist John Doe met guitarist Billy Zoom via a classified ad and singer Exene Cervenka at a poetry workshop. Adding Don J. Bonebrake on drums, the band became X in honor of Exene.

X-RAY SPEX The seminal English punk band was launched in 1976 by lead singer Poly Styrene (Marianne Elliott) and saxophonist Lora Logic (Susan Whitby). Best known for the song "Oh Bondage, Up Yours," they took their name from the novelty eyeglasses advertised in the back of publications like *True Detective* that supposedly gave the wearer the ability to see through clothing and other barriers.

XTC The band formed in Swindon, England, in the mid-1970s. They changed their name from the Helium Kidz after singer and guitarist Andy Partridge reportedly saw an old film in which Jimmy Durante discovered "the lost chord" and exclaimed, "Dat's it, I'm in XTC!"

THE XX The indie pop band formed in 2005 in the Wandsworth borough of London. According to guitarist Romy Madley Croft, their name "was always an aesthetic thing. It doesn't have a meaning. We just like X's. We made the name before the music, and I like that it's ambiguous and people can read into it if they want."

THE YARDBIRDS The band came together in London in 1963 and was originally called the Metropolis Blues Quartet. It was vocalist Keith Relf who, despite his initial reluctance to change the name, found the term "yardbird" in the liner notes for a Jack Kerouac record. A yardbird was a person, a hobo, who made his home around rail yards. It's worth noting that the group had its origins in two bands that played at the Railway Tavern in London. For a time, the band was billed as the Most Blueswailing Yardbirds. They did not name themselves after jazz great Charlie "Bird" Parker, as has been reported.

YEAH YEAH YEAHS The indie rock band formed in New York City in 2000. Despite rumors to the contrary, the band's name is not a musical reference, as in the Beatles' "She loves you, yeah, yeah, yeah." Singer and pianist Karen O explained: "It's something you'll commonly hear in New York City. I don't know if it's, like, a neurotic thing or if it's a remark, like 'Yeah yeah yeah, whatever,' you know?"

YES Yes formed in London in 1968. Singer Jon Anderson explained, "Yes got pulled out of the bag, I think. We wanted to display a strong conviction in what we were doing. We had to have a strong and straight title for the band."

YO LA TENGO The band's love for the New York Mets helped inspire their name when they formed in Hoboken, New Jersey, in 1984. The name has its origins in an anecdote from the team's first season in 1962 when, among other mishaps, centerfielder Richie Ashburn and shortstop Elio Chacón frequently collided chasing popups. Ashburn would yell, "I got it!" only to run into Chacón, who grew up in Venezuela and didn't speak English. Ashburn learned to shout "*Yo la tengo!*"—Spanish for "I have it," or "I've got her"—and was pleased to see Chacón back off in a game as a ball was hit in his direction. Ashburn got into position to make the catch only to have leftfielder Frank Thomas barrel into him. Thomas, who didn't speak Spanish, reportedly said to Ashburn after the collision, "What the hell is a yellow tango?"

THE YOUNGBLOODS Formed in Boston in 1965, the Youngbloods, who had a hit in 1969 with "Get Together," were named after founder Jesse Colin Young. Born Perry Miller, he took his name from Wild West figures Jesse James and Cole Younger, and Grand Prix racecar driver Colin Chapman.

THE YOUNG RASCALS The group formed in New York City in 1965. They planned to call themselves the Rascals until it was discovered that there was already a group called the Harmonica Rascals. Without their knowledge, Atlantic Records changed their name to the Young Rascals with the release of their first single in early 1966. In the spring of 1968 they convinced Atlantic that they could legally shorten their name to the Rascals. Their name had no connection to the TV show *The Little Rascals*.

"The name has its origins
in an anecdote from
the team's first season
in 1962 when, among other
mishaps, centerfielder
Richie Ashburn and shortstop
Elio Chacón frequently
collided chasing popups."

—YO LA TENGO

ZZ TOP After his psychedelic band the Moving Sidewalks broke up, guitarist Billy Gibbons started ZZ Top with bassist Lanier Greig and drummer Dan Mitchell in 1969. Later that year, the lineup was finalized when Greig was replaced by Frank Beard and Mitchell by Dusty Hill, both former members of the American Blues.

The band was not named after two leading brands of rolling paper, Zig Zag and Top, as has been rumored. Gibbons revealed, "We wanted somethin' real bluesy soundin', like B.B. King, you know? There was this R&B singer named Z.Z. Hill, and that seemed like a good place to start. We also wanted the name to suggest the best, the ultimate. For a while, we were just gonna call ourselves ZZ Brown. I thought that sounded pretty right. We knew ZZ King or ZZ Queen wasn't going to work! Then one day I was driving with a friend of mine and we passed by an old barn with the hayloft doors open, facing out. He pointed up at the two doors that had those old-fashioned Z-shaped beams on 'em and said, 'Look, ZZ Top!' I knew right then we had our name."